Graveyard
of
Champions

Library of Congress Control Number: 2001086648

ISBN 1-58150-066-1

Printed in the United States
First Edition: June 2002

Distributed to the trade by
National Book Network
4720-A Boston Way
Lanham, MD 20706
1.800.462.6420

a division of The Blood-Horse, Inc.
PUBLISHERS SINCE 1916

Graveyard of Champions

Saratoga's Fallen Favorites

BILL HELLER

ECLIPSE
PRESS

Lexington, Kentucky

To Anna and Benjamin

Contents

Foreword 6

1   The Graveyard of Champions 7
2   The Early Years 15
3   Unbeaten No More 29
4   The Up-Roaring Twenties 39
5   Jim Who?... 51
6   Like Father, Like Son? 65
7   Stymied 73
8   No Fooling 79
9   Three of a Kind 89
10   What Graveyard? 99
11   He Made Them Cry 115
12   Two of a Kind 139
13   Across the Street 151
14   One For How Many? 161
15   Triple Crown Lumps 183
16   Not a Secret Anymore 203
17   Come Back, Alysheba 211
18   Keep Off the Grass................................ 219
19   Don't Jump to Conclusions 229
20   Same Old Saratoga 235

A Chronology of Major Saratoga Upsets 244
Champions at Saratoga 247
Index 250
Sources 253
Acknowledgments 254
About the Author 255

Foreword

"Giant killer! Giant killer!" Julie Krone yelled jubilantly at Allen Jerkens while she dismounted from Classy Mirage, who had just beaten Inside Information, the 2-5 favorite who had stumbled badly at the start of the 1995 Ballerina Stakes at Saratoga. Inside Information had won five consecutive races and eleven of thirteen lifetime starts coming into the Ballerina.

Jerkens' record? Well, horses he trained had beaten Kelso three times, Secretariat twice, and Forego, Buckpasser, Skip Away, and Gentlemen once. At one point, Jerkens was the youngest trainer ever inducted into the Hall of Fame. None of the upsets matched the magnitude of Onion's victory over the 1-10 favorite Secretariat in the 1973 Whitney Handicap at Saratoga, a race that holds a special place in his heart.

Jerkens has been coming to Saratoga annually for more than fifty years.

Going back a ways, the track at Saratoga was a little different. Years ago, I remember Saratoga as a slow track. The first time I went was in the late forties. I didn't have much of a stable, three or four horses that used to run a mile and an eighth in 1:55 or 1:56. I had a horse, Admiral Vee, that won the Saratoga Handicap, a $50,000 race, in a slow time.

It's kind of hard to explain the upsets at Saratoga. It's the middle of the year when some of the horses are tailing off slightly, like the three-year-olds that have been running hard in the spring. That could be one of the reasons. The track, the feed, and the altitude are a tiny bit different. And there are so many horses from different parts of the country racing at Saratoga. Some of them coming in are better than we thought.

I think some horses just take to the climate. It's been hot at Belmont; then it kind of gets nice up there. The evenings are cooler. Some of the horses like the track. I always liked it, sure.

Allen Jerkens

1

The Graveyard of Champions

For six glorious weeks each summer, the charming Victorian city of Saratoga Springs in upstate New York becomes the center of the Thoroughbred universe.

Named by *Sports Illustrated* in 1999 as one of the top ten sporting venues in the world, Saratoga Race Course was called "the loveliest racetrack in the country" by *ESPN Magazine* in 2001. Saratoga's vast wooden grandstand with its pitched roof and gables, the whimsical woodwork and old-fashioned seats, the expansive shade trees and inviting paddock all add to the sense of timelessness that envelops the grounds.

Fans come from all over, lured not only by the high-profile meet and the beautiful track, but by Saratoga Springs' famed mineral water and baths, the Saratoga Performing Arts Center, the lush green trees and parks, and the crisp, cooler air.

Adding to the atmosphere are the once-a-year events such as the Saratoga yearling sales, the Hall of Fame inductions at the National Museum of Racing, and The Jockey Club Round Table Conference, which attracts industry leaders from all over the world.

But these are all peripheral events, framed around the six-week racing meet that draws the best horses in North America and the largest crowds. In 2001, Saratoga's 133rd season, attendance averaged more than 28,000, two thousand more than the city's population and a record for the fourth consecutive year..

At Saratoga, where racing dates to the Civil War, tradition rules. The days have a distinct rhythm, beginning with morning workouts and ending with dinner parties and late suppers.

The afternoons, of course, are spent at Saratoga Race Course, the site of many of racing's oldest and most famous stakes races: the Travers, the Alabama, the Whitney, and the Hopeful.

A victory in one of these high-profile stakes can help a horse win a divisional title or even Horse of the Year. A defeat can cost a horse a championship.

At Saratoga Race Course, many of the greatest horses in racing history have lost at prohibitively low odds, sometimes to the unlikeliest of opponents.

Saratoga Race Course is the Graveyard of Champions. It has never been, though it is often called, the Graveyard of Favorites.

Favorites do not lose more frequently at Saratoga. In the thirty-six-day meet in 2001, favorites won thirty-seven percent of the races, which actually is a little higher than the national percentage of winning favorites at all Thoroughbred racetracks.

After years of being inundated with questions about favorites losing at Saratoga, Tom Gilcoyne, the historian of the National Museum of Racing and Hall of Fame in Saratoga Springs, researched losing favorites from 1906 through 1992. He found favorites, nationally, won 35.4 percent during that time. Favorites at Saratoga won 36.3 percent of the time.

Saratoga's legacy is WHICH favorites lose in WHICH races and, occasionally, WHICH horses beat them.

Not only did Man o' War lose at Saratoga in the 1919 Sanford, it was the only loss of his gloried career. And the horse who beat him was named Upset.

Gallant Fox's loss in the 1930 Travers at odds of 1-2 was a shocker and the only race he did not win that entire year. When you consider that the horse who beat him by eight lengths, Jim Dandy, was 100-1 and did not win any of his other nineteen starts that year, Gallant Fox's defeat is even more amazing.

Secretariat was defeated at 1-10 in the 1973 Whitney Handicap by Onion, who had raced three days earlier, had never won a stakes before, and would never win another.

In 1982, the three separate winners of the Triple Crown races, Gato Del Sol, Aloma's Ruler, and Conquistador Cielo, converged in a five-horse field in the Travers and lost to a relatively unknown Canadian shipper, Runaway Groom, who had been a maiden all of four months before the Travers.

From 1936, when the Horse of the Year award was institut-

Barbara D. Livingston

Saratoga: "the loveliest racetrack in the country."

ed, through 2001, thirty-three Horses of the Year raced at Saratoga. Twenty lost at least once.

From 1970 through 2001, Horses of the Year made thirty-three starts at Saratoga and won just nineteen of them. Shocking losses, such as Man o' War's to Upset, still happen today at Saratoga.

These are the best horses losing the most important stakes, sometimes to the biggest longshot in the field.

"We call it the Graveyard of Champions because all the good horses run there," said Angel Cordero Jr., racing's fifth all-time leading rider (7,057 wins) and winner of fourteen Saratoga riding titles, including eleven in a row, before retiring in 1992. "When upsets happen at Saratoga, everybody knows. If it happens at Aqueduct, nobody knows."

Jerry Bailey, who won seven of eight riding titles at Saratoga from 1994 through 2001, offered his spin: "There's not that many more upsets at Saratoga, but the quality is so high with the horses it attracts, it's more 'headline-able,' if you will."

Retired jockey Eddie Maple, who still ranks twenty-fourth in

The yearling sales add to Saratoga's heady atmosphere.

Grand Victorian homes are part of Saratoga's charms.

all-time wins (4,398), agreed: "It's a short meet. It's condensed. It's jumping out at you, and the best horses come."

Annually, some of them lose. Cordero, now a jockey agent in New York for John Velazquez, has his own theories. "Saratoga is different than any track surface in America," he said. "I would say seven out of ten horses like Saratoga because of that, the facilities, and more open space. But three of them don't like it, and they don't perform good. Circumstances make a lot of favorites get beat. When you go to Saratoga with horses that have performed all year long, you can't expect them to keep running well all year round."

It's a sentiment shared by Hall of Fame trainer Phil Johnson, who has the incredible distinction of saddling at least one winner at Saratoga every year since 1961. "These horses are just played out," Johnson said in 2001. "Nobody really freshens up for Saratoga because there's too many big races before Saratoga. The horses are racing, racing, and racing, and as soon as they show anything, people say, 'Let's go to Saratoga.' They don't really plan for Saratoga."

When 1999 Eclipse champion older mare Beautiful Pleasure lost the 2000 Go for Wand Handicap at Saratoga as the 1-5 favorite, she was not breaking new ground.

"Favorites Upset in Saratoga Racing"

That was the headline on the front page of the sports section in *The New York Times*, not the day after Beautiful Pleasure's loss in the 2000 Go for Wand Handicap, but of an August afternoon ninety years earlier, when another champion mare, Maskette, went down at odds of 1-2 in the Delaware Handicap.

Champions have been losing at the 139-year-old queen of American racetracks almost from the very beginning. Their common bond is their apparent invincibility heading into a stakes race at Saratoga.

Other champions have raced at Saratoga and won, and even some of the champions that lost at Saratoga won other races there. But when you trace a line of history that includes:

- Hamburg's going down at 1-3 in the Grand Union Hotel Stakes in 1897
- Maskette's loss at 1-2 in the 1910 Delaware Handicap
- Man o' War's only loss at 1-2 in the 1919 Sanford
- Gallant Fox's defeat at 1-2 in the 1930 Travers
- Stymie's 1947 loss at 2-5 in the Whitney Handicap
- High Voltage's loss at 2-5 in the 1955 Alabama Stakes
- Lamb Chop's loss at 2-5 in the 1963 Alabama
- Secretariat's loss at 1-10 to Onion in the 1973 Whitney
- Davona Dale's loss at 3-10 in the 1979 Alabama
- Conquistador Cielo's loss at 2-5 in the 1982 Travers
- Manila's loss at 1-5 in the 1987 Bernard Baruch
- Steinlen's loss at 1-5 in the 1990 Bernard Baruch
- Inside Information's defeat at 2-5 in the 1995 Ballerina

and Beautiful Pleasure's defeat at 1-5, 103 years after

Hamburg's loss in the Grand Union Hotel Stakes, even the most skeptical racing fan would have to concede there seems to be a trend here.

It has been and remains a phenomenal trend. But to truly appreciate the magnitude of these historic upsets, they must be placed in context.

Saratoga is only open for six weeks a year. That's just thirty-six days of racing. Most of its preceding meets were even shorter. From 1898 through 1910, and from 1913 through 1946 (there was no racing at Saratoga in 1911 and 1912 and from 1943 to 1945), Saratoga's meet varied from fifteen to thirty days.

From 1947 through 1953, Saratoga raced thirty-six days. In 1954 and 1955, the meet was forty-two days.

From 1956 to 1990 — except for an experimental, twenty-seven consecutive-day meet with no dark days in 1982 — Saratoga raced only twenty-four days every year. Literally, four or five years of racing at Saratoga were the equivalent of a single year of racing at Belmont or Aqueduct. Even in 2001, with a thirty-six-day meet, Saratoga's dates were not even a third of Aqueduct's 134 or a half of Belmont's 92. These upsets were registered over a remarkably small number of racing dates.

And writers have been trying to explain them for decades. Noting Maskette's loss to Sir John Johnson and Textile's defeat of favored Semprolus the same day in 1910, *The New York Times* reported, "Both victories came in the nature of a surprise, but each race furnished high-class sport, and that atoned for the defeat of the more fashionable favorites."

Joe Mahar, a writer for the *Times Union* newspaper in Albany, explained Gallant Fox's loss in the 1930 Travers succinctly:

"The mighty have fallen"

In 1947 the Associated Press characterized Stymie's defeat in the Whitney as "one of the Spa's numerous upsets."

Eight years later, the Associated Press wrote of the 1955 Alabama: "The ceiling fell on the well-established system of form yesterday at Saratoga Race Track when, to the amazement of a crowd of 11,203, W. Arnold Hanger's Rico Reto raced to triumph in the seventy-fifth Alabama, the oldest race in the U.S.A. for 3-year-old fillies. It fell down so crashingly that those who bet on the Wheatley Stables entry of Misty Morn and High Voltage, prohibitive choices at 2-5, were still talking to themselves after the races."

Saratoga's reputation is so ingrained in the American sports culture that the editors of *Sports Illustrated* used this headline for Conquistador Cielo's 1982 Travers defeat:

"Another Body For The Graveyard"

When highly visible horses lose at Saratoga, it's news. The bigger the horse, the bigger the news. It's been that way for more than a hundred years.

2

The Early Years

Champions have been losing at Saratoga almost from the beginning of Thoroughbred racing there, which is a bit earlier than most people realize.

Thoroughbred racing is generally believed to have arrived in Saratoga Springs on the tails of John "Old Smoke" Morrissey in the early 1860s. An accomplished fighter turned New York City casino operator, Morrissey had decided to expand the scope of his business 175 miles northward as the Civil War raged on to the south. After establishing a casino in Saratoga Springs, which continued to be a popular summer resort destination during the war, Morrissey announced his next venture would be a racetrack for Thoroughbreds.

A track for harness horses already existed. Called the Saratoga Trotting Course, it was the site of Saratoga's first organized race, held August 14, 1847, in conjunction with the New York State Fair. Lady Suffolk, an amazing fourteen-year-old gray trotter immortalized by the song "The Old Gray Mare," defeated Moscow in three straight heats.

Morrissey announced that a four-day meet with two Thoroughbred races each day would commence August 3, 1863, at the existing track, which eventually was renamed Horse Haven and converted into a training track. Though the bloody battles of Gettysburg and Vicksburg had concluded just one month earlier, the war would drag on for another year and a half, continuing to drain the horse population and forcing the question: where would Morrissey find horses to race?

He sought help from three prominent businessmen: wealthy stockholder William R. Travers, sportsman and lawyer John R. Hunter, and Leonard W. Jerome, whose daughter Jennie would become the mother of Winston Churchill. Morrissey, Travers, Hunter, and Jerome formed a racing association and secured twenty-six horses to run in the eight scheduled races.

A newspaper ad touted the day:

Running Races!

At Saratoga

Cards of Admission, $1.00

All sections of the North and West, and some portions of the South will be represented by their best horses, and Canada will also contend for some of the various purses. Excellent racing is anticipated.

JOHN MORRISSEY,
Proprietor.

Saratoga's first race that August 3 was won by the three-year-old filly Lizzie W., who beat the three-year-old colt Capt Moore in two of three one-mile heats.

For more than one hundred years, Lizzie W. was credited with winning the first Thoroughbred race in Saratoga history. Her victory was even re-enacted at the 1963 Thoroughbred Racing Centennial in Saratoga Springs. But she was not Saratoga's first Thoroughbred winner. Diligent research by Landon Manning, author of *The Noble Animals* and a long-time Turf writer for *The Saratogian*, proved otherwise. The first Thoroughbred race had been held sixteen years earlier, during

The Blood-Horse

Since the start, Saratoga has been a fashionable racing venue.

that initial trotting meet of 1847. On September 16 of that year, Lady Digby won a one hundred dollar purse by defeating Disowned and Hopeful in three straight heats.

The considerable success of Morrissey's first Thoroughbred race meeting was documented in a front-page story in *Wilkes' Spirit of the Times*: "The meeting at Saratoga was a great success...It must have laid the foundation for a great fashionable race meeting at the Springs, like that at Ascot of England...It is now established that of the many thousands of people to be found at Saratoga this season of the year, there are but few who will not eagerly avail themselves of the opportunity for such amusement and interest as the sports of the turf afford."

But patrons complained the track was too narrow and the grandstand too small. So the racing association purchased 125 acres across the road and built a new racetrack. Brochure advertisements touted it as "The Most Classic Race Course in This Country, Located Among the Pines, Beautiful to the Eye, Rejuvenating to the Horse."

The new track opened August 2, 1864, and the four days of

racing included a stakes to honor the association's president, William Travers. His own horse, Kentucky, won that first Travers Stakes, beating favored Tipperary by four lengths.

Of course, a racetrack brought more tourists to Saratoga Springs, which was already saturated with visitors lured by its famed mineral spas and baths. They all needed a place to stay, and beginning in 1874, the richest visitors had two grandiose options a block apart: the Grand Union Hotel and the United States Hotel.

Originally named Union Hall, the U-shaped, five-story Union Hotel facing Broadway was purchased for $532,000 by Alexander Turney Stewart in 1872 and renamed the Grand Union Hotel. Stewart, the founder of America's first department store, spent an additional $500,000 to enlarge and refurnish the hotel, which already had private cottages, an interior courtyard shaded by elm trees, a main dining room seating a thousand, and an auxiliary dining room on the north piazza that could hold four hundred. By 1874, there were 824 refurbished guest rooms, crystal chandeliers, black walnut staircases, and a steam-engine elevator. In 1879, the Grand Union Hotel was the first building in Saratoga Springs to use electric lights.

The United States Hotel, also U-shaped, stretched more than a quarter of a mile in length when it opened in the summer of 1874. It boasted 768 rooms and cottage suites with marble washstands and cold running water. Hot water had to be ordered, and chambermaids served it to guests in covered containers. Each room had a rope attached to a hook in the wall in lieu of a fire escape.

A Saratoga stakes race was named for each hotel. First run in 1879, the Grand Union Hotel Stakes continued through 1959. The United States Hotel Stakes began in 1880 as a stakes for three-year-olds and up. The stakes was changed to a two-year-old race in 1901 and was last run in 1956.

One of the first great horses Saratoga patrons were privileged to see was Hamburg, a muscular bay son of Hanover bought by owner-trainer John Madden for $1,200. Madden, who was also successful with Standardbreds, would be America's leading Thoroughbred breeder for eleven consecutive years.

Hamburg arrived at Saratoga in 1897 with four wins and a third in his first five outings as a two-year-old. In his first Saratoga start, on opening day of the meet, he won the four-furlong Flash Stakes by a length and a half as the heavy favorite. A week later, he won the five-furlong Congress Hall Stakes at even money over Archduke, who carried fifteen pounds less than Hamburg's 134. Both two-year-olds returned three days later in the Grand Union Hotel Stakes at six furlongs with Hamburg carrying 129 pounds, only twelve more than Archduke. That is probably why Hamburg went off at 1-3, but Archduke, sent off at 16-5, upset him by a head. One account of the race said Hamburg "was sluggish away from the barrier and did not get to the lead until after a half-mile. Under 117 pounds, Archduke came on in the stretch with a powerful ride by whip-rider Fred Taral." The comment in Hamburg's race line was "poor ride." Madden decided to replace Hamburg's rider, Walter Willhite, for the horse's next start, the Generation Stakes at New York's Brighton Beach Racetrack, which Hamburg won.

Hamburg finished his two-year-old year with a record of twelve wins, two seconds, and a third in sixteen starts, an unheard of number of starts for a juvenile these days.

Madden sold Hamburg after the colt's two-year-old season to Marcus Daly for $40,001, then an American record for a Thoroughbred in training, the extra dollar so Madden could boast Hamburg sold for more than $40,000. Madden used the money to buy a large farm in Kentucky and called it Hamburg Place. Madden would breed 182 Thoroughbred stakes winners, including five Kentucky Derby winners, five Belmont Stakes winners, and the first Triple Crown winner, Sir Barton.

Widener Collection

Then as now, the paddock provided a close-up look of the contenders.

Hamburg earned Horse of the Year honors at three and concluded his career with sixteen wins in twenty-one starts and earnings of $60,380.

The next star to have her ups and downs at Saratoga was James R. Keene's precocious filly Maskette. Trained by James Rowe Sr., Maskette went off at odds of 1-4 in her debut, an allowance race at Saratoga on August 3, 1908, despite running against colts. She won by a half-length. The daughter of Disguise followed with victories in the Spinaway (also at Saratoga), Futurity, and Great Filly Stakes before running second to the colt Sir Martin in the Flatbush Stakes at Sheepshead Bay, a track at Coney Island that operated from 1884 until 1910.

Maskette rebounded to win the Matron Stakes in her final start at two, and then reeled off three stakes victories to begin her three-year-old season. She next was sent to Saratoga for the Alabama, which she won by a length and a half as the favorite. She tacked on a win against colts in the Pierrepont Handicap at Jamaica before suffering just her second career loss, again against males, in the Aqueduct Handicap, her final start that year.

As a four-year-old of 1910, Maskette sandwiched two handicap wins around a sixth-place finish in the prestigious Metropolitan Handicap. She was then second by a half-length to King James in the Sheepshead Bay Handicap. The Metropolitan and Sheepshead Bay were the only two starts in which she was not favored. She again headed for Saratoga, where she would again face colts, this time in the Delaware Handicap on August 6.

The Albany *Times Union* that morning had an interesting note about one of Maskette's opponents. Next to a story speculating about a trade of Ty Cobb or Larry "Nap" Lajoie to the Boston Red Sox for Harry Lord — wishful thinking for Red Sox fans — was the following note nestled under a headline:

"Some Saratoga Gossip"
"The rail birds are warning everybody to look out
for Sir John Johnson."

The railbirds were right.

Sir John Johnson, a five-year-old son of Isidor—La Tosca II, had finished fourth in the 1908 Travers and then won the Huron Stakes at Saratoga. As a four-year-old in 1909, he'd won three stakes, including the Merchants' and Citizens' Handicap at Saratoga.

In the 1910 Delaware Handicap, Sir John Johnson went off at 8-1. Maskette went off the favorite at 1-2 in the field of six despite concerns about her soundness. *The New York Times* noted the following day: "It was seen during the parade to the post that Maskette was slightly lame, but little attention was paid to that fact, for the reason that she supposedly greatly outclassed her field and the lameness was hardly noticeable."

Sir John Johnson, who carried 124 pounds to Maskette's 125,

broke on top and jockey Joe Notter kept Maskette in second in the mile handicap. "Both were going along under restraint, and it appeared as though the mare was capable of going to the big horse at any time," the *Times* reported. "Notter made the attempt to move up on the first turn, and it was then apparent that Maskette was not herself. She hung so badly that it was less than a furlong before she was well beaten."

Sir John Johnson won by a head over Stanley Fay. Maskette finished a distant fifth, beating one horse. She never raced again.

The end of the 1910 meet marked the start of a two-year hiatus for New York racing after the state declared gambling at racetracks illegal. Racing resumed at Saratoga in 1913, just in time for Andrew Miller's rugged two-year-old Roamer. The son of Knight Errant out of Rose Tree II by Bona Vista would make eighteen starts at Saratoga in his ninety-eight-race career, with nine wins, four seconds, and two thirds. At times at Saratoga, Roamer was brilliant. At other times, he was beaten. Figuring out which was which was a hazardous endeavor for bettors, particularly the 1915 Champlain Handicap.

Roamer made five Saratoga starts in 1913, finishing first, eighth, and second in handicap races, then winning the Saratoga Special by a length and a half at 7-1 before running fifth by two and a half lengths to Little Nephew at 4-1 in the Adirondack Stakes.

In 1914 Roamer was the even-money favorite in the Travers and won by ten lengths, the third-largest winning margin in the Travers' 132-year-old history, while setting a track record of 2:04 for the mile and a quarter. Roamer followed the Travers with a four-length victory at 1-2 in the Huron Handicap. His chart in both those races said he won "in a canter." Roamer had won twelve of his sixteen starts as a three-year-old and set track records at seven, nine, and ten furlongs.

As a four year old in 1915, he cantered to another Saratoga

victory, winning the Saratoga Handicap by ten lengths as the 3-1 favorite in a field of seven.

Roamer headed into the 1915 Champlain Handicap as the favorite and high weight, having won his previous three starts at Saratoga by ten, four, and ten lengths. This time, Roamer did not fire, finishing fourth by nine and three-quarters lengths to Star Jasmine, whom he had beaten by eleven lengths in the Saratoga Handicap. Roamer had spotted Star Jasmine twenty-five pounds in the Saratoga Handicap and beaten him easily. In the Champlain, he spotted him twenty-two. The comment in Roamer's past performance line said, "Never a threat."

Roamer atoned by winning his final two starts at Saratoga that year, the Merchants' and Citizens' Handicap by half a length as the 7-5 public choice, and the Saratoga Cup by eight lengths at 1-10. The following year at Saratoga, Roamer was third in the Merchants' and Citizen's Handicap as the 6-5 favorite and second by two lengths at 9-2 in the Saratoga Cup. In 1917, Roamer won the Saratoga Handicap by half a length

The Blood-Horse

The United States Hotel, which lent its name to a stakes race.

at 5-1 and was third, beaten just half a length, as the 3-2 favorite in the Delaware Handicap run at Saratoga. He started three times at Saratoga in 1918, winning the Saratoga Handicap at 7-2 (not the favorite), and then raced against time in a special five-thousand-dollar stakes when he outran the pacesetter from the start. In doing so, he raced a mile in 1:34 4/5, becoming the first horse to run a sub 1:35 mile around at least one turn. Roamer then lost the two-horse Saratoga Cup by five lengths to Johren, who was the favorite while carrying fourteen pounds less.

Roamer raced six times as an eight-year-old in the early summer of 1919, but never made it back to Saratoga. Overall in his marvelous career, Roamer won thirty-nine of ninety-eight starts, with twenty-six seconds and nine thirds. He died in the winter following his eight-year-old season in a paddock accident.

Racing at Saratoga in the second decade of the 1900s wasn't that different from Saratoga in the last decade of the 1900s: overflow crowds watching great horses; big races triggering major headlines in New York newspapers; and one and all scurrying for a place to sleep every night in over-priced lodgings.

The New York Times reported the opening day of the 1916 season under five sets of headlines, one proclaiming in part:

"Fervid Enthusiasm as Meeting Opens"

"It has been many years since the Saratoga Racing Association has had an opening like the one of this afternoon, which ushered in the 1916 racing season at the Spa. With the magic words of 'They're off!' 15,000 persons stood up at the start of the first race and shouted a rousing welcome to the thoroughbreds, while the band added to the general rejoicing by rendering as its initial effort, 'America.'

"Every box in the clubhouse and every available

seat in the grand stand were filled...A glance at the big grand stand, packed to the last inch, gave testimony to the hold of the sport of racing on the American public. A closer examination of the personalities in the big crowd would bring forth further evidence of the wide range of the sport's appeal. Rich and poor were there, and some of those present were names known the length and breadth of the nation. The rush to the track commenced at noon, and soon had assumed the proportions of a Russian advance. Union Avenue presented a risk of life to the pedestrian who desired to cross that picturesque thoroughfare."

Some things never change. Read on: "It is somewhat of a mystery where the thousands of visitors...are going to eat and sleep. Hundreds have been turned away from the hotels in the town and are seeking accommodation anywhere they can find it. The two principal hotels, the Grand Union and the United States, have been refusing bookings since last Thursday, and the small hostelries are asking exorbitant prices for cot room."

People were paying exorbitant prices for the opportunity to see champions race at Saratoga. But the champions did not always win.

Man o' War's first and only loss, in the 1919 Sanford Stakes, stands more than eighty years later as one of the most shocking upsets in racing history. But Man o' War was not the first famous undefeated horse to lose at Saratoga.

Regret, a filly owned and bred by Harry Payne Whitney and trained by James Rowe Sr., did little wrong in her historic three-year career.

A daughter of Broomstick, she was out of Jersey Lightning, a daughter of none other than Hamburg, an upset victim himself at Saratoga. As a two-year-old in 1914, Regret raced three times at Saratoga, mirroring her maternal grandfather. Unlike

Hamburg, she won all three, even though each was a stakes race against colts. She took the Saratoga Special by a length at 8-5 in her debut, the Sanford Memorial by a length and a half at 4-5, and the Hopeful Stakes by half a length at 8-5. Just three other two-year-olds have swept the Sanford, Saratoga Special, and Hopeful: Campfire (1916), Dehere (1993), and City Zip (2000).

While historic, the Saratoga sweep would not be listed first on Regret's resume. That came on May 8, 1915, at Churchill Downs, when she became the first filly to win the Kentucky Derby. As only Winning Colors and Genuine Risk have been able to match that accomplishment in the ensuing eighty-five years, Regret's accomplishment seems only more notable. But it did not come easily. In fact, she came perilously close to not even starting.

Rowe had not started a horse in the Kentucky Derby since winning it in 1891 with Hindoo. He had already come to peace with himself about making the Derby Regret's first start as a three-year-old, despite a nine-month layoff and the fact that she would be going a mile and a quarter while never having raced farther than six furlongs. But when she shipped poorly, went off her feed, and had two uninspiring workouts before the race, Rowe wondered whether he should run her. In addition, the day before the Derby, Whitney's brother-in-law, Alfred Gwynne Vanderbilt, died along with 1,197 others when a torpedo sunk the *Lusitania*. Vanderbilt had given his life jacket to a woman he did not know and then joined a group at one end of the ship. Together they sang, accompanied by the ship's orchestra, the last minutes before the ship went under.

Rowe, though, started Whitney's filly, and she won wire to wire by two lengths as the 5-2 favorite in a field of sixteen. Afterward, Whitney said, "I don't care whether she ever starts again. I told Rowe I didn't care if she ever won another race if she could only land this one. The glory of winning this event is big enough."

But Regret continued her winning ways. She beat males by a length and a half as the 1-3 favorite in the Saranac Handicap at Saratoga, upping her career record to five for five.

Regret returned to Saratoga to make her four-year-old debut against males in the $4,800 Saratoga Handicap, July 31, 1916, the opening day of the meet. For the second straight year, she was making her first start of the season in a mile and a quarter stakes race against colts.

Though she had not raced since August 17 of the previous year, Regret went off the .90-to-1 favorite in a distinguished field of eight that included August Belmont's entry of Stromboli and Friar Rock, along with The Finn and Short Grass, who held the American record for a one-turn mile.

Stromboli, a gelded son of Fair Play, had won the 1914 Saranac, Jerome, Manhattan, and Baltimore handicaps, and the 1915 Metropolitan, Kings County, Suburban, Belmont Park Autumn, Pimlico Fall Serial, and Bowie handicaps. He displayed his versatility by equaling the track record at Pimlico for six furlongs in the Fall Serial, and then missing the track record for one and three-quarters miles by two-fifths of a second while winning the Bowie Handicap by fifteen lengths in his next start.

In the 1916 Saratoga Handicap, the entry of Friar Rock, the winner of the 1916 Belmont Stakes and Brooklyn and Suburban handicaps, and Stromboli went off the 18-to-5 second choice. Short Grass, sent off the 5-1 third choice, carried high weight of 132 pounds. Leaving from the outside post, Regret, carrying 123 pounds, was gunned to the lead by her jockey, Joe Notter, who had ridden her in all her starts. Regret took a commanding lead, but could not maintain it when challenged by Stromboli. "She refused to make any further effort in spite of the strenuous riding of her jockey," according to *The New York Times*, and faded to last, sixteen lengths behind Stromboli, who beat Ed Crump by a length and a half.

Notter never rode Regret again, and Regret never stopped

Regret won the 1915 Kentucky Derby but stopped badly in the 1916 Saranac Handicap at Saratoga.

like that again. She won four of her five subsequent starts, her lone defeat coming against males in the Brooklyn Handicap. The comment in her racing line said, "Overconfident ride" by J. F. Robinson. Regret ended her career with nine victories and one second in eleven starts. Her only poor performance occurred at Saratoga. A few years later, her owner, Harry Payne Whitney, would be part of another memorable Saratoga upset.

3

Unbeaten No More

If Man o' War's appearance in the Sanford Stakes at Saratoga had happened in 1999 instead of 1919, there might have been Man o' War T-shirt or Man o' War beer stein giveaways. Instead, the only promotion of the most infamous race in Saratoga's history was an advertisement in the Albany *Times Union* on August 12, the day before the event. It was sandwiched between two other ads, one for a closeout sale of women's shoes for $1.95 and the other for "America's One Uniform Gas."

Saratoga's most infamous upset: Upset over Man o' War in the Sanford Stakes.

RACING AT
SARATOGA SPRINGS
Every Week Day at 2:45 p.m.
To-Morrow's Special Features Include

THE $5,000 SANFORD MEMORIAL
A 2-MILE STEEPLECHASE
THE WATERVLIET HANDICAP
Burnt Hills Handicap — And 2 Other Superb Contests
Affording a Delightful Afternoon's Diversion
Train leaves D. & H. Depot, Albany, 1:00 p.m.
Course also reached by trolley
Special race train Saturdays only at 12:30 p.m.
GRAND STAND AND PADDOCK $3.30,
LADIES $1.65, FIELD $1.10
Includes War Tax

(Eighty-one years later, in the year 2001, you could get into Saratoga Race Course for $2! Take note. It's the only price ever to decrease in Saratoga.)

On Wednesday, August 13, a mammoth crowd reported by *The New York Times* to be "about 20,000" expected to see unbeaten Man o' War win his next race. Only years and decades later would those race-goers realize they had seen racing history.

****

Just before midnight on March 29, 1917, the mare Mahubah foaled a chestnut colt, eliciting this entry the next morning in Major August Belmont's Nursery Stud foaling book: "Mch 29, 1917 — Mahubah foaled ch colt by Fair Play. Star, narrow stripe from right of star down center of nose. Height: 42. Girth: 33."

Eight days later, the United States declared war on Germany

and embroiled itself in the great conflict sweeping Europe.

Major Belmont planned to go abroad to help U.S. forces in World War I and decided to sell twenty-one of his yearlings, including the chestnut son of Fair Play. They were auctioned at Saratoga on August 17, 1918, and Samuel D. Riddle, owner of Glen Riddle Farm in Glen Riddle, Pennsylvania, purchased Man o' War for five thousand dollars, more than quadruple the sale's average yearling price of $1,107.

Trainer Louis Feustel was entrusted with Man o' War, whose color first earned him the nickname "Red" and then "Big Red" as he grew to more than sixteen hands.

Feustel patiently schooled and trained Man o' War at two Maryland tracks, Havre de Grace and Pimlico, in the spring of 1919. Man o' War made his debut at Belmont Park on June 6 and romped by six lengths at odds of 3-5 under Johnny Loftus, who would ride the colt in his first ten career starts.

Man o' War quickly jumped up to stakes company and easily won four stakes in succession: the Keene Memorial at Belmont Park by three lengths, the Youthful Stakes at Jamaica by two and a half lengths, the Hudson Stakes by a length and a half at Aqueduct, and the Tremont Stakes at Aqueduct by a length. Man o' War was the odds-on favorite each time, the last two at 1-10.

In his sixth career start, and first at Saratoga, Man o' War raced in the United States Hotel Stakes. Carrying 130 pounds, he beat Harry Payne Whitney's Upset, who carried 115 pounds, by two lengths. It was the first of six meetings between the two.

The second would be remembered forever.

A field of seven would contest the 1919 Sanford Memorial. Upset, a son of Whisk Broom II trained by James Rowe, would tackle Man o' War again. So would a fresh challenger in the Sanford, Mrs. Walter M. Jeffords' Golden Broom. Jeffords was the niece of Samuel Riddle's wife. Golden Broom, the $15,600 sale topper at Saratoga the year Man o' War was sold, had won the Saratoga Special in his last start and was given equal weight with Man o' War of 130. Bettors seemed to think enough of him to make him the 5-2 second choice to Man o' War's .55-to-1. Upset, again carrying 115 pounds, was the 8-1 third choice in the field of seven. Donnacona was 30-1, Armistice and The Swimmer each 50-1, and Captain Alcock 100-1.

The field in post position order was The Swimmer, Armistice, Golden Broom, Captain Alcock, Upset, Man o' War, and Donnacona.

Reports of the start of the Sanford Stakes vary and have been disputed for decades, except for the universal consensus that it was ugly and unfair. Regular starting official Mars Cassidy was ill and had been replaced by C.H. "Charlie" Pettingill, a former starter who had become a placing judge. Pettingill's worst start had been in the 1893 American Derby in which he took an hour and a half to dispatch the field.

Of course, there was no starting gate when Man o' War competed in the Sanford; rather, a single-strand rubber barrier stretched across the track. The starter pressed a button, activating a spring that would release the barrier forward and upward so horses wouldn't run into it.

Golden Broom broke the barrier prematurely three times, delaying the start for several minutes. What happened next has been disputed for decades.

The race chart said, "Man o' War began slowly," Captain Alcock "began slowly," and the overall start was "poor and slow."

The New York Times said that Upset, too, had tried to break through the barrier. The article also reported: "Man o' War acted very calmly but on his toes. Pettingill spent several minutes trying to get the horses lined up and then sent them away with only those near the rail ready for the start. The start was responsible for the defeat of Man o' War, it turned out." Other reports had Man o' War facing backward at the start of the six-furlong race.

In his Thoroughbred Legends book, *Man o' War*, distinguished author Edward L. Bowen came to this conclusion: "Man o' War was drawn next to the outside and got away poorly, but two of the field were away even worse. Almost certainly, he would not have been actually facing completely the opposite direction at the moment of the start, but the horror stories of his facing 'the wrong way' may well have meant he was turned sideways, or approximately so."

Tom Gilcoyne, the eighty-four-year-old National Museum of Racing historian, was told about Man o' War's defeat after the fact. "Most of the stories I heard came from my father, who embellished them to the benefit of Man o' War," Gilcoyne said. "So I'm not quite sure that some of those stories weren't a trifle fictional. But the idea was that he was beaten by the faulty start. If he had broken with the rest of the field, it never would have happened. Now, from what I've read since then in contemporary reports, he did get a bad start, but it wasn't the worst of the field. There were a couple that broke behind him."

Man o' War pictured with his connections, starting third from left, jockey John Loftus, owner Samuel D. Riddle, and trainer Louis Feustel.

The chart of the Sanford says exactly that, showing that Man o' War was fifth at the start, in front of both The Swimmer and Captain Alcock.

Golden Broom broke on top under Eddie Ambrose but was shadowed by Upset, ridden by Willie Knapp. Loftus had tried to compensate for Man o' War's poor start by saving ground on the inside of the turn, but that created an additional problem. Knapp felt confident in the stretch that Upset, not Golden Broom, was the stronger horse, and, sitting outside Golden Broom, saw no reason to rush by him with Man o' War on the inside behind Golden Broom.

"Man o' War didn't make his bid till we hit the turn, and then he churned up along the rail till his head bobbed into the corner of my eye," Knapp was quoted as saying in *Man o' War*.

"There he was tossing those 28-foot (sic) strides of his and tryin' to squeeze through on the inside of Golden Broom and

Upset. If I'd given so much as an inch, the race would've been as good as over, but jockeys don't ride that way. I could have breezed past Golden Broom any time I took my feet off the dashboard, but that would have let Man o' War out of his mouse trap and he'd have whooshed past us in half a dozen strides. When Johnny Loftus saw we weren't going to open up, there was nothing left for him but to pull up sharply and duck to the outside.

Upset's rider, Willie Knapp.

"That's what I'd been waiting for. That same moment I gunned Upset with my bat (whip)…Man o' War then had to come around and it cost him all of two lengths…he was chargin' like a jet plane, but Upset had just enough left to push his head down in front."

Actually, Upset's winning margin was half a length, according to the chart. *The New York Times* said: "Steadily Man o' War drew up on Upset. A hundred feet from the wire he was three-fourths of a length away. At the wire, he was a scant neck out of the first position and in another twenty feet he would have passed the Whitney horse."

The *Times* also noted that after the race "Man o' War received a fine ride from Loftus, who gave the colt every assistance within his power."

Yet less than a month later, on September 7, another *Times* story reported the opposite. "It was the fault of Loftus and not Man o' War that caused the colt to be left at the post," it read. "Man o' War could have won…but for a bungling ride in which Loftus found every pocket on the track."

A year later, both Loftus and Knapp were denied licenses by The Jockey Club with no explanation. Loftus had won the 1919 Triple Crown on Sir Barton and was the nation's leading money winner that year. Why he would have jeopardized his career at a time when he was on Man o' War, the best horse he had ever ridden, was a question never answered. Loftus and Knapp both became trainers. Knapp conditioned Exterminator for eight of his sixteen starts in 1921, including a one-length win carrying 130 pounds in the Merchants' and Citizens' Handicap and a walkover for his third of four consecutive victories in the Saratoga Cup.

To appreciate the enormity of Man o' War's loss in the 1919 Sanford one must be familiar with his amazing career and the incredible hold he had on the American public.

He took revenge on Upset in the Grand Union Hotel Stakes ten days later, then defeated him four more times: in the

Hopeful and Futurity at two, and in the Preakness and Travers at three.

Not only did Man o' War win twenty of his twenty-one starts, he always won by a minimum of a length. In the Lawrence Realization Stakes at Belmont Park, he defeated his only competitor, Hoodwink, by one hundred lengths while giving him ten pounds.

Five other times only a single horse entered against Man o' War. In the Jockey Club Gold Cup, which followed the Lawrence Realization, Man o' War defeated his lone opponent, Damask, by fifteen lengths.

Three other times, only two other horses raced against him.

Not only did he go off the favorite in every start, he was odds-on in every single one. His highest odds were .90-1 in the U.S. Hotel Stakes at Saratoga, his race before the Sanford.

In his final start, the mile and a quarter Kenilworth Park Gold Cup at Kenilworth Park in Ontario, Man o' War, then three, was challenged by four-year-old Sir Barton, winner of the Triple Crown the year before. Sent off at 1-20 in their match race while getting six pounds from Sir Barton, Man o' War won by seven lengths.

Man o' War retired with earnings of $249,465 and set world records winning the Dwyer Stakes at a mile and an eighth; the Belmont Stakes, then at a mile and three-eighths; and the Lawrence Realization at a mile and five-eighths. He set U.S. records taking the Jockey Club Gold Cup at a mile and a half and the Withers Stakes at one mile. He set track records for a mile and a quarter in the Kenilworth Park Gold Cup and in the Potomac Handicap at Havre de Grace in Maryland and equaled the mile and a quarter record at Saratoga of 2:01 4/5 when he won the 1920 Travers.

In his remarkable career, he won from five to thirteen furlongs (a mile and five-eighths) and on straight, clockwise, and counter-clockwise courses.

As a two-year-old, he won carrying 130 pounds six times; at three he won under 138 pounds in the Potomac Handicap.

In the 1947 volume of *American Race Horses*, legendary racing writer and historian Joe Palmer said of Man o' War, "He did not beat, he merely annihilated. He did not run to world records, he galloped to them. In 1920, he dominated racing as perhaps no athlete — not Tilden or Jones or Dempsey or Louis or Nurmi or Thorpe or any human athlete — had dominated his sport."

H.P. Whitney, owner of Upset.

John Hervey, another storied Turf writer and historian, wrote in the 1936 inaugural volume of *American Race Horses* that "Man o' War's renown is not confined to his own land. It has circled the globe and there is no doubt that he is the most widely famous horse in the world."

He still may be. Such is his legacy that in 2001 a question in "Trivia Quiz," a syndicated newspaper game, asked: "Upset was the only horse to upset this champion."

Indeed, Man o' War was proclaimed Horse of the Century by a panel of racing experts convened by *The Blood-Horse* magazine.

When Man o' War retired, owner Riddle was offered one million dollars for his horse. He declined. As a stallion, Man o' War sired sixty-four stakes winners, including Triple Crown winner War Admiral, and was visited by an estimated 1.5 million to more than three million fans who journeyed to Riddle's

Hinata Farm in Lexington, Kentucky, and then nearby Faraway Farms to see the legend.

Following Man o' War's death at the age of thirty on November 1, 1947, more than five hundred people attended his funeral, which was broadcast on radio. Man o' War was buried in a massive, lined casket. Joe Palmer wrote, "The American turf had lost, and perhaps would never have again, a single living symbol, a breathing, high-headed fiery horse which meant 'Racing!' to every man of racing, and to every wandering tourist from Portland, or San Diego or Athens, Ga."

They mourned a champion who lost just once in his life — at Saratoga. Years after he'd ridden Upset to win the 1919 Sanford Stakes, jockey Willie Knapp said, "Sure, I win the race all right — it was the biggest thrill of my life — but lookin, back at it now that's sure one horse which should of retired undefeated ... If I'd move over just an eyelash that day at Saratoga, he'd have beat me from here to Jalopy. Sometimes I'm sorry I didn't do it."

4

The Up-Roaring Twenties

Despite Prohibition it was easier getting a drink in Saratoga in the mid-1920s than it was getting a favorite home first in Saratoga's two oldest stakes, the Alabama and the Travers.

The Alabama, for three-year-old fillies, is run at the same testing mile and a quarter distance as the Travers for three-year-old colts. First run in 1872 and first won by August Belmont's Woodbine, the Alabama is the second oldest filly stakes in the country, predated only by the Ladies Handicap, which began in 1868.

In 1924 trainer Kay Spence targeted the Alabama as the major summer goal for Audley Farm Stable's Princess Doreen, a pretty bay who had an ugly pedigree, so to speak. Her grandsire was named Ugly.

A daughter of Spanish Prince II out of Lady Doreen, by Ogden, Princess Doreen was one of the remarkable mares in racing history, winning thirty-four of ninety-four starts at fifteen different racetracks and earning $174,745. Eighty-two of her starts were against males, including sixty-three of her final sixty-four races. Of those sixty-three, forty-eight were stakes and she won twelve of them.

She began her career at Saratoga against colts, finishing fourth in a field of nine on August 21, 1923. She was ninth in the Spinaway Stakes and then second by a nose in another maiden race against colts. After finishing fourth in the Tomboy Stakes and third in the Matron Stakes, she won her first race in her sixth start, also against colts. She made her first five starts in a span of twenty days, a display of durability she would show her entire career.

Princess Doreen arrived at Saratoga in the summer of 1924 as the nation's leading three-year-old filly. She'd won the Kentucky Oaks on the disqualification of the winner, Glide, and had also won the Coaching Club American Oaks at Belmont Park by two lengths "easing up," according to the chart.

Spence pointed Princess Doreen to the prestigious Alabama, and he prepped her for the stakes with a two-length handicap win over males as the even-money favorite.

Waiting for her in the Alabama was Belair Stud's Priscilla

Leading three-year-old filly in 1924, Princess Doreen fell prey to Saratoga in that year's Alabama.

Ruley, a daughter of Ambassador IV, who had won the Gazelle Handicap at Aqueduct and finished third behind Princess Doreen in the Coaching Club American Oaks. Others in the field were Latonia Oaks winner Befuddle, Initiate, Whetstone, Nellie Kelly, and Sunayr.

Rain pelted Saratoga Race Course from early morning until early afternoon the day of the Alabama, leaving the track in such condition that the stewards allowed owners to scratch horses without paying the usual penalty. Accordingly, forty-two of the eighty-eight horses entered overnight were declared out.

Only Princess Doreen, Priscilla Ruley, and Sunayr were left in the Alabama. Princess Doreen was sent off as the 2-5 favorite despite carrying 126 pounds, nine more than the other two fillies. Although Princess Doreen broke first, Priscilla Ruley quickly took over and managed to keep the favorite at bay virtually the entire distance, winning by a length.

Princess Doreen bounced back to win three more stakes that year and was named 1924 co-champion three-year-old filly with Nellie Morse. She earned champion older female honors the next two years. Racing against males as a five-year-old at Saratoga, she won the 1926 Saratoga Handicap by four lengths at 20-1; was fourth by four and a half lengths to Flagstaff as the 3-2 favorite in the Merchants' and Citizens' Handicap; and was third in the Saratoga Cup by seven lengths at 7-1 behind Espino and Display.

She retired as the richest filly up to that time.

In her defeat in the 1924 Alabama, Princess Doreen at least finished second in her three-horse field. Two years later, a future three-year-old filly champion, Edith Cavell, ran dead last in a field of six as the 6-5 favorite.

Walter M. Jeffords' Edith Cavell was a daughter of Man o' War—The Nurse, by Yankee. The bay filly, named for the martyred English nurse executed by the Germans during World War

Edith Cavell won the 1926 Coaching Club American Oaks (above) but was a badly beaten favorite in the Alabama.

I for helping Allied soldiers escape from behind enemy lines, had moved to the head of the three-year-old filly division with victories over W.R. Coe's Black Maria in both the Coaching Club American Oaks and Latonia Oaks. Earlier that year, Black Maria — not the same Black Maria who once won five four-mile heats in a single day in 1832 — had been a distant third to Harry Payne Whitney's Rapture in the Pimlico Oaks.

Ruthenia, Tattling, and Laura Dianti joined those three fillies in the 1926 Alabama. Black Maria was the 5-2 second choice; Rapture, the 12-1 fifth choice. Black Maria and Edith Cavell each carried 126 pounds, two more than Rapture.

Black Maria took control of the mile and a quarter race immediately, but was confronted on the first turn by Edith Cavell, who rushed up the inside. On the backstretch, Black Maria put Edith Cavell away, but did not have enough left to hold off Rapture, who won by two lengths under Pony McAtee. Ruthenia was third, ten lengths behind Black Maria, with Tattling and Laura Dianti straggling in. You needed a telescope to find Edith Cavell.

In his Alabama story in *The New York Times*, Henry Ilsley noted, "Rapture ran a brilliant race and simply rewarded the patience of Trainer James Rowe, Sr., who brought the Pimlico Oaks winner back fit to run the race of her career."

Tom Thorp, a writer for the Albany *Times Union*, examined the rash of defeats of favorites in an article that appeared under the following headline:

"Form Upsets And Poor Riding
Cause Talk At Spa
FAVORITES FINISH IN REAR"

Thorp wrote: "Many familiar faces are absent here today. The many upsets of the past few days have cut the list of players down considerably. The harvest that the oralists enjoyed through the poor running of many favorites has come from the public.

"The shrewd operators were well able to safeguard themselves. It is the unsuspecting public, those who pay the daily toll at the entrance gates, that had its bankroll picked by the disgraceful

Black Maria, co-champion three-year-old filly in 1926, lost the Alabama to longshot Rapture.

running of more than one supposedly reliable favorite."

Thorp was particularly upset that defeated Alabama favorite Edith Cavell had even been entered, calling it little short of scandalous: "This daughter of Man o' War never should have been sent to the post in that race. She was known to be 'short' by her trainer. The fact that she was a public choice should have made her owner withdraw her when he knew that she was not in proper physical condition to run the race that she was expected to show. That she was sent to the post was a direct violation of the trust that the public places in racing. They expect to receive at least honest treatment from owners who profess to be big class sportsmen."

Of course, nobody held a gun to people's heads to bet her. And, as history would reveal repeatedly, Edith Cavell was hardly alone as a disappointing heavy stakes favorite at Saratoga. Despite their mutual defeat in the Alabama, Edith Cavell and Black Maria were named 1926 co-champion three-year-old fillies. Black Maria was subsequently named 1927 and 1928 champion older female. One of her 1928 victories was in the Whitney Handicap over males.

It took all of four days after a daughter of Man o' War lost the Alabama for a soon-to-be-champion son of Man o' War to go down in the Travers Stakes — to another son of Man o' War.

THE
SARATOGA ASSOCIATION
For the improvement
of the
Breed of Horses

So read the cover of the August 14, 1926, "Programme" that offered the North American Steeplechase, the Spinaway, and Travers on the fourteenth day of the meet. The program reminded one and all that minors, dogs, and "pet animals of any kind" were not permitted on the grounds.

Fans traveling to the track from the state capital could catch the Delaware & Hudson Company's Saturday Special Train, which left Albany at 1:15, arrived in Saratoga at 2:15, and left for home at 6:15 after the races. A round-trip ticket cost $1.85. William Noller's Troy City Band provided the music, with renditions of everything from the "American Exultant" March to the overture to the "Old Timers Waltz."

Post time was 3 p.m. for a six-race card featuring the Travers with a guaranteed cash value of $15,000. A record crowd of 25,000 jammed Saratoga to see a showdown among Crusader, Boot to Boot, Pompey, Display, and Mars, forcing track president R.T. Wilson Jr. to open the infield to spectators. "They came from all directions in all sorts of conveyances," Henry Ilsley wrote in *The New York Times*. "They jammed the grandstand to suffocation, the free field was a solid mass of humanity, the lawns could hold no more. (Caterer) Harry Stevens packed his tables so closely on the clubhouse plaza, that it was hardly possible to move between them. Then the ladies insisted on more service, and he routed the men out of the lower plaza and served the ladies there, a thing unprecedented."

In the deeply contentious Travers field, Crusader seemed the one to beat. Sam Riddle's three-year-old homebred chestnut colt was from the second crop of Man o' War and out of the Star Shoot mare Star Fancy.

Crusader was not so highly regarded when he began his career the year before at Havre de Grace in Maryland. On April 16, 1925, Crusader went off at 39-1 in a maiden field of fourteen and finished eighth by seventeen lengths. He improved somewhat to be seventh in his second career start at Pimlico. Then he kept improving, winning his third career start by a head.

As a three-year-old, he followed a pair of seconds with victories in the Suburban Handicap by five lengths, the Belmont Stakes by one length, the Dwyer Stakes by a nose, and the Cincinnati Derby by three lengths.

He came into the Travers facing several top-class competitors, including Pompey, the 1925 two-year-old champion off his victories in the Hopeful Stakes and Belmont Futurity; the American and Ohio derbys winner Boot to Boot; Preakness winner Display; and the respective second- and third-place finishers in the Preakness, Blondin and Mars, the latter another son of Man o' War.

Trained by George Conway and ridden by Earl Sande, Crusader went to post as the 4-5 favorite after working the Travers distance of a mile and a quarter in 2:09, faster than Dangerous' winning time in the 1925 Travers. With a victory in the Midsummer Derby, Crusader would match his famous sire, winner of the Travers six years earlier.

Unfortunately, another of Man o' War's Saratoga performances had greater relevance: his historic loss in the Sanford .

Exactly seven years and one week after Man o' War's poor-starting defeat in the 1919 Sanford, Crusader was "practically left" at the starting gate, according to *The New York Times.* "It was most unfortunate that the running of the Travers was marred by a miserable start, in which Crusader, undoubtedly many pounds the best of his field, had not a chance. He was practically left at the post, made up a tremendous amount of ground to come to second position in the running only to tire by his magnificent effort under top impost of 129 pounds."

Crusader finished fourth by four and a half lengths.

Mars, who had started "none too well" himself, won by one and a half lengths at odds of 7-1 over Pompey and Display. All three carried 123 pounds, six pounds less than Crusader. Mars went on to win the 1926 Saranac Stakes and, as a four-year-old in 1927, the Dixie Handicap.

Crusader came back to win five of his next seven starts,

including the Jockey Club Gold Cup, and was named 1926 Horse of the Year and champion three-year-old colt. He raced until he was five years old, compiling a record of eighteen wins in forty-two career starts including losses in his final nine races. He was no Man o' War, but neither was any other horse.

That Was The Week That Was

The news at Saratoga from August 11 through August 18, 1928, was upsetting, and it wasn't confined to equine performances.

For openers, the first running of the Whitney Handicap produced a mild surprise when five-year-old Black Maria, the 3-2 second choice in a field of four, edged 9-10 favorite Chance Shot by three-quarters of a length. Then, in the Hermis Handicap, Tantivy, the 6-1 second choice in a field of seven, blew away even-money favorite Misstep, the Kentucky Derby runner-up, by five lengths.

That was a surprise, but not the biggest shock of the week. On the front page of its sports section, *The New York Times* on August 17 ran this item about the city famous for its racetrack and casinos:

"Shirt Sleeves Banned at Spa; The Attire Called 'Improper' "

"Shirt sleeves won't do at Saratoga. This was demonstrated this afternoon when three trainers were fined $10 each for permitting their attendants to appear on the race course in front of the judges' stand in 'improper' attire. The trainers were E.A. Burke, Matt Brady and James Healy, who had horses in the steeplechase. The attendants came on the track to lead back the horses after unsaddling."

Saratoga officials let the races continue that day, but chalk

Petee-Wrack's victory in the 1928 Travers came at the expense of Kentucky Derby winner Reigh Count, who finished last.

players may have wished otherwise. In the Grab Bag Handicap, odds-on favorite Shipmaster was second by half a length to 20-1 Lycidas. Then, in the sixth and final race, odds-on favorite Royal Stranger lost by a nose to longshot Verdi. "Form players were jolted when Royal Stranger went down to defeat," Bryan Field wrote in the *Times*.

Then came the Travers, hailed as "the greatest horse race of the year in the East," matching Mrs. John D. Hertz's Reigh Count and Harry Payne Whitney's Victorian.

As a two-year-old in 1927, Reigh Count had won the Futurity Stakes at Belmont Park and the Kentucky Jockey Club Stakes. The following spring he won the Kentucky Derby and the Miller Revival and would go on to win the Lawrence Realization and the Jockey Club Gold Cup over older horses Chance Shot and Display to be named 1928 champion three-year-old colt and Horse of the Year.

But Reigh Count was not the favorite in the 1928 Travers, despite a four-race winning streak. That role belonged to Preakness, Withers, Shevlin, and Champlain stakes winner

Victorian, who was sent off at 6-5 off three straight wins. Reigh Count went off at 7-5.

A prescient preview of the Travers in the *Times* noted: "Many famous horses have won in the past, yet veteran horsemen are of the opinion that tomorrow's revival will be the greatest of all. Despite the great favor in which Reigh Count and Victorian are held, it is not at all unlikely that both will be defeated. Misstep, second to Reigh Count in the Kentucky Derby and winner of the Fairmount Derby, cannot be counted out. Nor can Sun Edwin or Petee-Wrack."

Reigh Count, Victorian, and Misstep each carried 126 pounds, nine more than the lightweight in the field of seven, Petee-Wrack. Misstep, Sortie, and Diavolo all scratched when the track came up muddy, leaving a Travers field of just four. J.R. Macomber's Petee-Wrack was 8-1 and Sun Edwin 12-1. The small field allowed no show wagering.

Petee-Wrack, trained by Willie Booth, was sharp and had won twice at Saratoga in the previous ten days over softer competition. Earlier in the year he had finished fourteenth behind Reigh Count in the Kentucky Derby and seventeenth behind Victorian in the Preakness. By Wrack out of Marguerite, Petee-Wrack had a mud pedigree. But Reigh Count had won the Kentucky Derby on a muddy track and Victorian had won on wet tracks, too.

Jockey Laverne Fator put Victorian on the lead immediately and Sun Edwin took over second from Petee-Wrack, ridden by Steve O'Donnell. Reigh Count was rating in last under Chick Lang.

Heading into the far turn, Petee-Wrack passed Sun Edwin and went after Victorian. "A gasp went up from the crowd followed by an uproar as it was seen that Petee-Wrack was not giving ground but making up on Victorian," Bryan Field wrote in the *Times*.

Petee-Wrack took over the lead and held off Victorian by a length. Sun Edwin was another two lengths back in third and

Reigh Count a well-beaten last. The chart noted, "Reigh Count trailed the field for the entire trip, but had no mishap."

The same could not be said for those who backed him.

Two years later Petee-Wrack's half brother, Gallant Fox, would attempt to add the Travers Stakes to his Triple Crown.

5

Jim Who?

There seemed to be more than three thousand miles separating Gallant Fox and Jim Dandy, two three-year-old colts racing on opposite sides of North America in the summer of 1930.

In the East, Gallant Fox stood on the cusp of greatness following his victories in the Preakness, Kentucky Derby, and Belmont Stakes, run in that order that year. He had become just the second horse to win those three races, following Sir Barton in 1919. Gallant Fox's victories, though, inspired the designation of a Triple Crown.

Jim Dandy scored a shocking upset in the 1930 Travers Stakes.

Jim Dandy toiled in relative obscurity at Agua Caliente, a racetrack in Tijuana, Mexico. His lone brush with fame before the 1930 Travers happened the year before when he won the Grand Union Hotel Stakes at Saratoga at 50-1 on a heavy track. He'd won just one prior race, a maiden race at Churchill Downs a week before the 1929 Kentucky Derby. He finished his two-year-old season with just those two wins in nine starts, and he continued losing right through his three-year-old season. He would finish his career with just seven victories in 141 starts.

In 1930 Jim Dandy would win just one of twenty starts.

In 1930 Gallant Fox would lose just one of ten starts.

That they inflicted their aberrations on each other on the same afternoon at Saratoga is racing legend. That Jim Dandy, sent off at 100-1 in the 1930 Travers, beat Gallant Fox, the 1-2 favorite, by eight lengths only makes that race more remarkable.

That one afternoon will live forever in racing lore, for Gallant

Gallant Fox wearing the Kentucky Derby roses.

Fox had captured the attention of the nation. Maybe American sports fans, struggling through the Depression in 1930, wanted a hero. Maybe they wanted another Man o' War.

What they got was the Fox from Belair.

Gallant Fox was a homebred of William Woodward's Belair Stud. The colt was part of the first American crop of the imported French stallion Sir Gallahad III, who'd been brought to this country by a syndicate of Woodward, Arthur B. Hancock, Wall Street broker Robert Fairburn, and Marshall Field, a Chicago department-store tycoon. Sir Gallahad III, purchased for $125,000, stood his first season at Hancock's majestic Claiborne Farm near Paris, Kentucky, in 1926, and would be the nation's leading sire four times, 1930, '33, '34, and '40.

As a member of the syndicate, Woodward was entitled to breed at least one of his mares to Sir Gallahad III every year. That first year, 1926, Woodward bred Marguerite, an English-bred mare by Celt. He'd purchased her as a yearling for $4,700, and she had raced just once, finishing last after wrenching her back during the race. She joined the Woodward broodmares and immediately started an illustrious career. Her first foal, born in 1925, was Petee-Wrack, a son of Wrack, who would win the 1928 Travers.

On March 23, 1927, Marguerite foaled a bright bay colt with a wide white blaze. The colt had too much white around the pupil of one of his eyes, a characteristic that would later be described in his racing days as an "evil eye" that supposedly struck fear in his vanquished opponents.

If he had such power, he waited a year to show it. As a two-year-old in the patient hands of legendary Hall of Fame trainer Sunny Jim Fitzsimmons, Gallant Fox won only two of seven starts, the Flash Stakes at Saratoga and, in his final start in 1929, the Junior Champion Stakes at Aqueduct. In the rich Futurity Stakes at Belmont Park, Gallant Fox had finished third by three lengths at 20-1 to Harry Payne Whitney's Whichone. A son of Chicle, Whichone also captured the Champagne and Saratoga Special, finished second to stablemate Boojum in the Hopeful Stakes, and was named champion two-year-old male. But knee problems prevented him from competing in the spring of his three-year-old season.

Fitzsimmons knew he had a talented, late-developing colt, one with incredible curiosity, a characteristic that popped up continually after Gallant Fox passed horses during races and then slowed to look at the surroundings. Thus, he raced in almost completely cut away blinkers. "So long as he had competition, he would run like the wind," Fitzsimmons once said. "But as soon as he whipped everybody and got the lead, he would slow to a walk. He was a fire eater when he had the competition, though."

Fitzsimmons would use two, and sometimes even three, different horses in relays to work with the Fox. And mulling over Gallant Fox's upcoming three-year-old season, Fitzsimmons decided to change jockeys again.

James Burke, Danny McAuliffe, and Johnny Maiben had ridden the Fox at two. Fitzsimmons wanted the legendary Earl Sande, who had retired in 1928 and become a trainer after leading the nation in earnings in 1921 and 1927. Sande was convinced to come out of retirement for ten percent of Gallant Fox's three-year-old earnings instead of his usual $1,500-a-month retainer. Since Gallant Fox went on to win $308,270 at three, Sande earned $30,827 instead of the $9,000 he would have received for Gallant Fox's six-month campaign.

To say Sande fit Gallant Fox would be an understatement. In their first race together, the 1930 Wood Memorial at Aqueduct, Gallant Fox drew off to a four-length win over Crack Brigade as the 8-5 favorite.

Gallant Fox was even-money in a field of eleven in his next start, the Preakness, and was in trouble almost the entire way.

After being fenced in on the rail, Sande was forced to take Gallant Fox up sharply on the clubhouse turn. Sande then had to weave the Fox through traffic on the backstretch to advance from eighth to third. Crack Brigade looked home free, but the Fox ran him down late, winning by three-quarters of a length.

Just eight days later, the Fox won the Kentucky Derby by two lengths as the 1.19-1 favorite.

That set up a rematch in the Belmont Stakes June 7 between the Fox and Whichone, who was made the 7-10 favorite off his victory in the Withers. Gallant Fox was 8-5 in the field of just four that contested the stakes on a track described as "greasy" in the chart and officially labeled "good."

For the first time in his career, the Fox took the lead immediately. When Whichone, taken back to last by his jockey Raymond "Sonny" Workman, got within one length of him at the top of the stretch, the Fox scampered away to a surprisingly easy three-length victory over his rival. He did so by running the final quarter in a sparkling :24 3/5 to complete the mile and a half in 2:31 3/5, three-fifths of a second faster than Crusader's 1926 stakes record, though it should be noted that the 1930 Belmont Stakes was only the fifth one conducted at a mile and a half.

Fitzsimmons did not let the Fox rest on his laurels. Exactly three weeks after his Belmont Stakes victory, the Fox won the Dwyer Stakes by a length and a half at Aqueduct as the .13-1 favorite. Two weeks after that was the Arlington Classic at Arlington Park. The Fox won by just a neck over Gallant Knight as the .32-1 favorite, and Fitzsimmons decided to rest him until the August 16 Travers.

Whichone, meanwhile, took the Ballot Handicap, Saranac Stakes, and Whitney Stakes, named for Harry Payne Whitney's brother Payne. Whichone was especially impressive winning the Whitney by four lengths as the 1-10 favorite in a field of just three over Marine, a four-year-old who had won the Saratoga Handicap in his last start. "Whichone was hardly extended at any time," Joe Mahar wrote in the Albany *Times Union*.

Whichone's Whitney victory whetted the appetite of race fans everywhere for the rubber match between Whichone and the Fox in the Travers to resolve their 1-1 career record against each other.

In anticipation of the Travers, *The New York Times* magazine ran a lengthy feature on Gallant Fox under the headlines:

"GALLANT FOX RANKS WITH A KINGLY HOST"

"Race Horse With 'Evil Eye' and Moody Temperament Faces Greatest Test At Saratoga Track Saturday"

In his story, Bryan Field noted Gallant Fox's victories in the Wood Memorial, Preakness, Kentucky Derby, Belmont, and Arlington Classic, and concluded, "If he sweeps the field at Saratoga next Saturday he will claim a distinction of which not even the great Man o' War can boast."

Who was thinking about Jim Dandy?

The chestnut son of Jim Gaffney—Thunderbird, by Star Shoot, was bred and initially owned by W.S. Dudley. Jim Dandy broke his maiden in his second start at Churchill Downs, taking the four and a half-furlong race by one and a half lengths on a fast track and paying $40.20 to win.

In a story about Jim Dandy in the July/August 2000 issue of *The Backstretch* magazine, Debra Ginsburg wrote:

"Jim Dandy's maiden victory attracted the attention of trainer John B. McKee, who was on a buying trip to round up racing prospects for his young California client, Chaffee Earl.

Earl had inherited a family oil fortune on his 21st birthday
and sent McKee east with a blank check to buy what pleased
him — and Jim Dandy was one two-year-old that pleased him
greatly. With unlimited resources behind him, McKee did not
balk at the $25,000 price tag Dudley was asking for the colt."

It didn't seem like a bad deal after Jim Dandy pulled off his
shocking upset in the 1929 Grand Union Hotel Stakes at
Saratoga. Sent off under Johnny Maiben as the longest shot in
a field of eleven, Jim Dandy broke tenth, made steady progress
in the six-furlong race, moved up on the leaders three-wide
around the turn, and prevailed by a neck over Mokatam.
Caruso, the 4-5 favorite off his length and a half win over
Gallant Fox in the United States Hotel Stakes three weeks earlier, was third. Ironically, Whichone had been entered in the
Grand Union Hotel Stakes, but scratched. In winning the
Grand Union Hotel Stakes, Jim Dandy earned $13,725, more
than half his purchase price.

And then, to most racing fans, he disappeared.

Racing that winter at Agua Caliente just over the Mexican
border, Jim Dandy did little to distinguish himself, finishing
third once and dumping his rider at the start of the George
Washington Handicap. In his last start at Agua Caliente, Jim
Dandy received thirty-three pounds from a horse named
Brown Wisdom and finished several lengths behind him.

McKee was not discouraged and shipped Jim Dandy to
Tanforan, California, near San Francisco, for a deserved rest
with Naishapur, who had finished second to Clyde Van Dusen
in the 1929 Kentucky Derby.

McKee decided to ship both horses to Saratoga, and they
traveled first class. Landon Manning writes in his book, *The
Noble Animals*:

"Everything possible was done to assure that Jim Dandy and
Naishapur had a comfortable and even luxurious trip to
Saratoga. The two shared a car designed to carry 12 horses.

And to reach Saratoga in the shortest possible time, railroad officials were persuaded to hook Jim Dandy's car to The Californian, the crack Santa Fe Flyer, on the run from San Francisco to Chicago. As Jim Dandy boarded the train, McKee told Max A. Podiech, special passenger agent for Atchison, Topeka and Santa Fe Railroad, 'Now you see the winner of the Travers. He will beat them all whether the track is fast or muddy.' "

Jim Dandy gave no indication that he'd back up McKee's prediction, finishing last in an overnight handicap at Saratoga on August 8, eight days before the 1930 Travers. Yet his jockey, Frank Baker, who would become a trainer after retiring, told Manning years later that he felt he had a chance in the Travers: "Jim Dandy was a helluva colt, but he had what we call egg-shell feet, the walls being very thin, so that when the track was hard, it hurt him to run. He was really only able to run on a muddy track."

Actually, it was a possibility that Jim Dandy wouldn't even race in the 1930 Travers. Both he and Sun Falcon had also been entered in the race preceding the Travers, the Waterboy Handicap. Both wound up in the Travers, though Caruso, the

Gallant Fox was hopelessly beaten in the stretch.

58

only other horse entered to challenge Gallant Fox and Whichone in the Travers, would scratch.

In assessing the Travers field, the Albany *Times Union* reported: "Sun Falcon and Jim Dandy will probably scratch out to enter the preceding race where they are much better treated in the weights."

Despite McKee's contention of Jim Dandy's abilities to handle a dry or wet track, the weather and track condition would decide whether Jim Dandy would run in the Waterboy Handicap or the Travers.

"The weather had been good and the track was in great condition up until Friday night late, and it rained during the night and early Saturday morning, which changed the track into a sea of gumbo," noted Tom Gilcoyne, the historian of the National Museum of Racing and Hall of Fame in Saratoga. "Saratoga mud in those days was famous. A horse could almost get his foot stuck in it. It was so tough. When it came up gumbo, Jim Dandy was a late scratch from the other race. They knew that Jim Dandy was at his best on the worst kind of an off track, because he had won the Grand Union Hotel Stakes the year before against horses he could never have beaten in other circumstances. So they took their chances in the Travers."

How big was the 1930 Travers Stakes? Well, national radio covered it live, one of the first live national broadcasts of a horse race, with famed broadcasters Clem McCarthy doing the honors. New York Governor Franklin Delano Roosevelt and his wife, Eleanor, attended. Gene Tunney, the great boxer, made it. So did as many as 50,000 others, an estimate made by the *New York Herald-Tribune. The New York Times* estimated 30,000; the Albany *Times Union*, 35,000.

One of the fans was the National Museum of Racing's Gilcoyne, then fourteen, who went to the Travers with his dad. Gilcoyne had a rooting interest. "I was very much a Whichone fan," he said. "Not that I was against Gallant Fox, but I had thought this other horse was brought up to the Travers on a series of three good wins. He won against older horses in the Whitney. So I was watching for him."

Edward Hotaling wrote in his book *They're Off! Horse Racing at Saratoga* that the traffic was so bad into the track, that fans "abandoned motor cars two miles away. For the first time at Saratoga, Harry M. Stevens ran out of clam chowder, and there were so many requests for tables he had to serve lunch on the top deck of the clubhouse."

Then the weather began to clear. "By the time they got to the main race, whatever storm that had hit us had passed, and the weather wasn't bad at all," Gilcoyne said. He watched the race from in front of the grandstand.

The post position draw had given the rail to Sun Falcon. Immediately outside him were Jim Dandy, Whichone, and Gallant Fox, who was made the 1-2 favorite. Whichone was 8-5, Sun Falcon 30-1, and Jim Dandy 100-1 under Baker. Of the four, Sun Falcon would never get involved in the race.

Sonny Workman, riding Whichone, made certain there would be no replay of the Belmont Stakes in which he had tried unsuccessfully to catch Gallant Fox from behind. He gunned Whichone to the lead. And Sande sent the Fox with him. "And they ran the first mile as if there wasn't anybody else there, as if it was a match race," Gilcoyne said.

Bryan Field described the Travers in *The New York Times*:

"It was clear that Workman had been given instructions to run Gallant Fox off his feet. But he couldn't do it. Going around the bend, he was a neck or perhaps half a length to the good, but this was due as much to his shorter course along the rail as to any superior speed on the part of Whichone.

"In the first furlong of the backstretch run, Gallant Fox drew even. In the second furlong he went ahead. In the third furlong came the high point of the race. Going into the far turn, Whichone again closed on Gallant Fox and again got his head in front. Many thought Gallant Fox was beaten, but he was far from that. On he came, still covering ground on the outside, and he engaged Whichone on even terms."

The *New York Herald-Tribune* would describe their battle as "fit for the Gods of Sports."

But there was a caveat, a rather important one. Sande was renown for his trick of locking legs with a rival jockey if he got inside and close to him, and Workman was intent on keeping Sande and Gallant Fox as far outside on the far turn as he could. But the tiring Whichone took that turn wide, forcing the Fox even farther out.

Gilcoyne, watching their battle intently, lost the horses when they went into the turn because of the immense crowd, but coming out of the turn, he saw a horse on the inside in the lead. "Notice the colors of the silks," Gilcoyne said seventy years later. "Jim Dandy is white with blue diamonds. And Whichone is light blue. So you could mistake the colors, at

Hugh Miller

Whichone, a champion two-year-old in 1929, finished third in the 1930 Travers and suffered a bowed tendon.

least you could for an instant. I saw blue drawing clear, and I said to myself, 'Whichone's got it.' And then, in a second or two, I knew it wasn't Whichone. And it wasn't Gallant Fox. And I couldn't believe it was Jim Dandy. By that time, he had opened up five or six lengths and was just galloping along and continued to do so."

Jim Dandy had shot through the gaping hole on the inside of Whichone and the Fox to take command. He drifted out to the middle of the track after clearing them, but it didn't matter as Baker peeked once over each shoulder to make sure he was clear. He was — by eight lengths. "I was confident of winning the race in the backstretch," Baker said in Manning's book. "The colt ran nice and easy on the inside all the way. I was just galloping in the final furlong when I knew I had the race won."

Gallant Fox was a clear second, six lengths in front of Whichone, who had bowed a tendon. Workman said after the race that he felt Whichone's leg give way at the three-sixteenths pole. "He had gone lame in the running, but like a true thoroughbred had finished out the mile and a quarter," Field wrote in *The New York Times*. In doing so, Whichone finished third, three lengths ahead of Sun Falcon, to conclude his outstanding career with ten wins, two seconds, and one third in fourteen starts.

Sande was visibly shaken by Gallant Fox's defeat. "I'm sorry, more than you can imagine, for it hurts to lose on such a great horse," he told reporters.

Gallant Fox and Sande would not lose again, taking the Saratoga Cup against older horses by a length and a half, the Lawrence Realization at Belmont Park by a head, and the Jockey Club Gold Cup over older horses by three lengths at odds of .04-1. He had won ten of his final eleven races with one second and was named 1930 champion three-year-old colt and Horse of the Year.

Retired to stud, Gallant Fox became the only Triple Crown winner to sire a Triple Crown winner when Omaha, a member of his first crop, won the Derby, Preakness, and Belmont Stakes in 1935.

Jim Dandy did not win another race in 1930. "They took him to Havre de Grace (following the Saratoga meeting) and raced him on a hard track, so that his feet broke down to the point where his racing career was virtually finished," Baker said in Manning's book.

Yet Jim Dandy ran eight subsequent seasons, winning four of 112 starts. His career earnings of $49,570 were built on two stakes races at Saratoga, one of them so memorable that the key prep race at Saratoga for the Travers remains the grade II Jim Dandy Stakes (which was upgraded to grade I in 2001). First run in 1964, the mile and an eighth race has been won by such stars as Arts and Letters, Tentam, Affirmed, Private Account, Conquistador Cielo, Stephan's Odyssey, Fly So Free,

Jim Dandy after his first and only victory of 1930.

Louis Quatorze, Awesome Again, and Favorite Trick.

For his book, Manning asked Gallant Fox's trainer, Sunny Jim Fitzsimmons, about Jim Dandy's Travers. Fitzsimmons responded: "It was a fluke victory, by a fluke horse, who had no business in the race. Sonny Workman kept coming out on Gallant Fox, carrying him a sixteenth of a mile across the track on the far turn."

Damon Runyon offered his interpretation in the *New York American* the day after the 1930 Travers: "You only dream the thing that happened here this afternoon."

6

Like Father, Like Son?

Six years after Gallant Fox's stunning loss in the 1930 Travers, William Woodward's Belair Stud, trainer Sunny Jim Fitzsimmons, and a son of Gallant Fox named Granville were on the winning side of a Saratoga stakes upset.

Granville, out of Gravia by Sarmatian, mirrored his father. Gallant Fox had won two of seven starts as a two-year-old and had then become a champion at three. Granville won just one of seven starts as a juvenile — losing his first two starts at Saratoga — then blossomed at three and was named champion three-year-old colt and Horse of the Year in 1936, when the awards were officially inaugurated.

Granville relished a fight and was involved in seven photo finishes in a brief eighteen-race career of four allowance and fourteen stakes races.

As a two-year-old, he was third by a head in the Babylon Handicap at Aqueduct. At three he gave his connections one thrill after another.

Under a new rider, Jimmy Stout, Granville won his 1936 three-year-old debut in allowance company at Jamaica Racetrack by five lengths. The Wood Memorial was next, and Granville led late before being beaten by a nose by Teufel, who carried five pounds less. That set up Granville for the Kentucky Derby, but a horse forced into him during a rough

The Blood-Horse

Handicap heavyweight Discovery couldn't handle the younger Granville in the Saratoga Cup.

start caused Granville to stumble and lose his rider. As if that weren't hard enough to take, Granville then lost the Preakness by a nose to Kentucky Derby winner Bold Venture and the Suburban Handicap by a nose to Firethorn.

The next time, Granville got the photo right, taking the Belmont Stakes by a nose over Mr. Bones. He beat Mr. Bones again by two and a half lengths to win the Arlington Classic.

Granville headed for Saratoga, where he had finished third and second in his first two starts the year before. At three he won the Kenner Stakes by a neck over Memory Book, carrying three pounds less, and the Travers by a head over Sun Teddy, while spotting him five pounds over a muddy track.

That gave Granville a four-race winning streak, yet he would be an underdog in the mile and three-quarters Saratoga Cup against the seasoned veteran Discovery, even though the youngster would be getting ten pounds from him, on the closing day of the 1936 meet. There were no other entries. In previewing the race in *The New York Times*, Bryan Field wrote, "There are few who give Granville more than an outside chance."

Here's why: Alfred Gwynne Vanderbilt's five-year-old colt Discovery, the 1935 Horse of the Year, had been on a tear for nearly a year and a half, winning seventeen of twenty-five races and losing only to horses he had conceded great weight to, from fourteen to an ungodly forty-three pounds. The latter was the weight differential in his fifth-place finish to winner Esposa in the 1936 Merchants' and Citizens' Handicap at Saratoga.

Discovery atoned in grand fashion, winning his next start, the Whitney Handicap, for the third straight year. In 1934 he won his first Whitney by ten lengths as the 1-3 favorite. In 1935 he won by two lengths as the 1-10 choice. And in 1936 at 1-5, he beat Esposa by ten lengths while being eased. The difference from the Merchants' and Citizens' Handicap? In the Whitney, Discovery carried only 126 pounds and Esposa 121.

So with Discovery carrying 126 pounds on a sloppy track in the Saratoga Cup to Granville's 118, Discovery was the 2-5 favorite; Granville 9-5. Discovery had won two prior starts on sloppy tracks easily. Granville had won the Travers on a muddy track, but never raced on a sloppy course. Muddy tracks are deeper and provide some horses better traction than on sloppy tracks, which have more suface water.

Granville thrived on the slop. In sixteen prior races, Granville had raced on the lead just once, winning an allowance race at Jamaica. In the Saratoga Cup, he broke on top under Stout and stayed there. Discovery's jockey, Jean Bejshak, did not panic. "In the first quarter, he (Granville) opened three lengths and it was clear that Jean Bejshak aboard Discovery was content to let him do it," Field wrote in the *Times*.

Bejshak sent Discovery after Granville on the clubhouse turn, cutting Granville's lead to one length before the latter opened up again. Approaching the far turn, Discovery took another run at Granville, getting within a length of him before Granville again spurted clear. Bejshak tried coaxing a third try, but Granville was long gone, scampering home an eight-length winner.

Granville raced just once more, taking the Lawrence Realization at Belmont Park by two lengths at odds of .13-1. That gave him a record of seven wins and three seconds by a nose in eleven starts as a three-year-old, the lone poor performance when he lost his rider in the Derby. Granville was named 1936 Horse of the Year but shared co-champion three-year-old colt honors with Bold Venture.

After losing the Saratoga Cup, Discovery lost the Narragansett Special by a head at 3-2 to Rosemont while giving him nine pounds. Discovery's final start was on a sloppy track in the Havre de Grace Handicap. For the twenty-seventh consecutive time, Discovery went off the favorite, this time 3-5, but finished fifth to Roman Soldier, who, under 118, carried ten pounds less. Regardless, Discovery was named champion handicap horse. He had twenty-seven wins, ten seconds, and ten thirds to show for sixty-three career starts. Twelve of them came at Saratoga, where he had eight wins, a second, two thirds, and a fifth.

Discovery was not the only Horse of the Year or future Horse of the Year to lose or have a close call at Saratoga from the mid-1930s through the early 1940s.

Seabiscuit, the 1938 Horse of the Year, lost twice at the Spa as a two-year-old, then won his two Saratoga starts at three, the Mohawk Claiming Stakes and a handicap.

Challedon, the 1939 and 1940 Horse of the Year, narrowly avoided a high-profile Saratoga loss, taking the 1940 Whitney Handicap by a nose.

Calumet Farm's Whirlaway, fated to be the 1941 and 1942 Horse of the Year, lost the Grand Union Hotel Stakes as the 6-5 favorite in a field of six.

In two prior starts at Saratoga, Whirlaway had finished second by a neck to Attention in the United States Hotel Stakes and first by a length and a half over New World in the Saratoga Special. New World took revenge in the Grand Union, beating Whirlaway by a length and a half. The chart noted that Whirlaway, ridden by Johnny Longden, "trailed the field to the far turn, then began to move up, was caught in close quarters in the stretch and closed fast when clear."

Whirlaway won the Hopeful Stakes by a length over Attention seven days later. In 1941 Whirlaway won not only the Triple Crown but the Travers as well, and remains the only horse to do both, though 1978 Triple Crown winner Affirmed

Granville (above) was on the winning side of a Saratoga upset unlike his sire, Gallant Fox.

deserves an asterisk. He finished first in the 1978 Travers but was disqualified and placed second behind his nemesis Alydar for blatant interference on the backstretch.

Twilight Tear, the 1944 Horse of the Year, deserves an asterisk, too. She suffered a shocking defeat in a Saratoga stakes race, but the race was run at Belmont Park.

The Civil War didn't prevent Saratoga Race Course from opening its doors, and World War I did not shut them. But World War II did, as rationing of gas and tires restricted travel.

Granville spurted clear of Discovery in the 1936 Saratoga Cup.

Saratoga racing, though, continued in 1943, 1944, and 1945 at Belmont Park on Long Island. So did the upsets, none more stunning than Twilight Tear's defeat in the 1944 Alabama Stakes at odds of 1-20.

Bred and owned by Calumet Farm and trained by Ben Jones, Twilight Tear was a member of the first crop of Bull Lea. Calumet owner Warren Wright Sr. had purchased Bull Lea for $14,000 at the 1936 Saratoga yearling sale. Among his ten wins, the son of Bull Dog—Rose Leaves won the Widener Handicap and Blue Grass Stakes and earned more than $90,000. Bull Lea quickly established himself at stud with his first crop, which included not only Twilight Tear but also 1943 champion two-year-old filly Durazna and 1947 Horse of the

Year Armed. Bull Lea would lead the nation's sire list from 1947 to 1949 and again in 1952 and 1953.

Twilight Tear was out of the Blue Larkspur mare Lady Lark, who was purchased for $1,700. The striking, wine-colored bay was a terror on the track from day one, winning her first two races as the favorite at Washington Park in Chicago. Following a third-place finish and a win in allowance company, she was a game second to Miss Keeneland in the Selima Stakes on a muddy track at Pimlico. Jones kept her at the Baltimore track, and she won an allowance race easily, concluding her two-year-old season with four wins, one second, and one third in six starts.

For Twilight Tear's three-year-old debut, Jones put his filly in the Leap Year Handicap against older colts at Hialeah, and she was third, two lengths behind Mettlesome and Adulator.

Twilight Tear then ripped off eleven consecutive victories, seven of them stakes, including the Pimlico Oaks, Acorn, Coaching Club American Oaks, and the Princess Doreen. In beating colts in the Stokie Handicap at 3-10 at Washington Park, she stretched her winning streak to nine.

Jones then entered Twilight Tear in a non-wagering allowance race at Washington Park, again against males. The field included her stablemate, 1944 Kentucky Derby and Preakness Stakes winner Pensive, who had missed the Triple Crown by finishing second by a half-length to Bounding Home as the 1-2 favorite in the Belmont. Twilight Tear beat Pensive by a length and a quarter in the mile race.

To make sure everyone knew it was not a fluke, she beat Pensive again, winning the mile and a quarter Classic Stakes. She won by two lengths over Old Kentucky, who finished four and a half lengths ahead of Pensive in third. The entry of Twilight Tear and Pensive was the 1-10 favorite in the field of five.

That stretched Twilight Tear's win streak to eleven heading into the Alabama Stakes at Belmont Park, when she faced just three other three-year-old fillies. Twilight Tear went off at 1-20, Belair Stud's entry of Vienna and Thread o' Gold at 8-1, and Dare Me at 14-1. Of the $112,087 win pool, $94,455 was bet on Twilight Tear.

Jones elected to remain in Chicago. He was probably thankful he did not witness her loss.

Thread o' Gold broke first, while jockey Leon "Buddy" Haas kept Twilight Tear a close second "under the heaviest restraint," according to Bryan Field in *The New York Times*. Twilight Tear had no problem taking over the lead but did not have enough left to hold off Vienna, who rallied smartly from last under Jimmy Stout. Field described Vienna as "tired, wavering and staggering" in the drive to the wire, but she got there first, three-quarters of a length in front of the favorite.

After a seven-week freshening, Twilight Tear won a handicap race at Belmont Park by two and a half lengths and the Queen Isabella Handicap at Laurel Park by five lengths, her last start against fillies. On a muddy track, she was a distant fourth in the Maryland Handicap, but rebounded to win the Pimlico Special by six lengths. That made her three-year-old record fourteen wins, one second, one third, and one fourth in seventeen starts. She was named champion three-year-old filly, champion handicap mare, and Horse of the Year. Her racing career ended suddenly when she bled and was eased in her four-year-old debut in an allowance race against colts at Washington Park on August 28, 1945.

If not for the Alabama, she would have won fourteen consecutive races, two less than the modern record of sixteen set by Citation later that decade and matched nearly fifty years later by Cigar. But she could not escape Saratoga's Graveyard, even when it was nearly two hundred miles away.

7

Stymied

In the summer of 1945, ads in the Albany *Times-Union* encouraged Saratoga race fans to trek south to Belmont Park:

THEY'RE OFF!

Greater 1945 SARATOGA Race Meeting
Now...In full swing at Belmont Park...
The Saratoga Season of Famous Stakes Events

This is your invitation to
COME! ... THRILL! ... ENJOY!

Regularly scheduled train service from Pennsylvania Station and Flatbush Avenue, Brooklyn, direct to track ... Or you may take the 6th and 8th Avenue Subways to Parsons Boulevard Station, connecting with bus to track.

8 races daily — Including Steeplechasing
Admission $1.60 tax included

TODAY'S BEST BET! U.S. WAR BONDS!

Stymie, the 1945 champion handicap horse, may not have been as reliable as war bonds, but he was dependable, incredibly durable, and one great story. He was claimed for fifteen-hundred dollars in 1943 and retired six years later as the all-time leader in earnings at $918,485. He lost his first thirteen races, then won thirty-five of them. Along the way, in his 131 starts, he earned the distinction of being the only horse to lose as the favorite in the same Saratoga stakes race, the Whitney Handicap, at two different tracks, and to win as the favorite in that same stakes, too.

Foaled April 4, 1941, at Robert Kleberg Jr.'s King Ranch, the son of Equestrian—Stop Watch, by On Watch, gave trainer Max Hirsch no indication of early ability, though he had a nasty disposition. The combination prompted Hirsch to enter Stymie in a two thousand five-hundred dollar claiming race against winners in the colt's debut at Jamaica. Stymie was seventh in the field of nine and then finished eleventh in a straight maiden race at Belmont in his second start.

Max Hirsch next dropped Stymie into a fifteen-hundred dollar maiden claimer on June 2, 1943, and Hirsch Jacobs, the nation's leading trainer in victories eleven times, claimed the horse for his wife, Ethel. The decision did not appear particularly brilliant for quite a while.

Stymie ran seventh the day he was claimed and didn't find a

Stymie finished third and last to Rico Monte in the 1947 Whitney Handicap.

field he could beat until his fourteenth career start, when he won a three-thousand-dollar maiden claimer at Belmont. Subsequently, Stymie made three more appearances in five-thousand-dollar claimers without being taken. He finished a remarkably long two-year-old campaign with four wins, eight seconds, and four thirds in twenty-eight starts.

At three in 1944, Stymie won just three of twenty-nine races, though he was second by three lengths to Stir Up in a division of the Wood Memorial. Regardless, Stymie had just seven wins in fifty-seven starts and a record of zero for sixteen in stakes.

Then Stymie got a break — the first long rest of his career. Thanks to the government's ban on horse racing for the early months of 1945, Stymie received three days short of a six-month rest. And he came back a mature four-year-old.

Stymie was second by a neck in his four-year-old debut in allowance company, then won a handicap by three and a half lengths and finally won his first stakes, taking the Grey Lag Handicap by a half-length. After finishing second in both the Suburban and Queens County handicaps, Stymie won the Brooklyn Handicap, finished second in the Yonkers Handicap, and won the Butler Handicap.

That set Stymie up for his first "Saratoga" start in the 1945 Whitney Handicap at Belmont Park. A crowd of 45,576 took advantage of the lifting of gas rationing to attend, creating mayhem in the parking lots. "So great were the demands on parking facilities that the main gates were closed to automobilists long before the first race, and cars were parked here, there and everywhere on the streets adjoining the track," William D. Richardson reported in *The New York Times*.

In a field of six, Stymie was a slight 7-5 favorite over Walter M. Jeffords' entry of Trymenow and Pavot, sent off at 3-2, although Stymie was spotting them twenty-three and nine pounds, respectively. Trymenow won wire to wire by four

Gallorette finished a narrow second in the 1947 Whitney.

lengths over Pavot, while Stymie finished a dull third, another three lengths back.

Stymie recovered, winning five more stakes to earn championship honors in the handicap division.

In 1946 Stymie got another shot at Trymenow and at the Whitney Handicap. This time, the race was actually run at Saratoga Race Course. And this time, Stymie came out the winner. Sent off at 1-2 in a field of five, Stymie won by two lengths over Mahout with Trymenow another two lengths back in third. Later in the meet, Stymie was second in an allowance race and third in the Saratoga Handicap, though not favored in either one, before enjoying a walkover in the Saratoga Cup.

Stymie was at the top of his game when he returned to Saratoga a year later for the Whitney. He arrived having won the Metropolitan, Questionnaire, and Sussex handicaps, the Belmont Gold Cup, and, in his race before the Whitney, the Massachusetts Handicap.

Only four other horses entered the 1947 Whitney: Bridal Flower, Gallorette, Rico Monte, and Round View, who scratched. Bridal Flower, a tiny filly who weighed less than nine-hundred pounds, had finished second as the 6-5 favorite to Hypnotic in the 1946 Alabama. Argentinean import Rico Monte, who'd lost to Stymie in the 1946 New York and Gallant Fox handicaps, was winless in three starts in 1947.

The champion mare Gallorette, who had won the 1946 Metropolitan Handicap, was third to Stymie in the 1947 Met, though she'd beaten Stymie previously.

Then Bridal Flower also scratched, leaving the 1947 Whitney field at just three. Stymie carried 126 pounds, spotting Rico Monte and Gallorette thirteen and fourteen pounds, respectively. Stymie went off at .45-1. Gallorette was 2-1 and Rico Monte 9-2.

Gallorette set the pace under Eddie Arcaro, taking a two-length lead on Rico Monte early. Then Rico Monte, under Rupert Donoso, the "Chilly Chilean," closed in. He moved

Stymie won the 1946 Whitney as the favorite.

Rico Monte inside of Gallorette around the far turn and they battled the length of the stretch, with Rico Monte wearing down the mare by a head. Stymie had been eight lengths back early. He closed resolutely but ended up third and last, a length and a half behind the winner.

The Associated Press called the August 9 Whitney "one of the Spa's numerous upsets."

Rico Monte and Gallorette met again in the Saratoga Handicap, and Rico Monte won by a neck. Gallorette came back to Saratoga to win the 1948 Whitney as the 9-10 favorite.

Stymie won his next start after the 1947 Whitney, the Aqueduct Handicap, which he also won in 1948, along with the Metropolitan. He ran five times at the age of eight in 1949 before being retired.

In his prime four seasons of racing, Stymie's numbers were magnificent: twenty-eight wins, nineteen seconds, and twelve thirds in sixty-nine starts against the best competition he could find.

His final numbers were: 131 starts, thirty-five wins, thirty-three seconds, and twenty-eight thirds, earnings of $918,485 — then an all-time record for Thoroughbreds — and an infinite number of pleasant memories for race fans from all the battles he fought.

8

No Fooling

Undefeated seasons at the championship level of racing are rare, but Greentree Stable's Tom Fool posted one in 1953, a year after Alfred Gwynne Vanderbilt's Native Dancer went nine for nine.

Tom Fool won his first three starts and his final eleven in an outstanding thirty-race career. In between there were a few bumps in the road; three of them at Saratoga.

Trained by John Gaver and ridden in every start by Ted Atkinson, Tom Fool, a son of Menow out of Gaga by Bull Dog,

Alfred Vanderbilt's Cousin was a leading two-year-old of 1951.

Tom Fool went three for four at Saratoga at two, his only loss coming in Cousin's Hopeful.

made the first four starts of his two-year-old season at Saratoga in 1951. He debuted impressively with a rally from fifth to post a four-length maiden win as the 2-1 favorite in a field of twelve.

Tom Fool easily made the transition to stakes company, winning the Sanford Stakes by two and a quarter lengths as the 4-5 favorite.

Despite those two impressive victories, Tom Fool was not favored in his third start, the Grand Union Hotel Stakes. He went off at 2-1 in a field of five, one of only three times in his career that he was not the favorite. Alfred Gwynne Vanderbilt's Cousin was second choice to Jet Master in the Grand Union, even though the former was coming into the race off of five straight wins, three of them stakes. Tom Fool came from off the pace to win the Grand Union by a length, and the victory catapulted the colt immediately to the top of his class in the East, if not the country.

One week later while previewing the rematch for the $62,900 Hopeful Stakes, James Roach wrote in *The New York Times*: "At 4:11 P.M. last Saturday Greentree Stable's Tom Fool became the top ranking 2-year-old race horse in the East. That was the minute he won the Grand Union Hotel Stakes. More will be known about the ranking at approximately 5:20 P.M. tomorrow."

At six and a half furlongs, the Hopeful was a half-furlong longer than the Grand Union Hotel. Would it matter? Tom Fool and his entry-mate, The Minor, went off the 7-10 favorite. Cousin, ridden by Eric Guerin, went off at 6-5. Only three other two-year-olds entered: Hannibal, Thymus, and Paramount Pete.

It had rained the night before, and Roach described the track for the Hopeful as "wet on top, firm underneath. A jockey called it greasy. Cousin liked the going. Tom Fool apparently wasn't able to do his best on it. Cousin had mud caulks up front. Tom Fool wore steel plates."

Cousin reared in the starting gate, dumping Guerin. Guerin remounted, and Cousin got away slowly, as Thymus set the pace and Tom Fool stalked from third. Atkinson asked Tom Fool to move before the half and the colt fought his way to the lead, but could not withstand Cousin in the final two hundred yards. Cousin won by a length and a quarter.

After the Hopeful, Tom Fool finished second by four lengths to Hill Gail in a special weights race at Belmont Park after being bothered early. Tom Fool rebounded to win the Belmont

Futurity by a length and three-quarters at 5.75-1, by far the most generous odds of his career, and the East View Stakes at Jamaica. He earned the two-year-old colt championship with five wins and two seconds in seven starts. The only other race in which Tom Fool was not favored was the 1952 Jerome Handicap, a race he won by seven lengths at 5-2. That made him three for three when not the betting choice.

He was clearly one of the favorites for the 1952 Kentucky Derby, but he never made it to Churchill Downs. After wintering in Aiken, South Carolina, Tom Fool prepped for the Wood Memorial with a six-furlong allowance win at Jamaica. Racing on the lead for the first time, he went wire to wire to win by a neck over Primate, with his old rival Cousin just a neck back in third.

A massive field of fourteen entered the Wood Memorial, and Tom Fool was the 8-5 favorite. Tom Fool was second most of the way, took the lead near the eighth pole, and just failed to hang on, losing by a neck to Master Fiddle, while saving second by a half-length over Pintor.

Tom Fool came out of the Wood with a cough and missed not only the Kentucky Derby, but the Preakness and Belmont Stakes, too. Hill Gail won the Derby; Blue Man the Preakness; and One Count the Belmont Stakes over Blue Man. One Count had skipped the Derby and finished third in the Preakness.

Many in racing believed the best three-year-old was on the sidelines, and Tom Fool was given the opportunity later, at Saratoga, to prove them correct.

Tom Fool returned to racing off a nine-week layoff in the Rippey Handicap at Aqueduct, where he was second by a head at even money to Hitex. John Gaver shipped Tom Fool to Arlington Park, and Tom Fool ran out of the money for the only time in his career, finishing fourth of five in allowance company.

The Blood-Horse

Tom Fool returned to Saratoga at three only to lose the Travers.

If Tom Fool was going to contend for the three-year-old championship, he would have to win the Travers. Gaver decided on two prep races, both at Saratoga. In the Wilson Stakes on a sloppy track, Tom Fool ended his three-race losing streak with a four and a half-length romp at odds of .25-1.

The Travers was only eleven days away, but Gaver gave Tom Fool another start, a five-thousand-dollar allowance race at a mile and an eighth over a drying track rated slow. Sent off at 4-5 in a field of seven, Tom Fool was nosed by Count Flame, who had run fifth in the Kentucky Derby and eighth in the Preakness before winning the Choice Stakes at Monmouth Park. Roach described Tom Fool's performance in the *Times*: "He took the lead at the top of the stretch, was hit twice by Ted Atkinson when Golden Gloves (on the inside) and Count Flame (on the outside) charged up at him, and it appeared that he'd hold on for the decision. But right at the wire Count Flame leaped ahead."

Tom Fool had not vaulted to the head of the three-year-old colt division, raising more questions than answers with his fourth loss in five starts. And still the bettors believed in him, sending him off the 3-2 favorite in a field of eight in the Travers over a sloppy course described as "Spa Goo" in an Albany *Times Union* headline.

The Travers was not the only stakes the afternoon of August 16, 1952. Two-year-old Native Dancer dominated in the Saratoga Special, contested as a winner-take-all event two races before the Travers. The 7-10 favorite, Native Dancer won by three and a half-lengths under Eric Guerin.

Guerin would ride Mrs. Walter M. Jeffords' One Count, a son of 1943 Triple Crown winner Count Fleet, in the Travers. Guerin had not been aboard since the colt's debut in September 1951 at Belmont Park. It wasn't a pleasant memory. One Count broke slowly and finished eighteenth in a twenty-seven-horse maiden field.

Unlike Tom Fool, One Count had been the favorite only twice in his fourteen starts before the Travers, but he won both times. Idle since winning the Belmont Stakes, he was dispatched at 4-1 in the Travers while carrying high weight of 126 pounds, twelve more than Tom Fool.

Atkinson let Tom Fool set the pace, and although the fractions weren't quick on the slick surface (three-quarters in 1:14 4/5 and a mile in 1:40 1/5), Tom Fool had nothing left when confronted by One Count, who drew off to a three-length win over Armageddon. Tom Fool, carrying nine pounds less than Armageddon, was third, another length back.

With the Travers loss, Tom Fool had also lost any chance for the three-year-old title, which became a no brainer after One Count ran second in the Lawrence Realization and humbled older horses by winning the Jockey Club Gold Cup by two lengths and the Gold Cup at Jamaica by nine.

A month and a day after the Travers, his fifth loss in six

races, Tom Fool won the Jerome Handicap by seven lengths. He then won the Sysonby Handicap by a length and a quarter, was second in the Roamer Handicap, won the Grey Lag Handicap by a nose, and got nosed in the Westchester Handicap.

Tom Fool did not lose another race. He finished his three-year-old season with a head victory in the Empire City Handicap and then posted a perfect ten-for-ten record as a four-year-old, a performance that earned him Horse of the Year honors over Native Dancer, who was nine for ten as a three-year-old in 1953.

One of Tom Fool's four-year-old victories came in the Suburban Handicap, which he won by a nose over Royal Vale. He also gained a measure of revenge when One Count finished ten lengths back in the race. Tom Fool then carried 135 pounds to a two-length victory in the Carter Handicap and 136 to a length and a half win in the Brooklyn Handicap.

Such was his dominance that Tom Fool's final four races were conducted with no wagering. Two of them were at Saratoga: an eight-length romp in the Wilson and a three and a half-length score in the Whitney. That gave Tom Fool a career record at Saratoga of six wins, two seconds, and a third in nine starts, hardly a poor percentage by any measurement.

He was not the only champion to lose a stakes or two at Saratoga in the 1950s. Their reputations weren't destroyed, perhaps just dented a bit.

Walter M. Jeffords' Kiss Me Kate, a daughter of Count Fleet who won the 1951 Alabama at 4-5 on the way to the three-year-old filly championship, lost both the 1952 Diana Handicap, then run on dirt, at 4-5, and the Saratoga Cup against colts at even money.

Foxcatcher Farms' Parlo, the 1954 champion three-year-old filly and handicap mare, made three Saratoga starts, one in three consecutive years. After winning the 1954 Alabama

Stakes at 9-1, she returned to Saratoga the following year and finished third at 9-10 against colts in the Saratoga Handicap. In 1956, she finished last in a field of nine as the 6-5 favorite in the Diana Handicap, beaten twenty-three lengths by Searching.

Mrs. Jan Burke's Dedicate had the misfortune of being born in the same year as Nashua and Swaps, and he was unable to match their outstanding records. Nashua won twenty-two of thirty starts, and Swaps nineteen of twenty-five. Dedicate, who was sixth and second to Nashua in their two meetings, carved out his own successful career, winning twelve of forty-three starts with nine seconds and five thirds.

Rico Reto upset the 1955 Alabama in her only stakes win.

Bert Morgan/Belmont Park

Champion High Voltage was one of Rico Reto's victims in the Alabama.

At Saratoga, Dedicate won the 1956 Whitney Handicap as the 2-1 favorite, but lost the Saratoga Handicap as the even-money favorite by a head to Paper Tiger, who carried fourteen pounds less. In 1957 Dedicate finished fifth by eight lengths as the 6-5 favorite in the Saratoga Handicap, but was still named champion handicap horse.

At least Dedicate won a race at Saratoga. Reginald Webster's Quill did not. At two, she finished third as the 8-5 favorite in the 1958 Schuylerville and third in the Spinaway at 11-1. But those thirds were her only losses that year as she went on to be named champion two-year-old filly. Two years later, she was second as the 1-2 favorite in the 1960 Diana Handicap. She finished her career zero for three at Saratoga and fourteen for twenty-three everywhere else.

One of the most shocking upsets of the 1950s came in the 1955 Alabama Stakes. High Voltage, who had lost the Spinaway as the 9-5 favorite the year before but was still named 1954 two-year-old filly champion, and Misty Morn, who would be named 1955 champion three-year-old filly, were an entry favored at odds of 2-5. They finished seventh and third, respectively, to W. Arnold Hanger's 8-1 long shot Rico Reto. The Alabama was Rico Reto's first and only stakes victory. It was not even close to being the last, stunning upset in the Alabama. The early 1960s were full of them.

9

Three of a Kind

They were three of a kind: three consecutive three-year-old filly champions who came to Saratoga to contest the Alabama Stakes: Brookmeade Stable's Bowl of Flowers in 1961, Meadow Stable's Cicada in 1962, and William H. Perry's Lamb Chop in 1963.

But as odds-on favorites, all three lost, which is rather stunning given that they had won thirty-three of their combined fifty-three starts before their Alabama engagements and collectively had been out of the money just once: Lamb Chop's fifth on a sloppy track in the Selima Stakes as a two-year-old.

After seeing all three lose, one could only wonder which was the biggest surprise.

After running second in her May 13, 1960, debut at Aqueduct, Bowl of Flowers, a daughter by Sailor out of Flower Bowl trained by Hall of Famer Elliott Burch, nearly swept the rest of her two-year-old season. She posted six victories in eight starts. She won the Gardenia Stakes at Garden State Park under Bill Shoemaker and the Frizette Stakes at Aqueduct under her regular rider, Eddie Arcaro, to clinch the two-year-old filly championship.

She kicked off her three-year-old campaign by beating colts in a handicap race. She took the Acorn Stakes at 1-5 before finishing a close second to Funloving in the Mother Goose

Stakes at 4-5. In her final start before the Alabama, Bowl of
Flowers posted the largest winning margin of her entire career,
winning the Coaching Club American Oaks by five and a half
lengths at 2-5.

But the Alabama six weeks later would be no stroll down the
Saratoga stretch. Waiting for Bowl of Flowers was Darby Dan
Farm's Primonetta, whose only loss in nine previous starts was
a second to My Portrait in the Monmouth Oaks. Primonetta, a
daughter of Swaps trained by James P. Conway, had taken the
Prioress Stakes, Miss Woodford Stakes, and Delaware Oaks earlier in 1961.

This was an epic showdown matching the stretch-running
Bowl of Flowers with the brilliantly fast Primonetta. Better yet,
it was Arcaro, already a racing legend in his final year of rid-
ing, versus Shoemaker, still early in his journey to become rac-
ing's all-time leading jockey before being surpassed by Laffit
Pincay Jr. And for a bit of a twist, Arcaro had ridden
Primonetta to win her first two races as a two-year-old, and
Shoemaker had ridden Bowl of Flowers to win the Gardenia
Stakes as a two-year-old. Only four other fillies entered the
Alabama, and none of them had the early speed to make
Primonetta work on the front end.

Regardless, Bowl of Flowers went off the 1-2 favorite, and
Primonetta, carrying 121 pounds to Bowl of Flowers' high
weight of 124, was second choice at almost 5-2.

Primonetta, and Shoemaker, were magnificent. Shoemaker
doled out enough of Primonetta's speed to maintain a comfortable lead of one to one and a half lengths. Then, when
long shot Counter Call charged to within half a length of
her at the top of the stretch, Primonetta found another gear,
surging to a five-length win over Mighty Fair in a stakes-
record 2:03 1/5. Bowl of Flowers fell back to last in the field
of six before rallying mildly to finish third, a length behind
Mighty Fair.

**Darby Dan Farm's Primonetta works at Saratoga prior to her Alabama
win over champion Bowl of Flowers.**

"She just didn't run her race," Arcaro said afterward. "I hit
her at the five-eighths pole, and she just didn't respond. She
ran a little bit in the stretch, but she's got a much better punch
than that. This just wasn't her day."

Shoemaker knew. "I don't think Bowl of Flowers ran her
race," he said.

When Bowl of Flowers finished third in an allowance race at
6-5 in her next start, Burch added blinkers to help her focus.
They worked, as Bowl of Flowers avenged her Alabama loss by
taking the Spinster Stakes at Keeneland by three-quarters of a
length over Primonetta, who had followed her Alabama win
by running fifth in the Gazelle and third in the Beldame.
When Primonetta finished sixth at 4-5 in the Firenze
Handicap in her final 1961 start, Bowl of Flowers clinched the
divisional title.

In her final start, Bowl of Flowers tackled colts and was third
by a head behind Sherluck and Hitting Away in the Roamer

Handicap. That completed her career with a record of ten wins, three seconds, and three thirds in sixteen starts.

Primonetta got a title, too, the following year when she was named champion handicap mare, winning seven of ten starts, including the Regret, Molly Pitcher, and Falls City handicaps and the Spinster Stakes. One of her three losses as a four-year-old in 1962 came in the Beldame to a three-year-old named Cicada. The Beldame was Cicada's very next start after losing not only the 1962 Alabama, but the Travers as well.

Cicada, a bay filly by Bryan G. trained by J.H. "Casey" Hayes, was so precocious that she debuted February 23 of her two-year-old season in 1961. Sent off as even money as part of the field entry in a field of fourteen, she won a three-furlong race at Hialeah by four and a half lengths from the thirteen post.

Brookmeade Stable's Bowl of Flowers would be named champion three-year-old filly despite losing the Alabama Stakes to Primonetta.

She won four of her next eight starts, including a five and a half-length victory in the Blue Hen Stakes at Delaware, before taking her game to a new level. And she chose Saratoga to show it off, winning the Schuylerville by a length and a half and the Spinaway by a neck. When she tacked on victories in the Matron, Astarita, and Frizette, she was on the threshold of a championship. She left little doubt about her qualifications by concluding her season with a ten-length, eased-up victory in the Gardenia Stakes at Garden State on a sloppy track. That gave her eleven wins, two seconds, and three thirds in sixteen starts, and a feeling that she just might be as good as the two-year-old colts.

She began her three-year-old season with an easy allowance win at Hialeah, stretching her win streak to seven. She didn't make it to eight, running second as the 3-5 favorite to the four-year-old filly Smashing Gail in the Columbiana Handicap.

After winning an allowance race, she tackled colts in the Florida Derby at Gulfstream Park. Sent off at 2.45-1 under Bill Shoemaker in the mile and an eighth stakes, Cicada opened a four-length lead, surrendered it by half a length, and, while bearing out, came on again, getting nosed on the wire by Ridan. She beat third-place finisher Admiral's Voyage by six lengths in a gutsy performance.

Cicada resumed racing against fillies and won four straight stakes, all as the prohibitive favorite: the Kentucky Oaks Prep, the Kentucky Oaks, the Acorn, and the Mother Goose.

Cicada had never been better, but she could not maintain that form heading into the Alabama.

Sent off at 2-5 in the Coaching Club American Oaks, she was second by a half-length to Bramalea, a nose ahead of Firm Policy in third. At odds of 1-2 in the Delaware Oaks, Cicada was third by four lengths to North South Gal. Two weeks later in the Delaware Handicap, Cicada was second by a head to Seven Thirty.

**Casey Hayes trained Meadow Stable's Cicada to championships
in three consecutive years.**

Nevertheless, Hayes and Meadow Stable's owner, Christopher
Chenery, told reporters Cicada would race in the Travers
instead of the Alabama. Then they changed their minds.

Cicada's three-race losing streak and a jockey change from
Shoemaker — who was riding at Arlington Park that day — to
Bobby Ussery, who had ridden her in her first two career starts,
did nothing to deter the bettors. They made her the 4-5 favorite
in the field of nine contesting the 1962 Alabama on a muddy
track. Firm Policy, who had won two straight stakes, was 5-2.

Bramalea broke first but quickly yielded the lead to Cicada.
With three-eighths of a mile left in the eighty-second running
of the Alabama, Cicada had a two and a half-length lead. Then
the rest of the field closed in. Firm Policy, who had been rating
in third under Johnny Sellers, rolled to a one and three-

quarters-length victory over longshot Lincoln Center. It was another three and a half lengths back to Cicada, who saved third by a neck.

In a failed attempt to save the Saratoga season, Cicada was entered in the Travers. She was not the first modern-day filly to try colts in the Mid-Summer Derby. Bed o' Roses, the 1949 champion two-year-old filly, had been the 6-5 favorite in the 1950 Travers, but finished second to Lights Up.

Cicada finished seventh in the 1962 Travers, in which Jaipur gutted out a nose decision over Ridan after they battled head-to-head, gate-to-wire, for a mile and a quarter.

Cicada rebounded to win the Beldame Stakes against older fillies and mares and the Jersey Belle Stakes. At four, she won the Columbiana, Distaff, and Vagrancy handicaps, and, her lone grass start, the Sheepshead Bay Handicap, before suffering a season-ending stifle injury. She made one attempt to come back late the following year before being retired.

Cicada was the first and remains the only filly to win championships at two, three, and four.

Although neither Bowl of Flowers nor Cicada had lost the Alabama to a decided longshot, William Haggin Perry's ill-fated Lamb Chop would.

A daughter of Bold Ruler out of the Count Fleet mare Sheepsfoot, Lamb Chop was trained by Jim Maloney, who later saddled two-time champion filly Gamely and Broom Dance to win the 1967 and 1982 Alabamas, respectively.

Lamb Chop raced just five times as a two-year-old, beginning her career with a length and a half maiden victory at Saratoga at even money. She was fifth in the Selima Stakes at Laurel and then was shipped to California, where she won two of four starts, both minor stakes. Shipped back to New York, Lamb Chop won a division of the Comely Stakes by a length and a half over Spicy Living, before running third to that filly in both the Acorn and Mother Goose. Lamb Chop then beat

**Tona (on the inside) upsets champion Lamb Chop in the
1963 Alabama Stakes.**

Spicy Living by three and a half lengths in the Coaching Club
American Oaks and by a head in the Monmouth Oaks.

At Saratoga, Lamb Chop prepped for the Alabama by running
second to Barbwolf on a sloppy track in a division of the Test
Stakes. That made Lamb Chop zero for three on sloppy tracks,
though she'd won her lone start on a muddy track in California.

Lamb Chop's rival, Spicy Living, was nursing a bruised heel
at Rockingham Park. Without her in the Alabama lineup,
Lamb Chop, coupled with Perry's Batteur, would be the 2-5
favorite despite giving six pounds to Nalee and ten pounds to
the other seven fillies in the field.

Lamb Chop was ridden by Hall of Famer Braulio Baeza,
who'd won the Comely with her.

Thomas S. Nichols' Tona, a 21-1 longshot trained by N.R.
"Yorky" McLeod, was not listed with a rider in the track program. An agent's mix-up had Phil Grimm, who'd ridden Tona
in her last four starts, booked to ride the same day at Atlantic
City. Mike Sorrentino, who acted as his own agent, secured
the late mount just three days after he'd won the Bernard
Baruch Handicap at Saratoga with Endymion.

Tona, a daughter of Nashua out of the Tom Fool mare Evilone, had just one win as a two-year-old, at Saratoga. At three she'd won four allowance races; finished fifth behind Lamb Chop and Spicy Living in the Monmouth Oaks; run second to Spicy Living in the Delaware Oaks; and been fifth to Vitamin Shoot in the Pucker Up Handicap.

Nalee and Gay Serenade broke on top in the Alabama and were quickly joined by Vast Scope. Baeza had Lamb Chop a close sixth.

At the five-eighths pole, Tona shot up from eighth to join the three early leaders.

Baeza chose to save ground, then changed his mind. That decision cost him dearly. He abruptly angled Lamp Chop to the outside of the four-horse wall in front of him. If he had waited a bit more, he would have had a huge opening as Nalee, Gay Serenade, and Vast Scope collapsed from their early pace battle, leaving room on the inside of Tona, who had passed the leaders, but was drifting outside. Baeza had already committed Lamb Chop to the outside of Tona, and she

Lamb Chop lost the Alabama by a nose.

charged at the leader powerfully, missing by a nose and "forging to the front immediately after the finish," according to the Alabama story in *The Blood-Horse*. The story noted, "giving the Alabama winner 10 pounds, Lamb Chop lost no part of her reputation as the leading 3-year-old filly in the land."

After the Alabama, Lamb Chop won the Gazelle, was second by a nose against elders in the Beldame, won an allowance race, and then concluded her three-year-old season by winning the Spinster by eleven lengths, the Jersey Belle by twelve, and the Firenze Handicap by two.

Lamb Chop finished second in her four-year-old debut to Gun Bow in the second division of the San Fernando. But in her next start, on January 25, 1964, she broke down during the running of the Charles H. Strub Stakes at Santa Anita and had to be euthanized. She had badly fractured her left front ankle and veered into the rail heading into the backstretch. Before that race, she had won twelve of twenty-three starts with five seconds and four thirds. "It was a terrible thing to happen to a filly we loved so much," Maloney said.

10

What Graveyard?

N ot every champion who raced at Saratoga in the 1950s
and 1960s wound up a graveyard statistic.

Alfred Gwynne Vanderbilt's Native Dancer, "The Gray
Ghost of Sagamore Farm," was not only unbeaten at Saratoga,
but he nearly strung together three consecutive undefeated
seasons, just missing a perfect career record by the length of
24-1 longshot Dark Star's head in the 1953 Kentucky Derby.

Native Dancer was nine for nine as a two-year-old in 1952,
nine for ten as a three-year-old, and three for three as a four-
year-old before suffering a career-ending injury. That conclud-

Native Dancer was a perfect six for six at Saratoga.

ed the most brilliant record of any modern Thoroughbred who raced more than fifteen times: twenty-one victories and one second in twenty-two lifetime starts.

Included in that record was a perfect six for six at Saratoga, and none of the six victories were close.

The son of Polynesian—Geisha, by Discovery was bred by Vanderbilt, trained by Bill Winfrey, and ridden in every start but one by Eric Guerin. Native Dancer came to Saratoga in 1952 off two wins at Jamaica, a maiden victory by four and a half lengths in his debut and a six-length romp in the Youthful Stakes.

Four two-year-olds have swept Saratoga's three main juvenile stakes, the Sanford, Saratoga Special, and Hopeful. Native Dancer won four: the Flash by two and a quarter lengths, the Saratoga Special by three and a half lengths, the Grand Union Hotel Stakes by three and a half lengths, and the Hopeful by two lengths. (The Flash and Grand Union Hotel are no longer run.)

He extended his winning streak to eleven before losing the Kentucky Derby at 7-10 when, according to the chart, he was "roughed" on the first turn and wide afterwards.

Native Dancer never lost again. After taking the Withers by four lengths at 1-20, he beat Jamie K. by a neck in both the Preakness and the Belmont Stakes, and then added the Dwyer and the Arlington Classic before returning to Saratoga for the Travers.

Sent off at 1-20, the shortest Travers odds before or after in the race's 133-year history, Native Dancer won by five and a half lengths. He concluded his three-year-old season by taking the American Derby at Washington Park, but a stone bruise in his right front foot knocked him out for the rest of the year, derailing any chance of a much anticipated meeting with Tom Fool.

In 1954 Native Dancer won an allowance race and the

Metropolitan Handicap at Belmont Park, then an overnight handicap at Saratoga by nine lengths carrying 137 pounds on a sloppy track. When he came out of a workout at Saratoga a week later exhibiting soreness in the same foot he had injured, he was retired. Had he won the Kentucky Derby, he would have been perfect. Even so, he was perfect at Saratoga. His six-for-six record at Saratoga has endured as the best of any champion.

While three consecutive odds-on fillies, Bowl of Flowers, Cicada and Lamb Chop, failed in the Alabama to begin the 1960s, one unforgettable gelding and three champion colts journeyed to upstate New York and escaped untouched. And an outstanding mare of the late sixties nearly made it out of Saratoga with a clean record.

Kelso

Bred and owned by Mrs. Richard C. du Pont's Bohemia Stable, Kelso was Horse of the Year from 1960 through 1964 while carrying enough weight to slow an elephant. The son of Your Host—Maid of Flight, by Count Fleet was a plain dark bay gelding whose lone marking was a small patch of white hair on his right jowl, where he had been bitten as a yearling.

Looks didn't matter. Kelso compiled thirty-nine victories, twelve seconds, and two thirds in sixty-three starts while spotting the best horses in training considerable weight. Twice he won carrying 136 pounds, the most weight he was ever assigned. Kelso won at distances from six furlongs to two miles; on dirt tracks labeled fast, good, muddy, and sloppy; and on grass courses rated firm, soft, and hard. His career earnings of $1,977,895 were a record at the time and stood for fifteen years despite inflation and the drastic increases in purse money.

Veterinarian John Lee trained Kelso in his three starts as a two-year-old in 1959. Then Carl Hanford wove Kelso's magical career.

Beginning in 1962, Kelso made one start at Saratoga in each of four consecutive years, winning them all. He joined Henry of Navarre and War Admiral as the only champions to go four for four at Saratoga. Claiborne Farm's immense chestnut filly Moccasin, a full sister to Ridan, would match that record, getting her fourth win at Saratoga five months after Kelso retired in 1966. Seven champions went three for three at Saratoga: Sysonby and El Chico before Kelso, and Talking Picture, Desert Vixen, Easy Goer, Queena, and Dehere afterward.

Only Native Dancer and the brilliant filly La Prevoyante, who swept all five of her Saratoga starts in the early 1970s, topped Kelso's Saratoga record.

But Kelso's record was almost blemished.

The mighty Kelso (outside) had a perfect record at Saratoga, winning one start in each of four consecutive years.

He made his first Saratoga start on August 22, 1962, in an allowance race on the grass and won by a length and a half. The race was notable because it was the first time Kelso was ridden by Ismael "Milo" Valenzuela, who would be aboard Kelso in thirty-five of his final thirty-eight races. Previously, Eddie Arcaro and Bill Shoemaker had ridden Kelso most frequently.

Kelso returned to Saratoga in 1963 for the Whitney Handicap. Despite carrying 130 pounds, he won easily by two and a half lengths. The following year, Kelso's lone start at Saratoga was in another turf allowance race. Again he won handily by two and a half lengths. His final race at Saratoga, the 1965 Whitney, was a lot closer, too close for his fans.

Though he was eight years old and assigned 130 pounds, Kelso went off the 6-5 favorite in the Whitney.

"Kelso is not the horse he was at four or five," Kent Hollingsworth wrote in *The Blood-Horse*. "In his younger days, he had a kick, a burst of speed that could send him past any man's horse. Kelso at eight no longer has a sudden thrust. He had to be urged strongly to keep up during the early part and it takes all of Milo Valenzuela's considerable riding skill to bring out the most powerful run in racing today.

"To see Kelso wear down his adversaries in the stretch today is to see mature greatness. Kelso reminds of Ted Williams or Stan Musial in their final seasons, not the athletes of their younger days, but still better than rivals who were not even playing the game when the standouts first became champions."

Kelso, though, appeared to be in deep trouble with a half-mile left to run in the Whitney. He was still four lengths behind Malicious, who was carrying 114 pounds and showing no signs of stopping.

Valenzuela was concerned — for a moment. "He didn't seem to pick it up when I first asked him at the half-mile,"

Valenzuela said afterward. "He started at the three-eighths, and at the three-sixteenths he really started moving."

Kelso had to move, for he was still two and a half lengths back. But he was gaining, and he caught Malicious in the final two strides to win by a nose.

Hollingsworth offered his perspective of the five-time champion: "No horse in modern times has been so good for so long."

Late-running Buckpasser was even better than Kelso for a shorter time, winning fifteen straight races on the way to compiling a three-year record of twenty-five wins from thirty-one starts. He was a son of Tom Fool out of Busanda, who made her own headlines at Saratoga.

Busanda

Busanda, a daughter of War Admiral out of Businesslike, was an upset winner of the 1950 Alabama for Ogden Phipps, who derived her name from his Navy experiences while serving in the Bureau of Supplies and Accounts during World War II.

Busanda, owned by Ogden Phipps, handed Alfred G. Vanderbilt's champion filly Next Move a narrow defeat in the Alabama Stakes.

Trained by "Sunny Jim" Fitzsimmons, Busanda won just one of twelve starts at two. At three her major accomplishment heading into the 1950 Alabama Stakes was finishing in the money three times to the queen of the three-year-old filly division, Alfred Gwynne Vanderbilt's Next Move. Next Move had won the Prioress Stakes, Coaching Club American Oaks, Delaware Oaks, and the Gazelle, and had finished second in the Acorn and fourth against colts in the Wood Memorial.

In the Alabama, Next Move was the 7-10 favorite in a field of seven despite carrying 126 pounds. The entry of Busanda and Wheatley Stable's Antagonism, coupled because Fitzsimmons trained both fillies, was 4-1. Each of his fillies carried 108 pounds.

Next Move was versatile enough to win from off the pace, but preferred the lead. Six of her nine victories before the Alabama were wire to wire. Next Move's jockey, Eric Guerin, sent her to the front in the Alabama, but Ouija, ridden by Hedley Woodhouse, went to the front as well. They dueled head to head through an opening quarter in :23 2/5 in the mile and a quarter stakes. Next Move asserted her authority and cleared Ouija by a length and a half, getting a half-mile in :48 1/5. But Bobby Permane, referred to in the Albany *Times Union* as "the come-back kid," had Busanda rallying strongly from fifth. Busanda edged Next Move by a neck, giving Phipps his first Alabama victory. He would win a second, forty-four years later, with Heavenly Prize. The unusual comment in Next Move's past performance line from the Alabama was "weak ride."

Buckpasser

Phipps bred Busanda to Tom Fool and she produced Buckpasser, a beautifully balanced colt so dominant that he went off at less than even money in twenty-one consecutive races, even though he had a penchant for making his con-

Buckpasser had a close call in the Travers Stakes but kept his perfect record at Saratoga.

nections nervous. Fourteen of his twenty-five victories were by less than a length.

He was the favorite in all but two of his races, the first when he was a strong closing fourth at 5-1 to Lonely Gambler in his debut at Aqueduct. He then compiled twenty-four wins and two seconds in his next twenty-six starts.

Buckpasser was ridden in all but three of his thirty-one starts by Braulio Baeza. Bill Winfrey trained Buckpasser at two before Eddie Neloy took over the Phipps' stable when Winfrey retired.

As a two-year-old in 1965, Buckpasser arrived at Saratoga with a six-race win streak, though one of the victories was a dead heat with Hospitality in the National Stallion Stakes at Aqueduct. Coupled with stablemate Impressive, Buckpasser went off at .30-1 in the Hopeful Stakes on closing day at Saratoga. He broke last in the field of seven, but won easily by two and a half lengths over Impressive. The one-two finish by the entry produced a Saratoga record minus show pool of $10,247. That is how much the New York Racing Association had to pay out to ensure the minimum return for a two-dollar bet, which then was $2.20. Earlier that day, Kelso was cheered loudly after he zipped a seven-furlong public workout in 1:25 1/5 after the second race.

Buckpasser finished his two-year-old season with wins in the Arlington-Washington Futurity and Champagne Stakes. Sandwiched between was a second to the filly Priceless Gem in the Futurity at Belmont Park. That gave Buckpasser a record of nine wins, one second, and one fourth in eleven starts. He was named champion two-year-old colt.

At three Buckpasser ran second to Impressive in a non-wagering allowance race at Hialeah before winning the Everglades by a head over Stupendous and the Flamingo by a nose over Abe's Hope. Bill Shoemaker rode all three times.

A quarter crack kept Buckpasser out of the Triple Crown races, but he returned to the track on June 4, 1966, winning an allowance race at Aqueduct. Later that summer, he set a world record of 1:32 3/5 for the mile when he won the Arlington Classic over Creme dela Creme at Arlington Park.

For the second straight year, Buckpasser carried a winning streak to Saratoga. This time it was eight straight victories, but he had barely beaten Buffle by a head in the Brooklyn Handicap and Jolly by a neck in the American Derby in his two starts before the Travers.

One of his Travers' opponents, the speedy Stupendous, was coupled with Buckpasser because Neloy trained both colts. Only four other three-year-olds showed up for the Travers: Amberoid, Buffle, Abe's Hope, and Fast Count. Amberoid and Buffle had run one-two in the Belmont Stakes. The Buckpasser entry was 3-10, Abe's Hope 8-1, Amberoid 10-1, and Fast Count 23-1. Buckpasser carried 126 pounds, spotting Amberoid three and all the others six.

Buffle broke first, but Stupendous quickly took the lead. Amberoid settled in second and Buckpasser an unhurried fifth.

Amberoid took over the lead after three-quarters of a mile and opened a two-length lead at the top of the stretch.

But the others were closing in, none faster than Buckpasser under a confident Baeza, who split Abe's Hope and Buffle and went after the lead. Buckpasser had to work to get past Amberoid, but he did, winning the Travers by three-quarters of a length in 2:01 3/5, matching the stakes mark set by Jaipur in 1962.

Neloy was amazed at Baeza's poise riding Buckpasser. "He's too cool for me," Neloy said in the winner's circle. "Never play poker with Braulio Baeza."

Neloy was almost prescient. Buckpasser shouldn't have raced against a horse named Poker, who ended Buckpasser's fifteen-race winning streak in 1967 in the Bowling Green Handicap at Aqueduct, Buckpasser's only start on grass.

Damascus gave "the performance of a lifetime" in the 1967 Travers.

Previously, Buckpasser had been named 1966 Horse of the Year off of twelve victories and a second in thirteen starts. Buckpasser's standing in racing history, however, would be judged against two champions a year younger: Damascus and Dr. Fager.

Damascus and Dr. Fager

Damascus, the 1967 Horse of the Year, was bred and owned by Edith W. Bancroft and trained by Hall of Famer Frank Whiteley. The son of Sword Dancer out of Kerala by My Babu won eighteen of his first twenty-four starts. He raced just once at Saratoga, but it was the performance of a lifetime.

Racing fans hoped for a rematch of the brilliantly fast Dr. Fager and Damascus in the 1967 Travers. They had met just once, earlier that year in the Gotham Stakes at Aqueduct. Before a crowd of 50,522 on April 15, Dr. Fager, making the first start of his three-year-old season, held off Damascus by a half-length.

Thoughts of a Travers showdown were shot down two weeks before the race when Dr. Fager's trainer, Hall of Famer John Nerud, disclosed that Dr. Fager had suffered a viral infection and would miss training.

Still, 28,576 fans, then the second-largest crowd in Saratoga history, turned out August 19 to see Damascus take on three rivals in the Travers: Reason to Hail, Tumiga, and Gala Performance.

The track was sloppy from overnight rain, a development that didn't concern Damascus' jockey Bill Shoemaker, who turned thirty-six that day. "Not at all," Shoemaker said before the race. "It's still fast out there and we ought to go all right."

Damascus, the 1-5 favorite, did a little better than that. A downpour just before post time made the track even wetter, but it did not faze Damascus. Though he trailed front-running

Tumiga by fifteen and a half lengths at one point, Damascus won by a stakes-record twenty-two lengths over Reason to Hail. His winning time, 2:01 3/5 for the mile and a quarter, matched the stakes record shared by Jaipur and Buckpasser. "I didn't know we equaled the record or I might have let him run a bit more in the final furlong," Shoemaker said. "When I asked him to move to the leaders, just before we hit the half-mile pole, he took off. I hit him at the three-eighths pole because he looked like he wanted to loaf."

Damascus would get another shot at Dr. Fager, and his one and only meeting with Buckpasser, too, in the 1967 Woodward Stakes. Damascus beat Buckpasser by ten lengths with Dr. Fager another half-length back in third. Dr. Fager's chances were compromised by two speed horses, Hedevar and Great Power, entered by the trainers of Damascus and Buckpasser, respectively, to make front-running Dr. Fager work on the lead. They did, and Dr. Fager tired badly.

Damascus and Dr. Fager met twice more as four-year-olds. With a crowd of 54,336 at Aqueduct watching on July 4, 1968, Dr. Fager not only won the Suburban Handicap, beating Bold Hour by two lengths and Damascus by five, but equaled the track record of 1:59 3/5 for a mile and a quarter carrying 132 pounds, one less than Damascus. Their final meeting came just sixteen days later in the Brooklyn Handicap, and Whiteley again used Hedevar as a rabbit. Dr. Fager carried 135 pounds and Damascus 130. Hedevar did his thing and set up Damascus' late run, one he used to win by two and a half lengths over Dr. Fager in 1:59 1/5, breaking the track record Dr. Fager had just tied.

Damascus won two more stakes after the Brooklyn before finishing second twice and then bowing a tendon as the favorite in the Jockey Club Gold Cup. He finished the race last in the field of six, the only time in his thirty-two-race career he was out of the money. He'd posted twenty-one wins, seven

Dr. Fager won the Whitney Handicap by eight lengths and created a rare minus win pool.

seconds, and three thirds and earned nearly $1.2 million. He had split four meetings with Dr. Fager, leaving legions of fans of both horses to continue arguing who was better long after they both retired.

There were times, many times, in Dr. Fager's career when he seemed to be on a different level of speed and class than the poor horses chasing him.

Tartan Stable's Dr. Fager, the 1968 Horse of the Year, was a son of Rough'n Tumble out of Aspidistra, a mare of modest accomplishments on the track — two wins from fourteen starts. Aspidistra also was the dam of Ta Wee, the 1969 and 1970 champion sprinter.

Dr. Fager was freakishly fast with a nasty aversion to losing. He finished first in nineteen of twenty-two starts, though disqualified and placed fourth in one of them, with two seconds and one third.

But he was so much more than just a fast horse. He won the

The Blood-Horse

**Matching Native Dancer's Saratoga record, Gamely won all six of her
starts at Saratoga but was disqualified in the 1968 Diana Handicap.**

Brooklyn at a mile and a quarter. He won the mile and three-
sixteenths United Nations Handicap by a neck in his only
grass start. And he set records that defied belief.

Dr. Fager raced twice at Saratoga. He won an allowance race
by eight lengths at 9-10 in his second career start as a two-
year-old in 1966, getting six furlongs in 1:10 2/5.

Two years later in the 1968 Whitney Handicap, he drew off
to again win by eight lengths at 1-20 while carrying 132
pounds in a four-horse field. His popularity at the betting win-
dows created a rare minus win pool — no other betting was
allowed — and the New York Racing Association had to put
up the money for the new minimum payoff of $2.10. Dr.
Fager's winning time of 1:48 4/5 was just three-fifths of a second off the track record set by Stupendous in the 1967
Whitney Handicap while carrying 114 pounds.

Dr. Fager made just two more dirt starts after the Whitney.
On August 24, 1968, at Arlington Park, he carried 134 pounds
to a ten-length victory at 3-10 in the Washington Park

Handicap, setting a world record for the mile of 1:32 1/5.

After his gutsy victory in his grass debut in the United Nations Handicap, Dr. Fager concluded his brilliant career in the seven-furlong Vosburgh Handicap on November 2 at Aqueduct. He was astounding. Carrying 139 pounds as the 3-10 favorite in a field of seven, Dr. Fager set a pressured pace under regular rider Baeza. They went a quarter in :22 1/5, a half in :43 4/5, six furlongs in 1:07 4/5, and seven in 1:20 1/5, winning by six lengths. That track record held up for thirty-one years until Artax, the 1999 champion sprinter, won the Carter Handicap in 1:20 carrying 114 pounds. Dr. Fager was named 1968 Horse of the Year, handicap champion, sprint champion, and grass champion — the only horse to receive four titles in one year.

Gamely

Only one other champion threatened Native Dancer's six-for-six Saratoga record. She matched it, only to be disqualified from one of her wins.

Just three years after Lamb Chop's untimely death, owner William Haggin Perry and trainer Jim Maloney had their second great filly, Gamely. A daughter of Bold Ruler out of Gambetta by My Babu, Gamely won sixteen of forty-one career starts, with nine seconds, six thirds, and earnings of $574,961. She was 1968 champion handicap mare and split the 1969 award with Gallant Bloom.

Unraced at two, she started twice as a three-year-old at Saratoga in 1967. She won the first division of the Test Stakes by six lengths at 9-2 and the Alabama by two lengths at 9-10.

In 1968 at Saratoga, she won a handicap race by a half-length and the Diana Handicap by a neck, only to be disqualified and placed second for swerving into another horse. Green Glade was placed first.

Chapter 10

Gamely returned to Saratoga a year later and won an allowance race against colts by two and a half lengths at 1-2.

Then she took another shot at the Diana Handicap. Asked to carry 127 pounds, more than any previous winner since the race's inception in 1939 — and more than any Diana Handicap winner since, except Shuvee who carried 128 in 1971 — Gamely won by two and a half lengths over Obeah, who would produce the champion filly Go for Wand. This time, Gamely's number stood.

11

He Made Them Cry

S ecretariat arrived at Saratoga unnoticed in 1972. He
returned a year later to become the Graveyard's most
famous victim. Was there a difference between Secretariat's
1973 defeat and those of Man o' War and Gallant Fox?
Absolutely. Millions got to see it live on TV.

As Saratoga opened its 1972 season in late July, Penny
Chenery's Meadow Stable, trainer Lucien Laurin, and jockey
Ronnie Turcotte already had a star — Riva Ridge. Named
champion two-year-old of 1971, he followed with victories in
the Hibiscus, Blue Grass Stakes, Kentucky Derby, Belmont
Stakes, and Hollywood Derby, giving him a career record of
twelve wins in sixteen starts. Two of the losses occurred on
tracks labeled sloppy.

Riva Ridge, however, would not race at Saratoga in 1972.
Instead, he was shipped to New Jersey, where he ran fourth in
the Monmouth Invitational behind Freetex, King's Bishop,
and Cloudy Dawn. Riva Ridge skipped the Travers, but by
then people were already talking about his two-year-old stablemate, Secretariat, a magnificent copper-coated son of Bold
Ruler out of Somethingroyal by Princequillo. A Tony Leonard
photograph of Secretariat graces the cover of the *Daily Racing
Form* book *Champions*, catching him mid-stride, all four feet in
the air, as if he were truly flying.

"He was an amazing animal," Turcotte said. "His conformation, his balance, his stride...everything was exactly the way it should be. There was no more perfect horse."

Though Secretariat's record was not perfect on the racetrack, he and Riva Ridge gave Penny Chenery's ailing father, Christopher, much to smile about before his death in January of 1973.

Christopher Chenery was a prominent breeder in Virginia whose Meadow Stable, a 2,600-acre farm in Doswell, twenty miles north of Richmond, produced Hill Prince, his half brother First Landing, Sir Gaylord, and Cicada.

Hill Prince was the first colt ever to win championships at two, three, and four, a feat that has only been matched by Native Dancer, Cicada, Seattle Slew, Affirmed, and Spectacular Bid. First Landing was the two-year-old champion in 1958 after posting ten wins, one on a disqualification, and one second in eleven starts. Sir Gaylord, who had won four stakes at two and run third in the Champagne and Belmont Futurity, was one of the favorites for the 1962 Kentucky Derby. Two days before the Run for the Roses, Sir Gaylord suffered a hairline fracture of a sesamoid bone and was retired. A decade later, Secretariat would grab the glory he missed. And more.

At 12:10 a.m. on March 30, 1970, a large chestnut colt with three white feet and a narrow white stripe down the center of his face introduced himself to the world.

There's an old poem horsemen like to recite about foals with white feet:

> *One white foot, run him for life;*
> *Two white feet, keep him for your wife;*
> *Three white feet, keep him for your man;*
> *Four white feet, sell him if you can;*
> *Four white feet and a stripe on the nose;*
> *Knock him in the head and feed him to the crows.*

Secretariat was a keeper. He was on his feet in twenty min-

The Blood-Horse

Onion delivers a shocker in defeating Secretariat in the 1973 Whitney.

utes and began nursing twenty-five minutes later. His vora-
cious appetite would cause him to be a tad chubby in his
first year.

His name could have been Scepter, Royal Line, Something
Special, Games of Chance, or Deo Volente (Latin for "God
willing"). The Jockey Club rejected the first five names submit-
ted by Penny Chenery for the son of Bold Ruler. The sixth,
suggested by Elizabeth Ham, who was secretary to Christopher
Chenery, was approved.

Secretariat was shipped to Lucien Laurin at Hialeah on
January 10, 1972, with a handful of other newly turned two-
year-olds. Turcotte remembers the first time he saw
Secretariat. "I arrived at Hialeah from New Brunswick," he
said. "I'd been home for the holidays. I walked by the stall
and happened to glance at him. I said, 'Mr. Laurin, who is
this pretty boy?' He told me about his royal blood. Then he
said he was too good looking to be good on the track. He was
an awesome-looking animal."

Even so, Secretariat was clumsy at first. "He didn't know which leg to put down first," Turcotte said. "He didn't know what it was all about. But it didn't take him long to learn. He was very intelligent."

And he was in good hands with Laurin and Turcotte, two future Hall of Famers.

Lucien Laurin had just retired at the age of sixty when he got a phone call from his son, Roger, then training for Meadow Stable. Roger was about to leave Meadow Stable to train for Ogden Phipps, and, with Lucien's approval, convinced Penny Chenery to hire his father as his replacement.

Turcotte's serendipitous entrance into racing came only after he had dropped out of school in the eighth grade and spent his teenage years working as an undersized lumberjack alongside his father in Grand Falls, New Brunswick, Canada. Convinced that he did not want to spend the rest of his life chopping trees, the eighteen-year-old Turcotte ventured to Toronto looking for a construction job, unaware that the city was in the middle of a bitter strike involving carpenters, bricklayers, and roofers. Desperate for work, he washed dishes and collected worms for a bait company in the middle of the night on golf courses. About ready to give up and head home, Turcotte's life was changed by a single question from his landlord, "Have you ever thought of being a jockey?"

Turcotte, who had worked with horses as a lumberjack, went on to become a great jockey, riding such champions as 1965 Preakness winner Tom Rolfe, Shuvee, Fort Marcy, La Prevoyante, Key to the Mint, Northern Dancer, Desert Vixen, Our Mims, and Talking Picture, as well as Summer Guest, Upper Case, Fifth Marine, and L'Alezane.

He amassed 3,032 wins from 20,281 mounts. His last ride came on Flag of Leyte Gulf in the eighth race at Belmont Park, July 13, 1978. The filly was crowded coming out of the starting gate, clipped heels, and fell, hurling Turcotte to the ground. Turcotte landed on his back at an angle that left him paralyzed from the waist down for the rest of his life. But he had already made racing history on Secretariat.

Turcotte did so despite missing Secretariat's first two starts. On July 4, 1972, Turcotte had committed to ride Summer Guest in the Monmouth Oaks, a race he won for Hall of Fame trainer Elliott Burch. That left Laurin to find a temporary replacement for Secretariat's debut in a five and a half-furlong maiden race at Aqueduct. Laurin chose Paul Feliciano, an apprentice with a five-pound weight allowance.

Secretariat had the two post in a field of twelve and went off a tepid 3-1 favorite. He never had a chance. A horse named Quebec two stalls to Secretariat's right ducked in sharply at the break, sending the horse next to him, Strike the Line, into Secretariat. Feliciano settled Secretariat and then rallied him from eleventh, only to run into traffic on the far turn. Feliciano found room on the inside and Secretariat flew home, closing powerfully to finish fourth, a length and a quarter behind the winner, Herbull. Secretariat had made up seven and a half lengths by running his final one and a half furlongs in :17 2/5. The *Daily Racing Form* chart said he was impeded and full of run. "I saw the race many times," Turcotte said. "I think Paul Feliciano did a hell of a job getting him back sound. Some other kid could have panicked and ridden him hell-bent."

Laurin, though, was furious after the race. He eventually calmed down and gave Feliciano another chance when Secretariat made his second start on July 15 at Aqueduct in a six-furlong maiden race. Turcotte was out of action. Nine days earlier at Aqueduct, Turcotte had suffered contusions of his lungs, back, and chest when his mount, Overproof, had a heart attack during a race and went down.

Feliciano made the most of his second chance, as Secretariat broke eleventh, but won by six lengths in 1:10 3/5 as the favorite.

Secretariat made his only appearance in allowance company sixteen days later at Saratoga with Turcotte finally aboard, winning by a length and a half in 1:10 4/5 for six furlongs.

Laurin then upped the ante, entering Secretariat in the August 16 Sanford Stakes, the only race of Secretariat's career that he would not go off the favorite. Even so, he was bet down to 3-2 in a field of just five. The chalk was Neil Hellman's undefeated Linda's Chief, who was sent off at 3-5 off his five-for-five record. Hellman was a prominent business-man and philanthropist in Albany, twenty-seven miles south of Saratoga Springs.

The Sanford was not close, even though Secretariat was blocked at the three-sixteenths pole. Turcotte split two tiring pacesetters decisively, and Secretariat drew off to a three-length win over Linda's Chief in 1:10.

If the Sanford was a confirmation of Secretariat's ability, the Hopeful Stakes ten days later was a revelation. Sent off the favorite in a field of nine, Secretariat was dead last early, completely out of the picture on TV monitors, nearly fourteen

Secretariat with groom Eddie Sweat, trainer Lucien Laurin, jockey Ron Turcotte, and owner Penny Chenery.

lengths back. He was still last after a quarter of a mile in the six and a half-furlong race. He then circled the entire field six wide on the far turn, getting the lead by the head of the stretch by racing a second quarter in :23 4/5. He drew off to win by five lengths in 1:16 1/5. Horses rarely make middle moves that fast, let alone two-year-olds covering extra distance by traveling extremely wide around a turn.

Secretariat had swept three starts at Saratoga and was ready for new tracks and horses to conquer. He finished first in the Belmont Futurity by one and three-quarters lengths, then won the Champagne Stakes by two lengths, but was disqualified for interference and placed second, a decision that still rankles Turcotte. Secretariat won the Laurel Futurity by eight lengths and the Garden State Stakes by three and a half lengths over his stablemate Angle Light.

He not only was the champion of his division, but became the first two-year-old ever named Horse of the Year. Could he become the first Triple Crown winner since Citation in 1948?

Penny Chenery had other questions to answer. When her father died, she faced enormous estate taxes, so she syndicated Secretariat for $6,080,000, thirty-two shares at $190,000 each. Riva Ridge was syndicated for $5,120,000 shortly afterward.

Her tax problems were solved, but the syndication stipulated that Secretariat would be retired after November 15 of his three-year-old season, denying him the chance to prove he could carry great weight and still dominate horses. If Secretariat were to achieve greatness, he'd have to do it quickly. Laurin had little margin for error.

Laurin, who had started Riva Ridge's three-year-old campaign in Florida and then used the Blue Grass Stakes at Keeneland for the colt's final prep before winning the Kentucky Derby, chose a New York route for Secretariat, who had come to be known as "Big Red" around the barn.

Big Red opened his three-year-old season at Aqueduct by

winning the Bay Shore Stakes by four and a half lengths on a sloppy track and the one mile Gotham Stakes by three lengths in 1:33 2/5.

He had finished first in ten straight races and dominated his competition. The Wood Memorial, however, included a fresh face, Sham. Trained by Hall of Famer Frank Martin, Sham had won the Santa Anita Derby over Linda's Chief, his fourth victory in his last five starts.

Secretariat, coupled with Angle Light, was 3-10 in the Wood; Sham 5-2.

Turcotte knew something was wrong with Secretariat in the post parade. "He was throwing his head," Turcotte said. "I had no idea what was making him do it."

There wasn't a heck of a lot of time to find out. Turcotte could only hope Secretariat was good enough to overcome what was bothering him.

Angle Light, ridden by Jacinto Vasquez, set a slow pace: three-quarters of a mile in 1:12 1/5. Secretariat was struggling in fifth before beginning to rally on the final turn.

But he was not doing enough. Angle Light bravely held off fast-closing Sham by a head. Secretariat was four lengths back in third. What Turcotte did not know at the time was that Secretariat was racing with an abscess in his mouth, a sore discovered by New York Racing Association veterinarian Manuel Gilman the morning of the Wood. Gilman told Laurin of the abscess. Laurin treated it and never told Turcotte, who learned of it a week after the race. The abscess explained Secretariat's erratic performance in the Wood. Every time Turcotte pulled on the reins, it hurt.

Syndicate members who had just spent hundreds of thousands of dollars to be part of Secretariat's future four months earlier may not have slept during the two weeks between the Wood and Kentucky Derby, but Turcotte was confident Secretariat would redeem himself. The abscess had cleared, and Secretariat worked sharply for the Derby. Then he ran the fastest mile and a quarter in Kentucky Derby history, rallying from eleventh in the thirteen-horse field to a two and a half-length win over Sham in 1:59 2/5 as the 3-2 favorite while coupled with Angle Light.

In doing so, Secretariat had run his five quarter miles progressively faster: :25 1/5, :24, :23 4/5, :23 2/5, and :23, the fastest final quarter in Derby history.

Horses just don't do that. They get tired. Secretariat got quicker.

The Preakness had ended Riva Ridge's Triple Crown bid a year earlier when he lost to longshot Bee Bee Bee on a sloppy track. Turcotte took criticism for that ride, even from Laurin, who said Turcotte had been preoccupied watching Key to the Mint, Riva Ridge's rival. The truth was that Riva Ridge could not handle most wet tracks, as he subsequently demonstrated again by running fourth in the Woodward and seventh in the Metropolitan.

The 1973 Preakness was run on a fast track on a sunny day. In a masterful move Turcotte asked Secretariat, who had broken fourth in the field of six, to go after the leaders heading into the first turn at Pimlico. "I went to drop inside on the first turn, and I looked up and saw everybody taking back," Turcotte said.

So he let Secretariat roll, and Big Red shot past horses to gain the lead by the time the field reached the backstretch. The normally staid *Daily Racing Form* called it "a spectacular run to take command."

Even Turcotte was amazed: "I went from last to first in a quarter of a mile on the first turn," he said. "That's unheard of. That is the proudest move in my racing career. I did what I thought should be done at the time."

Secretariat, sent off at 3-10, cruised on the lead to an identical two and a half-length win over Sham, with Our Native the same eight lengths back in third, as he had been in the Derby.

The time of Secretariat's victory has been disputed. Pimlico's malfunctioning electronic timer gave Secretariat's time for the mile and three-sixteenths as 1:55, well off Canonero II's 1:54 Preakness record set two years earlier. The *Daily Racing Form* clockers, however, caught Secretariat in 1:53 2/5. ABC-TV verified the *Form*'s time by playing Canonero II's and Secretariat's Preaknesses simultaneously on tape. Secretariat won by three lengths, the equivalent of three-fifths of a second. Pimlico officials, though, would only settle on a compromise, listing Secretariat's time as 1:54 2/5, which deprived Secretariat from setting records in all three Triple Crown races. The *Form* has continued to note its own Preakness clocking underneath the official one in Secretariat's charts.

Secretariat was a race away from becoming racing's first Triple Crown winner in twenty-five years and would go off at odds of 1-10 in his attempt. In the three weeks between the Preakness and Belmont Stakes, Secretariat was featured on the covers of *Time*, *Newsweek*, and *Sports Illustrated*.

The Belmont Stakes would be the defining moment of Secretariat's career, and he turned in a performance so stunning that it still defies belief, not only his thirty-one-length winning margin, but his world record time of 2:24 for a mile and a half. There have been 133 runnings of the Belmont Stakes, and the closest any winner has gotten to 2:24 is the 2:26 posted by Easy Goer in 1989 and A.P. Indy in 1992. Two seconds is the equivalent of ten lengths. Riva Ridge had posted the third-fastest Belmont when he won in the 1972 running in 2:28. That's a difference of twenty lengths.

After dueling Sham into defeat through a head-to-head six furlongs in 1:09 4/5, a suicidal split halfway through a mile and a half stakes, Secretariat simply drew off from the field, winning by a sixteenth of a mile to the screaming delight of 67,605 fans at Belmont Park and millions more watching on

TV. In the brightest spotlight ever focused on a Thoroughbred, thanks to *Newsweek*, *Time*, *Sports Illustrated*, and the twenty-five-year gap between Triple Crown winners, Secretariat crossed the line from being a great racehorse to being an American sports hero, one that ESPN ranked as the thirty-fifth greatest athlete of the twentieth century.

Accordingly, Penny Chenery felt obligated to share Secretariat with fans around the country, and she considered sending Secretariat to Chicago for the $125,000 Arlington International just three weeks after the Belmont Stakes. Other three-year-olds have been exhausted from competing in the Triple Crown races and taken months to return to racing. Yet Laurin told Chenery that Secretariat had recovered from the Belmont Stakes quickly, so off he went to the Windy City. Arlington officials rounded up three other three-year-olds and Big Red eased to a nine-length win on June 30.

Riva Ridge, meanwhile, seemed inspired by his stablemate.

Associated Press

Another view of the 1973 Whitney, but the same result.

Eight days after Secretariat's Belmont Stakes, Riva Ridge equaled Whirlaway's 1942 track record for a mile and an eighth at Suffolk Downs, winning the Massachusetts Handicap in 1:48 1/5. In his next start, the July 4 Brooklyn Handicap at Aqueduct, Riva Ridge set a world record for a mile and three-sixteenths, winning by a head over True Knight while spotting him ten pounds to become racing's newest millionaire. Riva Ridge, carrying 127 pounds, recorded a time of 1:52 2/5.

There was no hotter stable in America, no hotter trainer or rider, and certainly no better horses than Secretariat and Riva Ridge.

Then they went to Saratoga.

Waiting to test Secretariat was trainer Allen Jerkens, known as "The Giant Killer" for the numerous upsets his horses have inflicted on other trainers' champions.

Jerkens has been at the top of his profession for decades. He started his career at twenty-one and accomplished enough in the next twenty-four years to become the youngest trainer ever inducted into the Hall of Fame, in 1975. By then, he had upset five-time Horse of the Year Kelso three times with Beau Purple. Beau Purple took down Kelso at 3-5 in the 1962 Suburban Handicap, at even money on grass in the 1962 Man o' War, and at 2-5 in the 1963 Widener Handicap. Jerkens then upset Buckpasser, the 7-10 favorite, with Handsome Boy by eight lengths in the 1967 Brooklyn Handicap.

While the historic upsets continued for Jerkens through 2001 — when Bohemia Stable's Shine Again, the 21-1 longshot in a field of five, won the Grade I $250,000 Ballerina Stakes at Saratoga — Jerkens said he wouldn't mind terribly if people stopped referring to him as the Giant Killer. "It was fun for a while," he said. "But it's a little worn out now. There's a lot of other guys that have beaten just as many good horses, like Ron McAnally."

Jerkens has also trained good horses, including Belong To Me, Blessing Angelica, Classy Mirage, Devil His Due, Dixie Flag, Kelly Kip, Missy's Mirage, Never Bow, November Snow, Sensitive Prince, 1994 champion older mare Sky Beauty, Vertee, and Virginia Rapids.

Jerkens' biggest break came in 1962 when he began training horses for Wall Street investor Jack Dreyfus Jr., who races under the name of Hobeau Farm and supplied the trainer with Beau Purple, Kelly Kip, Onion, and Prove Out. "Mr. Dreyfus has been so good to train for," Jerkens said. "I've trained for him for thirty-nine years. He always lets me do what I want all the time, which is really a big help to me."

Consistent success can do that for a relationship, and Jerkens works hard to maintain the high standards he set for himself. His work ethic and attention to detail are unerring, and he has changed with the times, which is why he finished sixth in the nation in earnings in 1993 and nineteenth in 1997 despite racing a relatively modest-sized stable. Jerkens was leading trainer of the 1996 Belmont fall meet and of the 1998 Aqueduct spring meet, the latter at the age of sixty-nine. He was New York's leading trainer four times, in 1957, 1962, 1966, and 1969, and won the Eclipse Award in 1973.

Yet with all that he has accomplished, if you asked serious racing fans to name a horse that Jerkens trained, at least some would answer, "Onion."

Jerkens trained Onion's sire, Third Martini, to win the 1964 Queens County Handicap. "Onion's father was as generous as a horse could be," Jerkens said.

Unraced at two, Onion, a Hobeau Farm homebred out of the Beau Gar mare With a Flair, raced eleven times as a three-year-old in 1972, winning four, with three seconds, one third, and earnings of $36,320.

Two of Onion's victories in 1972 were at Saratoga in a pair of seven-furlong allowance races under jockey Ernest Cardone.

Secretariat in the Saratoga paddock.

On August 12, 1972, Onion blew away 1971 Kentucky Derby and Preakness Stakes winner Canonero II by six lengths in a quick 1:22 2/5.

Onion visited the Saratoga winner's circle again ten days later, sizzling seven furlongs in 1:21 4/5 to defeat Loud by four lengths

As a four-year-old, Onion advanced to stakes company, running second to North Sea in the Paumonok Handicap, third behind Traffic Cop and North Sea in the Roseben Handicap, and second to King's Bishop in the Carter Handicap.

Jerkens was encouraged enough to consider future stakes engagements. Jacinto Vasquez was Onion's regular rider, and after the Carter, Vasquez's agent, Fats Weiscman, bumped into Jerkens on the Belmont Park backstretch. Weiscman asked Jerkens when he was going to run Onion again. Jerkens said, "The Whitney," and Weiscman laughed. But Jerkens was serious. "When I was training for Mr. Dreyfus alone, we used to save horses for Saratoga," Jerkens said. "With Onion, we started freshening him up in May. He didn't race in June or July."

That allowed Onion to arrive at Saratoga with a 1973 record of two wins, six seconds, and one third in nine starts. But if Onion were going to step forward to take on Secretariat, who was already listed as a probable starter against older horses in the Whitney Handicap on Saturday, August 4, Jerkens wanted proof that Onion deserved that opportunity. Jerkens targeted an overnight allowance race at six and a half furlongs on July 31, just four days before the Whitney. It would be an unorthodox training move, asking a horse to run the best race of his life on three days' rest, but Jerkens was never much on conventional thinking. "I knew if Secretariat decided to run in the Whitney, it would make a very small field," Jerkens said. Still, Onion would have to win his race impressively to start in the Whitney.

In the interim, Secretariat turned in not only the most remarkable workout in Saratoga history, but perhaps the greatest workout of any horse, anywhere, anytime.

With Ronnie Turcotte using an exercise saddle, meaning Big Red carried more than 135 pounds, Secretariat broke two track records while galloping out on a sloppy track on July 27, eight days before the Whitney. He worked a mile in 1:34 4/5, faster than the Saratoga track record, and galloped out a mile and an eighth in 1:47 4/5, two-fifths faster than Stupendous' 1967 track record of 1:48 1/5, and still only four-fifths of a second off Tri Jet's 1974 track record of 1:47, which has held up for twenty-seven years. The memory of Secretariat's workout still warms Turcotte years later. "He was doing it like he was in the Belmont," Turcotte said. "All on his own."

Secretariat had set incredible fractions: :11 1/5, :22 4/5, :33 3/5, :45 2/5, :57 2/5, 1:09 1/5, and seven furlongs in 1:21 3/5.

How could anyone think Secretariat was vulnerable? He had

finished first in fourteen of his last fifteen races, the lone blip a third in the Wood Memorial, which became more and more a fading memory as Secretariat piled one tremendous perform-ance on top of another.

But Jerkens stuck to his plan. And in the six and a half-fur-long allowance race the Tuesday before the Whitney, Onion set his own record. With Eddie Maple subbing for Vasquez, Onion dominated the field, which included six-furlong track record holder Spanish Riddle, by eight lengths in 1:15 1/5, two-fifths of a second faster than Bold Lad's nine-year-old track record for six and a half furlongs. "Vasquez couldn't ride Onion because he had a previous call," Jerkens said. "That's why Maple rode him. Afterwards, Vasquez' agent said, 'Let me ride him back.' " Jerkens did. In the Whitney.

The headlines of the front page of the Albany *Times Union* sports section the next day, three days before the Whitney, read:

"Onion Romps in Spa Feature Turcotte Has Riding Triple"

July could not have ended much better for Turcotte, who, on the 31st, won the fourth race with Nice To Have, the fifth race with Ghost Train, and the eighth on Rokeby Venus.

But a lot can change in a day.

Secretariat's final workout for the Whitney, scheduled for 7 a.m., Wednesday, August 1, was announced the day before. Albany *Times Union* executive sports editor Tom Cunningham wrote in his column that morning:

"The king will work out today. Secretariat is scheduled for an early morning half-mile trip around 7 o'clock over the main track.

"This horse has to be something else. The times on the dirt have been very, very slow so far. That's why Secretariat's dou-ble-record performance in a workout last week is so amazing."

The official estimate of the crowd that morning was five

thousand. "Fans began to congregate at 5 o'clock, two hours before the listed time for the half-mile work," Joe Nichols wrote in *The New York Times* the next day. "At 7 a.m., there was a traffic jam extending several blocks as latecomers tried to get a chance to see the champion run. The spectators included a complete cross-section from John Hanes (a member of the New York Racing Association Board of Trustees) and Alfred G. Vanderbilt to grooms and swipes, not to mention casual vacationers and babes in arms.

"With Turcotte, his regular rider in the saddle, Secretariat paraded in front of the stands, while an announcer on the microphone described the colt's progress."

Most of the witnesses thought they'd seen a maintenance work, four furlongs in :48 1/5. Jerkens saw something else. Perhaps. A chink in the armor. "I was right there on my pony," Jerkens said. "People said he went easy, but I saw Turcotte moving his arms a little bit."

Turcotte, who had noticed Jerkens, was forced to chirp to Secretariat to do his work. "He was dead, real dead," Turcotte said. "It was like three full seconds slower than what he would have done. I told Mr. Laurin Secretariat wasn't right. He said, 'That's just what I wanted.' I said, 'Mr. Laurin, this horse is sick.' "

Separately, Jerkens and Turcotte pondered the same question. Had Secretariat's sensational workout the week before been too much, even for him? "He didn't want to have the 1:34 workout," Jerkens said. "I've had it happen to me, when they work too fast."

Turcotte said, "Secretariat was not himself. I might have cooked him the week before. After all, he was only flesh and blood, and he had a lot of hard races, even though he makes them all look so easy."

While he struggled to find an answer before the Whitney, Turcotte turned his attention to his mounts Wednesday afternoon. One was Riva Ridge, who would go off a 1-2 favorite in a field of seven in a mile and a sixteenth allowance race on grass. Riva Ridge had won the Mass 'Cap and Brooklyn Handicap in his two previous starts, but he had only raced once on turf. In the Washington, D.C., International on a soft course at Laurel the previous year, he'd finished sixth by thirty-eight lengths in a field of nine. In the Saratoga allowance, Riva Ridge disputed the pace through a grueling three-quarters in 1:09 4/5, eked out a one-length lead at the head of the stretch, and could not hold off 56-1 longshot Wichita Oil, who won by a length and a quarter. The five-year-old shipper from Delaware Park carried eleven pounds less than Riva Ridge and paid $114.40 to win. Though he'd done little in his career to that point, Wichita Oil, trained by Pete Howe, went on to win two grass stakes in 1974, the San Bernardino Handicap and a division of the Camino Real Handicap.

The next morning Laurin entered Secretariat in the forty-sixth running of the $53,850 Whitney Handicap, where the colt would carry 119 pounds in his first start against older horses. Only four others entered the mile and an eighth stakes: Onion, with Vasquez back up, carrying 119; Rule By Reason at 119; and the highweights, Haskell Handicap winner West Coast Scout at 126 and True Knight, who'd been runner-up to Riva Ridge in the Brooklyn Handicap, at 122. There would be win betting only, and Secretariat would go off at 1-10. Onion was the second choice at 5-1. Maple, who didn't have a mount in the Whitney, thought Onion had a chance: "Onion loved Saratoga, and you have a horse coming around with Allen Jerkens training him."

The track, sloppy the day before, was drying out Saturday, August 4, and officially listed as "fast," though the inside seemed deep. A record crowd of 30,119 packed Saratoga Race Course early. Fans were shoulder to shoulder trying to wedge their way into a coveted spot on the fence to see Secretariat when he went by. They got an unexpected treat when racing officials decided to have the Whitney starters saddled on the infield turf course in full view of the grandstand, as well as the CBS cameras, which were showing the Whitney live.

Earlier that day Turcotte had asked Laurin to scratch Secretariat. Turcotte's request went unfulfilled, most likely due

Saddled, Secretariat heads for one of racing's greatest upsets.

to the aura of invincibility Secretariat had created. A Secretariat at ninety percent was still better than just about any other horse in training.

Turcotte wished Secretariat was anywhere near ninety percent as he warmed up the 1-10 favorite after the post parade. "When I warmed him up, he was dead," Turcotte said. "He was a sick horse. I don't know how he got past the vet. Usually, the vet takes the temperature in the morning. Maybe he didn't have the fever then. But this horse had no energy. He was not himself."

And then he showed it, banging his head on the door of the starting gate, snapping the door open before the start, hardly a good omen.

Onion showed his blazing speed by easily taking the lead from the four post under Vasquez, who had upset Secretariat in the Wood Memorial aboard Angle Light. In the Whitney, Vasquez set as slow a pace as he could while keeping Onion well off the rail, which, he had told Jerkens before the race, was tiring.

Secretariat sat fourth early, then moved on the inside to pass West Coast Scout and Rule By Reason on the backstretch after six furlongs in 1:11. Turcotte kept Secretariat on Onion's inside and moved ever closer to him heading into the far turn, cutting a half-length deficit to a head. Onion, however, had plenty left, surprising even Vasquez. "I thought he would just go right on by," Vasquez said. "About the eighth pole, I thought, 'this is not the same Secretariat today.' "

Allen Jerkens, the Giant Killer.

By then, everybody knew.

Turcotte had resorted to using his whip on Secretariat for the first time since the Kentucky Derby. Through the stretch, Turcotte whipped Secretariat ten times left-handed. Vasquez merely showed Onion the whip at mid-stretch, hit him once right-handed at the eighth pole, and tapped him left-handed just before the wire, which he crossed a length in front of Secretariat in an unremarkable 1:49 1/5. Secretariat held second by a half-length over Rule By Reason. "I really cannot explain what happened to him," Turcotte told reporters. "He just never fired. The pace was slow, and when I tried to set him down he just wasn't the same horse."

Then Turcotte, a proud man seldom inclined to reveal his emotions, broke into tears walking back to the jockeys' room. "I asked Mr. Laurin Saturday morning not to race Secretariat," Turcotte said twenty-seven years later. "That's why I was crying going back. It hurt more because I knew he shouldn't have run."

Then a veterinarian confirmed Turcotte's concerns. A virus had, indeed, infected Secretariat. He came down with a fever and was forced to skip the Travers, which Turcotte won anyway on Annihilate 'em on the way to taking the Saratoga riding title with twenty-seven victories, not a single one from Riva Ridge or Secretariat.

Turcotte took abuse for keeping Secretariat on the inside in the Whitney, but he won the very next race, the finale that day, on the rail on Wildcat Country. "There was nothing wrong with the rail," Turcotte said.

Nor with Turcotte's riding. Just three days after the Whitney, Turcotte won five races from six mounts. In Saratoga's long, gloried history, only John Velazquez, who rode six winners (from nine mounts) on closing day of the 2001 Saratoga meet, has won more. Four riders have won five in one day: Cordero from seven mounts in 1968, Julie Krone from six mounts in

1993, Mike Smith from nine mounts in 1996, and Velazquez, who also won five from seven mounts on a separate afternoon in 2001.

Secretariat's sickness did absolutely nothing to diminish the incredible performance by Onion. "It was such an unbelievable thing," Jerkens said. "We were happy to be in the money. Vasquez rode a brilliant race on him. The men from the barn were there. We just couldn't believe it. We were jumping up and down."

Dreyfus was not there, so Jerkens, tearful as he did so, accepted the trophy.

About a week and a half later, Jerkens purchased a horse for Hobeau Farm named Prove Out. "For $65,000, right in the middle of the meet," Jerkens said. "Buddy Hirsch was a good friend of mine. He said, 'You can have him.' "

In his first start for Jerkens, twenty days after the Whitney Handicap, Prove Out won an allowance race at Saratoga by six and a half lengths. The 3-5 favorite in the race, another three-quarters of a length back in third, was Forego. "Of course, Forego was not Forego then," Jerkens pointed out. "Nobody knew." Forego would go on to be the Horse of the Year in 1974, 1975, and 1976, and race just one more time at Saratoga. At the age of seven, on a sloppy track he could not handle in the 1977 Whitney, Forego ran last in a field of seven at 4-5 to Nearly On Time, spotting him thirty-three pounds. Jerkens didn't train that upset winner, but he did take another shot at Secretariat in 1973 with Prove Out.

Big Red had bounced back from his illness with a spectacular three and a half-length victory over Riva Ridge in the first Marlboro Invitational Handicap, getting a mile and an eighth in a world record 1:45 2/5, still a Belmont Park track record.

Both Riva Ridge and Secretariat were nominated to the mile and a half Woodward Stakes at Belmont Park on September 29, Laurin figuring Secretariat would race instead of Riva Ridge if it looked like rain. The track came up sloppy, and Laurin started Secretariat. Only four opposed him: Cougar II, who'd been third in the Marlboro, Prove Out, Amen II, and the filly Summer Guest, whom Turcotte had ridden to win the 1972 Monmouth Oaks. Secretariat and Amen II would carry 119 pounds, seven less than Cougar II and Prove Out and four less than Summer Guest. Secretariat was 3-10. Prove Out was the longest shot on the board at 16-1 under Jorge Velasquez.

Prove Out and Secretariat dueled for a mile and a quarter before Prove Out surged clear, running a final quarter in :24 to win by four and a half lengths. Secretariat was eleven lengths in front of Cougar II in third.

Secretariat had lost for the third time in 1973 in three stakes all beginning with the letter "W." But he closed his career with easy victories in his only two grass starts, taking the Man o' War by five lengths over Tentam in a Belmont Park track record 2:24 4/5 for the mile and half on grass and the Canadian International by six and a half lengths with Eddie Maple subbing for Turcotte, who had drawn a five-day suspension earlier in the week at Aqueduct.

Secretariat's career ended with sixteen wins, three seconds (including the disqualification), one third, and one fourth in twenty-one starts. "The saddest part was that we hadn't seen the best of Secretariat," Turcotte said. "He'd gotten to the point where he was like a deer on his feet. He'd just float. If he'd raced as a four-year-old, God knows what he'd have done."

Turcotte thought Secretariat could have become the first U.S. horse to win the Prix de l'Arc de Triomphe had he raced as a four-year-old. His fans could only wonder.

Onion never had a chance to prove his Whitney win was not an aberration, bowing a tendon and missing his entire five-year-old season. He resurfaced at age six and eight to win five of twenty-seven starts while finishing his career in claimers. "He was not the same horse," Jerkens said.

Chapter 11

Onion had won fifteen of fifty-four career starts; earned just under a quarter of a million dollars, and, on one August afternoon at Saratoga, captured the attention of the world.

12

Two of a Kind

Two outstanding filly champions of the 1970s, Carl Rosen's Chris Evert and Calumet Farm's Davona Dale, entered the Alabama Stakes at Saratoga wearing similar cloaks of invincibility: each had only two career losses. Chris Evert, named for the famous tennis star, had won eight of ten starts before the 1974 Alabama. Five years later Davona Dale entered the starting gate for the Alabama having won ten of twelve starts.

When each finished second in the Alabama, at odds of 1-2 and 3-10, respectively, their connections attempted a quick fix, taking on colts in the Travers Stakes exactly one week later. That didn't work out well either.

Carl Rosen, a New York sports apparel manufacturer, paid $32,000 for Chris Evert, a daughter of Swoon's Son. He named her for the classy tennis star who was on her way to accumulating eighteen Grand Slam singles titles.

The equine Chris Evert could be just as dominating. She wasted little time making an impact in her two-year-old season, winning her September 14, 1973, debut and an allowance race under Laffit Pincay Jr. before jumping up to grade I stakes company. In the fourteen-horse Frizette at Belmont Park, Chris Evert reared at the start under Marco Castaneda and then rallied to finish second by half a length to Bundler. Chris Evert later beat Bundler by a length and a quarter in the Golden Rod Stakes at Churchill Downs. Chris Evert finished her two-year-old campaign by winning the Demoiselle Stakes. That victory gave her a record of four wins and one second in five starts, but the Eclipse Award for champion two-year-old filly went to Talking Picture, who had won five of eleven starts and lost to Chris Evert when fifth in the Frizette, their lone meeting.

After running third in the Comely Stakes in her three-year-old debut under her new rider, Jorge Velasquez, who would ride her the entire year, Chris Evert won the New York Filly Triple Crown. She took the one-mile Acorn by three-quarters of a length, the mile and an eighth Mother Goose by a half-length on a sloppy track, and the mile and a half Coaching Club American Oaks by three and a half lengths in 2:28 4/5, two-fifths of a second faster than Little Current's winning time in the Belmont Stakes two weeks earlier.

If there was any lingering doubt about the leadership of the division, Chris Evert shattered it in a $350,000 winner-take-all match race at Hollywood Park against Aaron U. Jones' Miss Musket, who went off as the favorite. Normally a stalker, Chris Evert went wire to wire by setting incredible fractions of :21 4/5, :44 3/5, and six furlongs in 1:08 4/5 in the mile and a quarter race, winning in 2:02 by fifty lengths. That's not a typo. Fifty lengths. The $350,000 payday upped her career bankroll to $602,801, a tidy sum for a $32,000 yearling.

When she then drilled four furlongs in :46 and five furlongs in :59 1/5 two days before the 1974 Alabama — just after the human Chris Evert won Wimbledon — her trainer could not have been happier. "She did what we wanted her to do," Trovato told Lindy Strout, the Turf writer for the Albany *Times Union*. "She's ready and we'll have no excuses Saturday."

Rosen, though, sounded a note of caution: "Everybody is just assuming she'll win it, but we certainly aren't assuming anything."

The blaze-faced Quaze Quilt upset the odds-on favorite Chris Evert in the 1974 Alabama in stakes-record time.

Most everybody assumed Miguel Rivera would be riding one of Chris Evert's challengers in the Alabama, Fred W. Hooper's Quaze Quilt. But Rivera became ill early on the day of the Alabama, and Hooper secured Heliodoro Gustines, the regular rider of Horse of the Year Forego, as a last-minute replacement. "I asked (the steward) who was available and he came back with a list of six or seven names," Hooper told William H. Rudy of *The Blood-Horse*. "I crossed this one off and then that one, and I ended up with Gustines."

Gustines was not riding a Horse of the Year in Quaze Quilt, but she was not a longshot either. Unraced at two, she won the Kentucky Oaks before finishing fourth in the Acorn and third in the Mother Goose. The homebred daughter of Specialmante prepped for the Alabama by taking a division of the Test Stakes at Saratoga in 1:22 2/5, one and a fifth seconds faster than Maybellene's winning time in the other division.

Quaze Quilt would be coupled in the mile and a quarter Alabama with Special Team, and the Fred Hooper entry went off the 5-1 third choice in the field of eight. Chris Evert was 1-2 off a career record of eight wins, one second, and one third in ten starts. Both fillies carried 121 pounds.

Fred W. Hooper's Quaze Quilt had already added the Kentucky Oaks and the Test Stakes to her resume.

Quaze Quilt and Chris Evert raced first and second from start to finish. Setting moderate fractions, Quaze Quilt maintained a length to a length and a half lead through brisk fractions. Quaze Quilt ran a final quarter in :26, fast enough to hold Chris Evert off by a neck while setting a stakes record of 2:02 3/5 in the ninety-fourth running of the Alabama.

"Boy, what a pick-up!" Gustines said after the race. "She's one game filly. They told me to set the pace, steal it or make a false pace. She ran so easy. I had no trouble and we didn't have to use her too much too early, and she had a good kick left in the stretch."

Velasquez offered his insight to reporters after the upset: "I don't have anything to say. She just couldn't catch the leader in the stretch."

Chris Evert was a clear second, five lengths in front of Fiesta Libre.

Chris Evert's connections also sent her against colts in the Midsummer Derby. Sent off at 9-5, Chris Evert disputed the pace and weakened to third. She finished four and a half lengths behind Holding Pattern, who edged Preakness and Belmont stakes winner Little Current, the even-money Travers favorite, by a head.

Chris Evert was given a four and a half-month rest and returned to win the Conniver Stakes at Aqueduct on the final day of 1974. Shipped to Santa Anita, she concluded her career by gamely taking the La Canada Stakes by a nose before running out of the money for the only time when eighth as the 7-5 favorite in the San Margarita Handicap. She had won ten of fifteen starts, with two seconds and two thirds.

Bred to Secretariat, Chris Evert produced the stakes winner Six Crowns, the dam of 1984 champion two-year-old male and 1985 Travers winner Chief's Crown. Chris Evert died at age thirty on January 8, 2001, in Kentucky. Just four days later, another Triple Crown winner, Affirmed, died in Kentucky, too. He was twenty-six.

Davona Dale, a daughter of Best Turn out of the Tim Tam mare Royal Entrance, would win two Triple Crowns for fillies. She was exceptional early in her career, winning ten of her first twelve starts for trainer John Veitch and Jorge Velasquez, her only jockey in an eighteen-race career. Her debut at two was delayed until she overcame splints and minor ailments. After winning her maiden race on October 23, 1978, and the

Holly Stakes at The Meadowlands, Davona Dale finished fourth against colts as the 6-5 favorite in the 1979 Tropical Park Derby at Calder Race Course.

Undefeated Candy Eclair, on the way to the two-year-old filly championship, beat Davona Dale in the six-furlong Shirley Jones Stakes at Gulfstream Park wire to wire for her seventh straight victory. The two fillies met again in the seven-furlong, non-wagering Bonnie Miss Stakes two weeks later. This time, Davona Dale nailed Candy Eclair late, winning by three-quarters of a length in a stakes-record 1:21. Candy Eclair's three-quarters-of-a-length loss would be the closest another filly got to Davona Dale for more than five months as she strung together an awesome eight-race winning streak.

Davona Dale won the Debutante Stakes at Fair Grounds by seven lengths and followed with a victory in the Fantasy at Oaklawn Park by two and a half lengths.

Before the New York Racing Association renamed its three races for three-year-old fillies the Triple Tiara, there were two different filly Triple Crowns, the traditional one encompassing the Kentucky Oaks at Churchill Downs, Black-Eyed Susan at Pimlico, and Coaching Club American Oaks at Belmont Park, and the New York version consisting of the Acorn, Mother Goose, and Coaching Club American Oaks.

Davona Dale won both crowns at prohibitive odds. And none of her five victories were close.

After taking the Kentucky Oaks by four and a half lengths, Davona Dale won the Black-Eyed Susan by the same margin, the Acorn by two and a quarter lengths, the Mother Goose by ten lengths, and the Coaching Club American Oaks by eight lengths.

Veitch shipped her to Saratoga and mulled the pluses and minuses of racing Davona Dale in the Alabama, a stakes he had won two years earlier with Calumet Farm's Our Mims, or taking on colts in the Travers a week later. Initially, he entered Davona Dale in the 1979 Alabama, where a talented filly was waiting to challenge her leadership in the three-year-old filly division. Harbor View Farm's It's in the Air, purchased for $300,000 the previous September, was trained by Laz Barrera, who would be inducted into the Hall of Fame two days before the Alabama.

Veitch's and Barrera's names will be linked forever in racing history through the two colts they raced against each other. Harbor View Farm's Affirmed, trained by Barrera, remained, through the year 2001, the last Triple Crown winner. Calumet Farm's Alydar, who became the first horse to finish second in all three Triple Crown races, was his gallant rival over the course of two years. Affirmed won seven of their first nine meetings, in 1977 and 1978. Six of those seven times, Alydar was second. When Alydar won twice, Affirmed was second. They met for the final time in the 1978 Travers, attracting a record crowd of 50,122. Nothing was resolved as Affirmed won by a length and three-quarters over Alydar, but was disqualified and placed second for blatantly cutting off Alydar on the backstretch. Veitch handled Alydar's defeats with unerring

Chris Evert had won the New York Filly Triple Crown and was named champion three-year-old filly despite her loss in the Alabama.

Harbor View Farm's It's in the Air defeated Filly Triple Crown winner Davona Dale in the Alabama Stakes in 1979.

class and dignity, but, surely, Barrera wouldn't beat him again in the 1979 Alabama. Right?

While not matching Davona Dale's dominance, It's in the Air, a daughter of Mr. Prospector out of A Wind Is Rising by Francis S., had shared the 1978 two-year-old filly championship with Candy Eclair. At three a throat infection sidelined her for ten weeks. She returned to defeat older fillies and mares in the Vanity Handicap at Hollywood Park by a neck before Barrera shipped her east.

It's in the Air arrived at Saratoga with a career record of six wins, five seconds, and two thirds in thirteen starts. Barrera prepped It's in the Air for the Alabama with an allowance race at Saratoga. She won by eight lengths under Jeff Fell, who would also ride her in the Alabama.

Only three other fillies contested the Alabama: Croquis, Poppycock, and Mairzy Doates. Davona Dale was 3-10; It's in the Air 3-1.

Rated superbly on the front end by Fell, It's in the Air got away with soft fractions: a half in :49, and three-quarters in 1:12 4/5. Then she made it nearly impossible for the stalking Davona Dale to catch her.

It's in the Air ran her fourth quarter in :24 flat and her final quarter in :24 3/5, setting a new stakes record of 2:01 3/5 for the mile and a quarter. Davona Dale, who had fallen three lengths off the pace, made up half of the deficit, losing by a length and a half.

"I had just as much horse as Jorge did, and when it counted, I had more," Fell said.

Velasquez said, "No excuse. She had absolutely no excuse. What more can I say?"

Veitch tried to salvage the 1979 Saratoga meet by entering Davona Dale against colts a week later in the Travers, which would be missing superstar Spectacular Bid, who was resting for his fall campaign. His absence begged the question: Would he have won? For General Assembly, a son of Secretariat who had run second to Spectacular Bid in the Kentucky Derby, chose the 1979 Travers to run the race of his life, going wire to wire on a sloppy track in a stakes record 2:00 to win by fifteen lengths. Davona Dale, sent off the 5-2 favorite in the field of seven, was far back in fourth.

Davona Dale would start just four times more in her career. Though she ran fourth behind Blitey and It's in the Air in the Maskette, she was named champion three-year-old filly off a record of eight wins, two seconds, and three fourths (two of them against colts) in thirteen starts. It's in the Air, who also won the Delaware Oaks and Ruffian Handicap before finishing fifth by eleven lengths on a sloppy track in the Beldame, had a record of five wins, three seconds, and two thirds in eleven starts for the year.

But Davona Dale had a score to settle, just as she did with Candy Eclair. And Veitch was fated to lose another Alabama Stakes with the favorite.

In her first start at four, Davona Dale was third at 7-10 in an allowance race at Belmont Park.

She had now lost four straight races, but Veitch pointed her to the seven-furlong Ballerina Stakes at Saratoga anyway. It's in the Air also suffered four straight losses before winning the Vanity Handicap. Barrera pointed her to the Ballerina, too.

In a star-filled field of four — the other two were Misty Gallore, a gritty filly who had won five stakes that year, and Jedina, who was two for two in 1980 — It's in the Air went off the 6-5 favorite and Davona Dale second choice at 9-5.

Jedina led narrowly over Misty Gallore with It's in the Air a close third and Davona Dale right there on the outside in fourth. The quartet dueled through a quarter in :22 and a half in :44 1/5. At one point early in the stretch, the four were almost dead even in a magnificent battle. Jedina reluctantly gave in late, and Davona Dale lost momentum when she jumped a footprint near the sixteenth pole. It didn't matter. Davona Dale surged past It's in the Air to win by a length. Misty Gallore beat It's in the Air by a nose for second and Jedina was another one and three-quarters lengths back in fourth. Davona Dale started just once more, running fourth by seven and a quarter lengths as the 6-5 favorite in the Maskette behind Bold and Determined, Genuine Risk, and Love Sign. It's in the Air won just four of thirteen races following the Ballerina.

Veitch didn't have long to savor Davona Dale's upset in the Ballerina Stakes. The very next day Calumet Farm's Sugar and Spice, who had won the Mother Goose, lost the Alabama at 6-5 to Stephen C. Clark Jr.'s Love Sign, who also knew both sides of a Saratoga stakes upset. The daughter of Spanish Riddle, whose 1972 six-furlong track record of 1:08 still stands at Saratoga, compiled a record of three wins in six Saratoga stakes for trainer Sid Watters.

As a three-year-old in 1980, Love Sign was the upset winner

of both the Test Stakes and the Alabama. Sent off the 6-1 fourth choice in a field of six in the Alabama under Ruben Hernandez, Love Sign battled Weber City Miss on the front end, lost the lead, and then gamely spurted again in the final eighth, winning by one and three-quarters lengths in 2:01, an Alabama record. Weber City Miss was second, one and three-quarters lengths ahead of Sugar and Spice.

Despite compiling a three-year-old record of eight wins, one second, and one third in eleven starts, Love Sign was denied an Eclipse Award, which went to 1980 Kentucky Derby winner Genuine Risk, who was also second in both the Preakness and Belmont Stakes. Genuine Risk would show up at Saratoga in 1981 in an allowance race, which she won by eight and a quarter lengths.

Love Sign also returned to Saratoga in 1981, where, at 7-2, she would upset a 2-5 favorite (Highest Regard) in the Ballerina Stakes and then lose a handicap at 2-5 just twelve

Davona Dale turned the tables on It's in the Air in the Ballerina Stakes the following year.

149

days later. In 1982, she would finish fourth in the Ballerina as the even-money favorite. That made her zero for three as a favorite at Saratoga and three for three when she wasn't the favorite, all in stakes. Go figure.

13

Across the Street

At most Thoroughbred racetracks around the world, the last contest on the card signals the end of an afternoon at the races. But not necessarily in Saratoga Springs. There you can exit Saratoga Race Course through the clubhouse gate, cross Nelson Avenue, and take in an evening of harness racing at the beautifully manicured Saratoga Equine Sports Center, formerly known as Saratoga Harness. That is, if you can endure a doubleheader.

Is the quality of racing the same? Not even close. Does it prevent great Standardbreds from racing at the Sports Center? No. Bunny Lake, the 2001 Horse of the Year, is stabled there. Two of the sport's greatest trotters, Nevele Pride and Mack Lobell, journeyed to the Saratoga track and won. So did the 2000 Horse of the Year, Gallo Blue Chip, and the 1981 Horse of the Year Fan Hanover. Do they ever lose there? One champion did, and he may have been the greatest harness horse of all. His name was Niatross. He came to Saratoga Harness undefeated and was lucky to walk out alive. It's impossible to write a book about the Graveyard of Champions and not include him, even though he raced across the street.

Niatross' sire, champion Albatross, won fifty-nine of seventy-one starts in the early 1970s with eight seconds and three thirds. Niatross' dam, Niagara Dream, was a large mare who won six races in her career. Niatross was bred and owned by Elsie Berger of Grand Island, New York, near Buffalo. Hall of Famer Clint Galbraith drove and trained her horses, and they became equal partners of the tall and rangy 1977 foal.

Galbraith began training the dark bay Niatross in the fall of 1978 and immediately liked what he saw. "Niatross was a very smart colt," Galbraith said. "I think he was one of the smartest horses ever to race. He learned quickly. He always did every thing so easily."

Galbraith liked to start his two-year-olds at Vernon Downs, a three-quarter-mile track between Utica and Syracuse in central New York. Right at the start, Niatross did more than what was expected of him. In his debut, June 22, 1979, a two-year-old pace worth a paltry $250, Niatross left from the rail and raced on the lead. He surrendered the front heading to the three-quarter-mile mark and could have been content to sit in the pocket in second. Instead, he regained the lead and won by three lengths in 2:02 3/5.

Sensing he might have a top two-year-old, Galbraith didn't rush Niatross. He gave him two more conditional races, which he won comfortably, before his stakes debut at Vernon Downs. Niatross won by three lengths in 1:57 3/5. How good was this colt?

Galbraith decided to find out. He entered Niatross in the $862,750 Woodrow Wilson Pace, the showcase stakes for two-year-olds at the New Jersey track, The Meadowlands, which had taken precious little time to become the country's number one harness racing meet and facility after opening its doors September 1, 1976. Horses had to earn their way into the rich Woodrow Wilson final by qualifying the week before in elimination heats. Niatross won his by three-quarters of a length in 1:56 2/5. Then he won the final, wire to wire from the nine post (The Meadowlands starts ten across its one-mile oval) in 1:55 4/5. In his next start, a stakes at Liberty Bell in

Courtesy Horseman and Fair World

Niatross tumbles over the rail at Saratoga Harness.

Philadelphia, Niatross won by seventeen and a quarter lengths. He was more than halfway through a perfect thirteen-for-thirteen two-year-old season that culminated with his being named Horse of the Year.

He came back even stronger at three, winning stakes at Vernon Downs, the Battle of Brandywine at Brandywine Raceway in Delaware, a stakes at Buffalo Raceway, and an effortless victory in two heats in the Cane Pace at Yonkers, winning back-to-back races, the first by three and a quarter lengths in 1:57 3/5 and the second by one and a quarter lengths in 1:57 4/5 an hour and a half later.

That made him nineteen for nineteen.

Niatross was harness racing's greatest attraction, and Galbraith was intent on giving fans from all over the United States and Canada an opportunity to see him. The Grand Circuit, a series of major stakes races at tracks all over North America, made it easy to do so. Top two- and three-year-old pacers and trotters would battle at one track, hit the road, and do it all over again a week or two later at another.

The Grand Circuit included Saratoga Harness, which offered the Battle of Saratoga, two $100,000 races for three-year-old pacers and trotters. This was twenty times the top overnight purse of five thousand dollars offered for the best horses on the grounds. The Battle of Saratoga pace was named the Harold M. "Hap" Haswell Memorial in honor of the former racing secretary there.

In the 1980 edition of the $100,000 Harold M. Haswell Pace, Niatross faced horses he had already beaten many times. One of them was Trenton Time from the powerful stable of Hall of Famer Billy Haughton, harness racing's dominant driver and trainer for more than three decades. Haughton was the nation's leading driver in earnings twelve times and the leader in victories six times. He was followed into the sport by three of his sons, Tommy, Cammie, and Peter.

Trenton Time had finished second to Niatross by three and

Niatross only lost two races in his career and became quite an ambassador for the sport of harness racing.

three-quarters lengths in the Battle of Brandywine, but only lost to him by a length and a quarter in the second heat of the Cane Pace. Was Trenton Time closing the gap?

"We were awful close to him in ability," said Haughton's son Cammie, who trained and groomed Trenton Time. "It seemed like we couldn't pass him, like Niatross would hang in there."

Trenton Time, who had won thirteen of nineteen starts for the year, was taking another shot at Niatross in the Haswell Memorial, but even Billy Haughton doubted he could upset the champion. "Niatross would have to be sick or something," Haughton said the day before the race. "That's the only thing I can think of. He's an awful-nice horse."

The post position draw, vital on a half-mile track like Saratoga, worked to Trenton Time's advantage, as he drew the rail. But Haughton was disappointed that Niatross drew the three post in the field of nine rather than an outside post. "My horse looks like he's second best," Haughton said. "He'd be the one to beat Niatross, if there was one, but I don't think he can. It'd be different if Niatross didn't draw the three (post)."

It would be hard to imagine any person more excited about Niatross' upcoming race at Saratoga than Virginia O'Brien. The den mother of the Saratoga Harness press box would spend summer mornings and afternoons giving free tours of the backstretch for children and adults. Now eighty-two and still going strong as the director of the Saratoga Harness Hall of Fame, she maintains a deep, passionate love of horses and was particularly fond of Niatross. "I gave dozens of tours that week, periodically every hour, for literally hundreds of people," she said. "I would bring crowds of people over to Niatross. I showed so many kids Niatross on the tour. And Niatross loved it. He was so calm and passive, just a beautiful horse."

Saratoga Harness allowed no win, place, or show betting on

the Haswell Memorial Pace, the ninth of ten races on the afternoon card, but did have quinella and late daily-double wagering, using the eighth race as the first half and the Haswell as the second.

The morning of July 5, 1980, broke unseasonably cold and damp in Saratoga Springs, almost as if a day in late October had been misplaced. Intermittent rain did not help. Only 7,065 fans turned out to see Niatross, and the track was a muddy mess, so bad that track officials ordered an extra fifty minutes between the seventh and eighth races. That allowed a maintenance crew to scrape and resand the track, which was upgraded from "sloppy" to "good."

In the paddock, Cammie Haughton, now the presiding judge at The Meadowlands, spotted something he thought was unusual. "All the horses were standing in the paddock waiting to go on the track," Haughton said. "And I noticed that Niatross had a lot of blankets on him for some reason. Now it's good to keep a horse warm, especially if there's a delay, for their muscles might tighten up. But they had three coolers on him. I thought it was rather peculiar. So did my dad."

That was a prelude to quite possibly the most peculiar harness race ever.

Almost all harness tracks then had a two-foot-high hub rail, ostensibly to keep horses from going into the infield. That day at Saratoga, it did not work.

Saratoga's leading driver, Jean-Paul Morel, sent longshot Danielles Romeo to the lead from the four post. Galbraith was in quick pursuit with Niatross, who took over, and then eased to the quarter in :30 and a poky half of 1:01 2/5, which elicited boos from the crowd hoping to see Niatross break Sundance Skipper's 1:56 track record or Falcon Almahurst's 1:55 2/5 world record on a half-mile track.

Instead, Niatross had reached the half only three-fifths of a second faster than the horses in the preceding race, a three-thousand-dollar conditional pace.

Haughton jerked Trenton Time to the outside at the half and went up to engage Niatross head to head.

They paced a third quarter in :28 4/5 as a team, reaching the three-quarters in 1:30 1/5 with Niatross maybe a nose in front on the inside.

Haughton knew he had the champion beat. "I knew I could have gone by him at the three-quarters," Haughton said. "I saw he was laboring. He just wasn't right."

Niatross had never been beaten, but Trenton Time was going by him at the head of the stretch. Galbraith tried to rally Niatross by using his whip right-handed.

A startled Niatross, who had never been whipped before, bore to his left, away from the whip. Racing on the rail, there was nowhere to go but over. Niatross tumbled over the hub rail, taking Galbraith and the sulky with him. Galbraith was hurled to the infield.

Upstairs in the press box, Virginia O'Brien fainted momentarily. "I was so devastated," she said twenty years later. But she was okay.

Amazingly, so were Niatross and Galbraith.

Niatross somehow managed to completely twist his body as he fell. He landed, then quickly got up on all four legs facing the opposite direction, the sulky still attached. He had not been seriously injured. Galbraith, too, escaped injury.

"The colt is all right, and I'm all right," Galbraith said. "It's the first time I hit him. He went sideways and jumped the rail."

Then Galbraith left the paddock, crying, as other horsemen tried figuring out what had just happened. Morel's view was better than anyone else's, sitting right behind Niatross on the rail. "That horse is not used to being hit with the whip, not hard in the stifles," Morel said. "He got scared. He made a U-turn."

Watching a replay of the race in the paddock, one driver said, "The more he hit the horse, the more he bore in."

Trenton Time won the race by a length over Justin Passing in 1:59 3/5, but hardly anyone was watching. With Niatross out of the money, the winning quinella paid $312.20 and the late double $186.60.

Billy and Cammie Haughton walked Trenton Time up the track from the winner's circle in eerie silence as people's eyes stayed riveted on Niatross, wondering whether he and Galbraith were all right. Billy Haughton handed Trenton Time's reins to Cammie, and then went over to console his friend Galbraith, who was sitting by himself on the steps of the racing office, still obviously shaken. Haughton sat down and talked with Galbraith. "Billy felt almost as bad as I did because of what happened to the horse," Galbraith said. "We were good friends."

To this day, Galbraith, who is still driving and training horses, is unsure of what happened to Niatross that afternoon at Saratoga. "He was going to get beat that day even before he fell over the rail," Galbraith said. "Maybe he had a touch of virus. I just don't know what was wrong with him that day."

Niatross had suffered superficial injuries and Galbraith pointed him to the one-million-dollar Meadowlands Pace. Similar to the Woodrow Wilson, the Meadowlands Pace had eliminations a week earlier to qualify for the final. In one of three $25,000 elimination heats, Niatross, for the only time in his career, made a break (going off-stride). Most breaks take a horse out of contention completely, but Galbraith got Niatross back on gait and he rallied to finish fourth, barely qualifying for the twelve-horse final.

The super horse had two straight losses, but he was never defeated again, not only taking the Meadowlands Pace Final, but every single major stakes left for three-year-olds, including

Monica Thors

Even after he retired to a successful stud career, Niatross toured tracks to promote harness racing, but never again visited Saratoga.

the Little Brown Jug, the Messenger, and the Prix d'Ete at Blue Bonnets in Montreal. One of the fans rooting for him in Canada was Virginia O'Brien, who had driven more than two hundred miles to see Niatross.

He had won the Pacing Triple Crown (the Cane Pace, Messenger Stakes and Little Brown Jug), and would finish his career with a record of thirty-seven victories in thirty-nine starts at nineteen different tracks in the United States and Canada.

But before he concluded his three-year-old season, he left another measuring stick of his greatness. Much as Secretariat had done by taking the Belmont Stakes in a time a full two seconds faster than any other three-year-old ever, Niatross displayed his awesome speed, too, in a time trial at Lexington's The Red Mile.

Top harness horses do time trials to take a speed mark. To simulate a race and to maximize the horse's effort, one or two Thoroughbred prompters are harnessed to carts and asked to keep up with the horse doing the time trial while not passing him at any time.

When Niatross walked onto The Red Mile on October 1, 1980, he was hoping to lower the 1:52 all-time mark set by Steady Star in 1971. It was the fastest time ever by a Standardbred.

Niatross time trialed in 1:49 1/5, the equivalent of fourteen lengths faster than Steady Star.

Upon retirement, Niatross had an incredible first crop of foals, led by Nihilator, who won thirty-five of thirty-eight starts for Billy Haughton and was the 1985 Horse of the Year.

As if he had not done enough for the sport, Niatross gave more. At the age of nineteen, he went on a tour of tracks throughout the country to promote harness racing. The response was so positive that he did the tour again in 1997. His appearances were a tremendous success, as were most of his racing appearances.

Except at Saratoga. He never went back to Saratoga.

14

One For How Many?

For one whole summer, the Graveyard of Champions became the Graveyard of Stakes Favorites. Maybe it was an epidemic or the mineral water. It had to be something, because, even by Saratoga standards, the 1981 meet was unreal. Favorites lost the first fifteen dirt stakes. There were only sixteen during the whole twenty-four-day meet. Only seven of the fifteen favorites even finished second. And who beat them? Big balloons! Horses at 36-1, 26-1, and 18-1.

The 1981 meet also featured the following oddities:

• Appearances in the Daily Double on separate days by 1980 Kentucky Derby winner Genuine Risk and the horse who beat her in the 1980 Belmont Stakes, Temperence Hill.

• Losses by the two horses that accounted for the three 1981 Triple Crown races.

• A New York-bred hero winning the Whitney Handicap long before state-breds were competitive in open company.

• Former maiden claimers taking the Alabama and Hopeful Stakes.

• An upset perpetrated by a two-year-old colt named Conquistador Cielo and trained by Hall of Famer Woody Stephens. This colt would be on the other end of a historic upset the following year.

Stephens was hoping to jump-start his meet by sending out

Trove and Dame Mysterieuse, the respective favorites in the $57,200 Schuylerville for two-year-old fillies on opening day and the $56,900 Test Stakes for three-year-old fillies the following afternoon. Each filly lost.

Rain caused five turf races to be switched to the main track opening day as twenty-three horses were scratched in the nine races. The track, listed as sloppy, played wet-fast initially but slower as the day progressed. Trove, who was two for two heading into the Schuylerville, was third as the 4-5 favorite to Houston businessman Ed J. Hudson's Mystical Mood, an 8-1 longshot she'd beaten by five and three-quarter lengths in her last start. Mystical Mood paid $18.20 after winning by four lengths in a pedestrian 1:11 4/5. "The off track helped my horse," Mystical Mood's jockey, Jacinto Vasquez, said. Mystical Mood's win gave trainer Del Carroll his second consecutive Schuylerville.

The very next day, favored Dame Mysterieuse was fifth in the Test. Undefeated Discorama, the 2-1 second choice, was third to Cherokee Frolic, who beat 30-1 longshot Maddy's Tune by a length and three-quarters under Gary Cohen. Trained by Bill Cole, Cherokee Frolic was owned by Charles Friedfertig's Carolsteve Stable in Hollywood, Florida. Friedfertig, who invented an offset printing process, had claimed Cherokee Frolic for $25,000 in her second career start.

The Horse for the Course

If every horse entered in the 1981 Whitney Handicap had actually started, it would have made for one of the best races of the year. It was anyway, but for a very different reason.

Heading the list of scratches in the fifty-fourth running of the $175,500 Whitney was 1980 three-year-old champion Temperence Hill, 1980 Eclipse champion older mare

Glorious Song, and 1981 Carter Handicap winner Amber Pass, who came down with gastritis.

Who was left?

Well, Winter's Tale, Noble Nashua, The Liberal Member, Ring of Light, and four outsiders, one of whom had enjoyed remarkable success at Saratoga: a six-year-old gray New York-bred named Fio Rito.

Winter's Tale had won five of seven starts in 1980 but finished seventh by fourteen lengths behind State Dinner in the 1980 Whitney. In 1981 Winter's Tale had won just one of five starts, an allowance race.

The Liberal Member had run third in the 1979 Whitney chasing Star de Naskra and Cox's Ridge. Following a year and a half layoff, he had run third in an allowance race and then finished second to Hechizado in the Brooklyn Handicap.

Noble Nashua, who would become the most expensive stallion ever to stand in New York at $55,000, had won the 1981 Jerome Handicap, Dwyer Stakes, and Swaps Stakes.

As a five-year-old, Ring of Light had taken the 1980 Massachusetts Handicap and the Excelsior Handicap at Aqueduct. In 1981 he'd run second in the Suburban.

Fio Rito was an afterthought to many. Long before the New York breeding program had reached a competitive plateau in open company — before Saratoga Dew, L'Carriere, Victory Speech, Thunder Rumble, Say Florida Sandy, and Critical Eye were even foaled, let alone winning open graded stakes — a six-year-old New York-bred winning a grade I stakes such as the Whitney stretched the imagination. Kelso, Dr. Fager, Key to the Mint, Alydar, and Fio Rito?

But Fio Rito was no ordinary New York-bred, especially at Saratoga, and the Whitney was not a careless fling by his Finger Lakes-based connections, trainer Mike Ferraro and fifty-eight-year-old owner/breeder Ray LeCesse, a bowling alley owner in Rochester who raced a stable of nine at nearby Finger Lakes.

Ferraro, a former candidate for Mr. America, had been the leading trainer at Finger Lakes for six years. Fio Rito's jockey, Les Hulet, had been the leading rider for six years.

At age five, Fio Rito, a giant of a horse at 17.1 hands and 1,300 pounds, had won nine of twelve starts, one of them a five and a half-length win carrying 138 pounds in the mile and a quarter Wadsworth Memorial Handicap. He was second in two other races. His lone poor performance came as the favorite in the mile and three-sixteenths Queens County Handicap at Aqueduct, when he led early and weakened to fifth.

After the winter Fio Rito returned to Finger Lakes. Ferraro and LeCesse quietly pointed him to the Whitney, giving him a second chance to prove he belonged in open New York stakes company at Saratoga, where he had posted three victories and one second in four starts.

Fio Rito's 1981 record before the Whitney, four wins and one second in five starts, did nothing to discourage Ferraro.

Fio Rito gave the New York breeding program a boost when he upset the 1981 Whitney field.

"We figured if he ever was going to prove he belongs with the best, I think it would be here at Saratoga," Ferraro said. "He won't embarrass us in any way. He's a racehorse. He's a genuine racehorse."

Ferraro was less concerned about Fio Rito's credentials than his physical condition. Fio Rito had bruised his left foot two days before the Whitney. "We're not really sure how bad it is," Ferraro said at the time. "We want to run, but if he's not one hundred percent, there's no way we'll start him."

By Saturday afternoon Fio Rito's foot was okay. But he might have been scratched anyway when he broke through the starting gate, if not for a miraculous, diving catch by assistant starter Jim Tsitsiragos. "When he broke through the gate, I thought we blew it," Ferraro said.

They hadn't. Now all Fio Rito had to do was run the race of his life. He had his favorite track and his regular rider, Hulet, and went off at 10-1, even though he was getting eight pounds from 121-pound highweight Winter's Tale, the 3-2 favorite. The Liberal Member was 3-1, Noble Nashua 4-1, and Ring of Light 6-1.

Hulet rode Fio Rito daringly on the front end, taking on all challengers and putting them away one after another. First 50-1 longshot Blue Ensign engaged Fio Rito. They dueled head to head, exchanging the lead twice before Fio Rito inched out to a half-length lead on the inside of Blue Ensign, who faded.

Then, Ruben Hernandez, riding Ring of Light in third, took his shot. So did Eddie Maple aboard Noble Nashua and Jeff Fell on Winter's Tale, who got through along the rail. Hulet gave Fio Rito a steady tattoo of the whip right-handed, and he proved unwavering, holding off Winter's Tale by a neck. Ring of Light was a length behind Winter's Tale in third, a head in front of The Liberal Member.

"Please, don't talk to me. I don't believe it," Hernandez said afterward to reporters.

There was nothing fluky about Fio Rito's victory. He had covered the mile and an eighth in 1:48, just one second off Tri Jet's 1974 still-standing stakes and track record and, at the time, the fourth-fastest winning time since the Whitney had been shortened from ten furlongs to nine in 1955.

Fio Rito returned to the winner's circle to considerable applause. "He's a truly great horse," Hulet said. "He really proved himself today. That's for sure."

As Fio Rito pawed the winner's circle with his right front foot, Ferraro struggled to find words. "This is unreal," he said. "It's just...it's a Cinderella story."

Well, Cinderella paid $22.20 to win in becoming one of the few New York-breds ever to win a grade I or major stakes (major stakes were not graded until 1973). New York-bred Silent Screen won the 1969 Champagne Stakes before it was made a grade I.

The next day at Saratoga, the winner of the 1981 Belmont Stakes, Summing, finished last in a roughly run edition of the Jim Dandy Stakes.

Summing, making his first start since denying Pleasant Colony the Triple Crown by winning the Belmont Stakes, was the surprising 9-5 second choice in a field of eight as the 128-pound highweight. Summing battled on the lead with Prince Fortune and faded to last. The 7-5 favorite, Sportin' Life, was a troubled fourth.

And the horse who beat all of them was Willow Hour, trained by Jim Picou and ridden superbly by Eddie Maple. Willow Hour, a son of 1966 Hopeful Stakes winner Bold Hour, had been a well-beaten fourth and fifth in his previous two starts, explaining his 18-1 odds. Maple waited for Summing to put away Prince Fortune before moving. Willow Hour opened a length and a half lead at the top of the stretch and then was all out to hold off Lemhi Gold by half a length.

Lemhi Gold's rider, Angel Cordero Jr., claimed foul against

the winner in two different spots, torture for Willow Hour's connections because the colt had been disqualified from first the year before in the Nashua Stakes at Aqueduct.

But the stewards let Willow Hour's win in the Jim Dandy stand. Lemhi Gold had indeed been bothered on the first turn, but it was a chain reaction triggered by Silver Express, who bore out sharply into Sportin' Life, who in turn banged into Lemhi Gold.

The 1981 Belmont Stakes winner had been defeated, but the horse who would win the 1982 Belmont Stakes on the way to becoming Horse of the Year, speedy Conquistador Cielo, fared better the next day in the Saratoga Special. Sent off at 8-1 and racing from behind, Conquistador Cielo upset Lejoli, the 2-1 favorite.

Again it was Eddie Maple at the controls, and, again, Maple had to survive not only a foul claim, but a steward's inquiry, too. "It seems these things are getting pretty tough," he said afterward.

The steward's inquiry and an objection by Cash Asmussen, who finished second by a half-length on Herschelwalker, focused on contact between his horse and Conquistador Cielo through the stretch, particularly at the eighth pole after they had both rallied from off the pace. Matt Graves reported in the Albany *Times Union* the next day that Conquistador Cielo seemed to bear in a little bit and Herschelwalker bore out a bit. That's the way the stewards saw it, leaving the order of finish up. Timely Writer was third and the 2-1 favorite, Lejoli, fourth after being blocked badly coming out of the starting gate.

Conquistador Cielo was a $150,000 yearling purchase by Henry de Kwiatkowski. De Kwiatkowski owned a New York-based aircraft firm and was affiliated with an aviation club called Les Conquistadors de Cielo (Conquerors of the Sky). Cielo did perfectly fine on earth.

In the race before the Saratoga Special, 1977 champion grass horse Johnny D., owned by Dana S. Bray Jr. of Glens Falls, a city ten miles north of Saratoga Springs, attempted a come-back in an allowance race. Sent off the 2-1 favorite despite a layoff of nearly four years, he was last in a field of nine, anoth-er beaten favorite in a meet already full of them after just one week. The only stakes-winning favorite in opening week was Thrice Worthy, who won the Lovely Night Steeplechase Handicap.

Second Week: Bigger Longshots

The day after Highest Regard lost at 2-5 in the $54,000 Ballerina Stakes to the 7-2 second choice, Love Sign, Accipiter's Hope's lit up the tote board, paying $54.20 after winning the $115,600 DeWitt Clinton Stakes for New York-breds under apprentice sensation Richard Migliore.

Migliore, who rode without his five-pound weight allowance because it was a stakes race, would break Steve Cauthen's single-season earnings record for an apprentice the following day.

Getting through on the inside of tiring pacesetters Prosper and Knightly Spiced, Accipiter's Hope was all out to hold off Adirondack Holme, the 8-5 favorite and 126-pound high-weight, by a nose. Adirondack Holme, ridden by Ruben Hernandez, was bred and owned by the pioneering late presi-dent of the New York Thoroughbred Breeders Inc., Dr. Dominick DeLuke, who was a prominent orthodontist in nearby Schenectady, New York.

Accipiter's Hope's win was extra sweet for the seventeen-year-old Migliore, not only because it was his first victory in a $100,000 stakes but also because of the winner's trainer, Steven L. DiMauro. DiMauro's father, Steve, also a trainer in New York, had been personally responsible for developing Migliore's jockey skills during the past year. "I always felt the kid (Migliore) was a natural, and he proved it," the elder DiMauro said. Accipiter's Hope, a homebred, had been entered in a sale and retrieved for $10,000 when nobody wanted him. After the DeWitt Clinton, everybody wished they had him.

A Better Day for Luis Barrera

Summing's loss in the Jim Dandy Stakes was disappointing for his trainer, Luis Barrera. But Summing had given Barrera the biggest win of his career in the Belmont Stakes earlier that summer, less than three years after he started training on his own. He had been working as an assistant to his brother, Laz, from 1970 through 1978. "I had to make that decision," he said. "I had no chance to show myself. I was in my brother's shadow."

Barrera would be placed in the spotlight again with Happy Valley Farm's Prismatical, a filly who started her career as a $25,000 maiden claimer. She won by seven and a quarter lengths and, fortunately for Barrera, wasn't claimed. A foot injury ended Prismatical's two-year-old season, and Barrera tempted fate by entering her in a $47,500 claimer at three.

Again Prismatical was not claimed, and she won six of seven starts, though she was disqualified from one of her victories. "Every time she races she gets better," Barrera said. Her lone loss was a fifth in a stakes race after breaking poorly.

Barrera gave Prismatical another shot in the Monmouth Oaks, and she won by two and a quarter lengths. That put her on track for the 101st running of the Alabama Stakes, which had seldom been a payday for former maiden claimers.

But Prismatical, the 7-2 third choice in a field of six under Eddie Maple, took Banner Gala, the 7-5 favorite under Angel Cordero Jr., to the limit in the mile and a quarter stakes before 32,291, one of the largest crowds in Saratoga history.

Test Stakes winner Cherokee Frolic set the pace in a strung-out field in the Alabama, with Banner Gala second, Discorama third, and Prismatical fourth. Maple was following Barrera's instructions. "Luis said the speed would come back, and I'd have enough filly to get there," Maple said. "He was right."

So he didn't panic as Prismatical fell behind by fifteen lengths.

Cordero moved Banner Gala with less than a half mile to go, and she quickly disposed of front-running Cherokee Frolic, opening a three-length lead. Discorama tried darting to the inside to stay with her, but could not. Maple, though, had Prismatical rolling on the outside, and she was quickly head to head with Banner Gala. The two fillies slugged it out shoulder to shoulder through the stretch, each jockey hitting left-hand-ed. In the final strides, Prismatical pushed her neck in front, giving Maple his third major stakes win in seven days, following the victories of Willow Hour and Conquistador Cielo. "Banner Gala was tough and wouldn't give up," Maple said. "But my filly hung tough, too, and fought it out."

Cordero was also proud of Banner Gala. "My filly ran big, very game," he said. "We have no excuse. What more do you want when two fillies run so hard and fast?"

There was an even faster filly out at Saratoga two days later. Her name was Genuine Risk, and she would start the Monday racing program in an allowance race to begin the Daily Double. Native Courier, sent off at 9-2 under Maple, and Great Neck, the 6-5 favorite under Cordero, had taken Sunday's grass stakes, the two divisions of the Bernard Baruch Handicap. A stakes favorite still hadn't won on dirt.

Genuine Risk, owned by Bert and Diana Firestone and trained by LeRoy Jolley, had made racing history in 1980, becoming only the second filly to win the Kentucky Derby before finishing second to Codex in a controversial Preakness Stakes in which she was carried extremely wide by Codex, who survived a claim of foul, and a game second to

Temperence Hill in the Belmont Stakes. She was nosed by Bold and Determined in the Maskette Handicap, then concluded her 1980 season with a nose victory over Misty Gallore in the Ruffian Handicap.

Genuine Risk won her four-year-old debut, an allowance race at Aqueduct, by nine and a half lengths. Jolley then tried her on turf, and she finished a tiring third by two lengths in an allowance race.

She had been off two and a half months when she entered the starting gate at Saratoga for the first time. Jolley might have had a flashback. Four years earlier his stakes winner Honest Pleasure lost in an allowance race at Saratoga. Genuine Risk, though, gave Jolley no anxious moments, easing to an eight and a quarter-length, wire-to-wire win under Jeff Fell, getting seven furlongs in a snappy 1:21 2/5 and paying $2.20 to win. "I'm always nervous when she runs," Jolley said afterward. "But she ran super. I couldn't be happier."

Kentucky Derby winner Genuine Risk escaped the "graveyard" jinx in her only start at Saratoga but never raced again.

She never raced again. Two days before she was scheduled to face males again in the Woodward Stakes at Belmont Park, Genuine Risk took several bad steps. Convinced she had a chronic knee injury, Jolley and the Firestones retired her.

Monday's feature was the $58,600 Adirondack Stakes for two-year-old fillies and an opportunity for Trove to redeem herself after losing the Schuylerville. Absolute Value won the race before the Adirondack Stakes at 36-1, paying $75.20. It was the highest win payoff of the day. Barely.

Trove went off at 6-5; Thrilled N Delightd was 36-1. She'd lost her first four starts, but won her maiden at Saratoga eight days before the Adirondack for trainer Joe Pierce Jr. and his wife, Sheila, Thrilled N Delightd's owner and breeder.

Ninth after a quarter of a mile in the six furlong stakes, Thrilled N Delightd rallied to a length and a quarter win under Jorge Velasquez and returned $74.80. Apalachee Honey, who was eighth at the head of the stretch, beat Trove by three-quarters of a length for second. Schuylerville winner Mystical Mood was fourth.

The meet was half over and a stakes favorite still hadn't won on dirt. If one horse couldn't get the job done, maybe two could, as an entry in Wednesday's Sanford Stakes.

Two for the Price of One

The entry of Shipping Magnate, ridden by Jeff Fell, and Lejoli, with Angel Cordero Jr. up, went off the 2-1 favorite in the $58,800 Sanford Stakes on Wednesday, August 12. And they nearly got the job done before a weekday record crowd of 31,104 that was treated to a four-horse blanket finish.

The photo involved Nick Zito's speedball Mayanesian.

Zito had decided to make an equipment change after Mayanesian had opened huge leads in his first three starts and caved in each time. Zito added blinkers, and Mayanesian

responded with a four-length maiden win at Saratoga under
new rider Jacinto Vasquez.

In the Sanford, Mayanesian figured to be severely tested,
and he was. Conquistador Cielo and Herschelwalker, the horse
Conquistador Cielo narrowly upset in the Saratoga Special
nine days earlier, each went off at 7-2 in the field of ten.
Mayanesian was 10-1.

Breaking from the nine post on a speed-favoring, drying-out
track labeled "good," Mayanesian streaked to the lead, opening up a two-length lead by zipping the first quarter mile of
the six furlong stakes in :21 3/5. He increased his lead to three
lengths by running the half in :45. Then the field closed in.

Shipping Magnate had been stalking Mayanesian the entire
way, and Fell took to the inside and whittled away
Mayanesian's advantage, gaining with every stride. Outside of
Mayanesian, Lejoli and Conquistador Cielo were flying, but
Mayanesian was unwavering, gutting out a head victory over
Shipping Magnate, with Lejoli a nose back in third and
Conquistador Cielo just another nostril back in fourth. Once
again, there was an inquiry centering on bumping in the
stretch between Lejoli and Conquistador Cielo, but the stew-
ards took no action.

"He's a fast sucker and has just that one style," Vasquez said
afterward. Mayanesian got the six furlongs in 1:11 1/5, leaving
the string of defeated favorites in dirt stakes intact.

The $57,000 Empire Stakes for two-year-old New York breds
two days later did nothing to alter the landscape. Salute Me
Sir, who was tenth by fifteen lengths in a maiden race in his
last start, making him zero for three in his career, beat the
speedy filly Cupecoy's Joy by a length at 6-1. The 8-5 favorite,
Bright Rex, was another length back in third in the field of
nine. The winner was trained by Johnny Campo, who figured
he could end the drought of winning stakes favorites the next
day when he saddled Pleasant Colony in the Travers Stakes.

Chapter 14

And Then It Poured

Torrential rain produced a sloppy track, August 15, 1981, but did nothing to impact what was a magnificent 112th running of the $226,000 Travers Stakes before a crowd of 39,146, the track's second-largest crowd. They were treated to a battle of wills between Willow Hour, a virtual unknown before his upset victory in the Jim Dandy Stakes thirteen days earlier, and Pleasant Colony, the Kentucky Derby and Preakness winner who missed the Triple Crown when he was third behind Summing and Highland Bid in the Belmont Stakes.

Pleasant Colony had been switched to Campo's barn after finishing fifth by thirteen lengths to Lord Avie in the Florida Derby in his second start as a three-year-old under trainer Lee O'Donnell. Previously, Pleasant Colony had beaten Lord Avie by a head in his three-year-old debut when he was second by a nose to Akureyri in the Fountain of Youth.

Campo freshened Pleasant Colony, and the bay colt responded by winning the Wood Memorial by three lengths, a prelude to his near sweep of the Triple Crown.

Campo decided to bring Pleasant Colony up to the Travers on works alone, and he did an incredibly fine job, one documented by David L. Heckerman in the August 22 edition of *The Blood-Horse*:

"Campo used the first two of the 10 weeks between the Belmont and the Travers as a rest and recuperation period for Pleasant Colony, which had lost weight and much of the bloom in his coat during the Triple Crown campaign. The colt's shoes were pulled off, and he was wormed. His only exercise for 14 days came in morning walks around the shed row.

"Campo then sent the colt back to the track for a series of progressively longer gallops. Pleasant Colony's first serious work was at six furlongs in mid-July and was followed by a series of once-a-week, one-mile drills. The colt breezed a mile

**Longshot Willow Hour (3) narrowly defeated dual classic winner Pleasant Colony
on a sloppy track in the 1981 Travers.**

Bob Coglianese/NYRA

at Saratoga on July 25 in 1:40 2/5 and then was clocked at
1:36 4/5 on Aug. 1 and 1:36 2/5 on Aug. 8. In each of the last
two works, Campo used the 3-year-old Fictional Chief, which
had been competing in $35,000 claiming races, as a target for
Pleasant Colony during the last five furlongs. The tactic result-
ed in quarter-miles that were the fastest of the drills. Pleasant
Colony's preparation was completed with an easy five furlongs
over the Oklahoma Training Track in 1:02 2/5 on the
Wednesday before the Travers.

"In the early weeks after the Belmont, Pleasant Colony
gained 75 pounds, then trimmed 15 of that away during the

final tightening period. The colt's coat was lustrous again on Travers day."

And very wet. As were those of his protagonists, who included Belmont Stakes winner Summing, Jersey Derby, and Haskell Invitational winner Five Star Flight, Lord Avie, Noble Nashua, Lemhi Gold, and the horse who had won the Jim Dandy, Willow Hour. The field of ten was completed by Prince Fortune, an entry-mate rabbit of Pleasant Colony's added to prevent a slow pace, and extreme longshots Fairway Phantom and Dorcaro. Of the ten, one horse had a win over the track, Willow Hour. He went off at 24-1, most bettors figuring the addition of nine pounds from the Jim Dandy and the huge step up in competition would mitigate his chances. Willow Hour had been a distant fifth to Noble Nashua in the Dwyer Stakes and a non-threatening fourth to Five Star Flight in the Jersey Derby. But his jockey, Eddie Maple, who had won the 1980 Travers on Temperence Hill at 7-2, expected a good showing from Willow Hour in the Travers. "I had a lot of confidence in this little horse today," Maple said afterward.

The bettors had a lot more confidence in Pleasant Colony, sending him off the 8-5 favorite under a new rider, Cordero. Both Lord Avie, under Pleasant Colony's former rider, Jorge Velasquez, and Five Star Flight, ridden by Craig Perret, were 7-2. Noble Nashua was 6-1 and Summing 8-1.

Willow Hour broke on the lead, but was quickly joined by Fairway Phantom, Five Star Flight, and Prince Fortune, who sprinted four wide to make the front. Maple let Willow Hour settle into second around the clubhouse turn, two to three lengths behind Prince Fortune. Five Star Flight and Fairway Phantom raced together third and fourth and Pleasant Colony was farther back in fifth. Lord Avie, meanwhile, was floundering far back in last. "At one point, I made him 29 lengths back," *Daily Racing Form* chart man Jack Wilson told *The Blood-Horse's* William H. Rudy afterward.

Prince Fortune took the field the first three-quarters of a mile before Maple sent Willow Hour up for the lead, which he garnered quickly. Behind him, Pleasant Colony was closing with a breathtaking rush, shooting past Five Star Flight, Fairway Phantom, and Prince Fortune in just seconds. Pleasant Colony's momentum carried him up to Willow Hour's head midway around the far turn.

"Pleasant Colony made such a move at him, I thought he'd go right by," Willow Hour's trainer, Jim Picou, said.

But Willow Hour wasn't even close to being done, and he gamely held off Pleasant Colony. "He never got in front," Maple said. "I don't think he ever got ahead."

In the driving rain — Cordero said he went through seven sets of goggles that day — the two three-year-olds drove to the wire together in the middle of the track.

"When they came into the stretch and my horse was still there, I said, 'He's not going to get by him today,' " Picou said.

Willow Hour held on by a head. "I thought we were going to get him, but we just couldn't," Cordero said. "My horse ran great, but he couldn't get there."

Behind Willow Hour and Pleasant Colony, Lord Avie had made a sensational rally from last, more than twenty-three lengths off the lead with just half a mile left. But Velasquez compromised his chances by veering Lord Avie to the deeper inside part of the track at the sixteenth pole, inside of Willow Hour and Pleasant Colony, and he finished third, a length and three-quarters behind Pleasant Colony.

Campo handled Pleasant Colony's agonizing defeat with class: "My horse ran super, just super. We have no excuses."

Willow Hour paid $50.20 to win, still the highest Travers win payoff.

Pleasant Colony rebounded to win the Woodward Stakes by a length and three-quarters in his first start against older horses as the 9-5 favorite, then ran fourth by six and a half lengths

as the even-money favorite in the final start of his life, the
Marlboro Cup Handicap, behind Noble Nashua, Amber Pass,
and Temperence Hill. Regardless, Pleasant Colony was
deservedly named three-year-old champion of 1981.

But a favorite still had not won a dirt stakes at the meet,
though the day after the Travers, De La Rose and Eddie Maple
won the Diana Handicap on grass as the even-money favorite
for trainer Woody Stephens. On dirt the following day,
Ballerina Stakes winner Love Sign ran second at 2-5 to Jameela
in a four-horse field in the $55,900 Mahubah Handicap.

The Final Week

If Genuine Risk could open up a daily double at Saratoga,
so could Temperence Hill, who had skipped the Whitney,
and The Liberal Member, who had been a close fourth in the
Whitney. Temperence Hill and The Liberal Member both
showed up in Wednesday's opener, a $35,000 mile and
three-sixteenths allowance race on turf. Temperence Hill had
run twice on grass, finishing third by a length and three-
quarters at 8-1 in an allowance race at Belmont Park, and
seventh by sixteen lengths in the 1980 Turf Classic at
Aqueduct at 2-1. The Liberal Member had started eight times
on grass and won once. In a field of six, The Liberal Member
and Temperence Hill finished third and fifth at odds of 3-2
and 5-2, respectively. Manguin, the 4-1 third choice, beat
Scythian Gold by a nose.

The feature Wednesday was the $55,500 Yaddo Stakes for
New York-breds, then run at seven furlongs on dirt. Cupid's
Way, the 3-2 favorite with Cordero, ran bravely on the front
end under pressure inside and outside before weakening to
third, a length and a quarter behind Czajka, a 7-1 winner with
Ruben Hernandez.

That extended the favorites' dirt stakes losing streak to fourteen. There were only two stakes left in the four-week meet, the Hopeful and the Spinaway that Saturday and Sunday. Just for good measure on Friday, though, Adlibber, the 3-2 favorite in the $86,550 West Point Handicap for New York-Breds on grass, checked in third behind Naskra's Breeze, the 12-1 winner for Hall of Fame trainer Phil Johnson and jockey Jean-Luc Samyn.

It seemed like the cosmos were getting involved to preserve the stakes favorites' oh-fer on dirt.

Undefeated Monmouth Park-based Out of Hock was being pointed to run in the $500,000 Arlington-Washington Futurity on August 29 in Chicago. However, an air-controllers strike made shipping that far risky. So trainer Stanley Rieser shipped to Saratoga instead for the $85,650 Hopeful Stakes on August 22. Out of Hock, a chestnut gelding by No Robbery out of Sweet Simple Girl, a daughter of Jaipur, had been dominant winning his first four starts at Monmouth. The speedster won his first two starts by identical eleven-length margins and then won the $32,525 Tyro Stakes by five lengths and the $150,990 Sapling by seven lengths on a sloppy track. He had been in front at all but one call in his four races and signaled his intentions for the Hopeful with a blazing work two days before the race, three furlongs in :34 1/5, galloping out four in :46 1/5.

A super match-up of undefeated two-year-olds in the Hopeful, Out of Hock versus Canada-based Deputy Minister, who was six for six, failed to materialize because Deputy Minister's Coggins test for equine infectious anemia had expired. His connections didn't find out in time for a new test to be processed before the Hopeful. He was out. Mayanesian, that "fast sucker" who won the Sanford, was in.

Now Handicapping 101 tells us that when two speed horses hook up, a suicidal duel is a distinct possibility. Yet Out of Hock and jockey Don Brumfield went off the 9-10 favorite in the field of eight, which included Timely Writer and Lejoli, the third-and fourth-place finishers, respectively, in the

Saratoga Special. Timely Writer, a $13,500 yearling, was a geld-
ing owned by Peter and Francis Martin, trained by Dom
Imprescia and based at Suffolk Downs. Timely Writer won his
first start by eight lengths in a $30,000 maiden claimer at
Monmouth Park.

Mayanesian, not Out of Hock, was the quickest two-year-old
in the Hopeful, and he led by a length over Out of Hock
thanks to a dazzling first quarter in :22 1/5. Out of Hock shadowed him on the outside in second through a quick half in
:44 4/5. Brumfield inched Out of Hock closer to Mayanesian
on the turn, and Out of Hock took the lead, opening a two-
length lead. But Timely Writer, kept well off the pace by Roger
Danjean, had Out of Hock measured and exploded past him
to win by four and a half lengths. Out of Hock held second by
two lengths over Lejoli, who literally walked out of the gate at
the start. "We can't make any excuses," Rieser said. "We got
beat by a nice horse."

A very nice horse. Timely Writer went on finish third in the
Belmont Futurity and win the Champagne in 1981, then the
Flamingo and Florida Derby in 1982 before he was tossed out
of the Triple Crown chase when an intestinal blockage forced
him to undergo emergency abdominal surgery that April. He
returned to action with a victory in the $78,300 Yankee
Handicap at Suffolk Downs August 14 at 3-10. But Timely
Writer's return was a prelude to tragedy as he was euthanized
after shattering his left foreleg a half-mile from the finish line
in the Jockey Club Gold Cup that fall.

Before Dawn on the Last Dawn

There was one dirt stakes left, the $88,200 Spinaway Stakes
on Sunday, August 23. Out of Hock hadn't delivered. Could
Calumet Farm's Before Dawn, an undefeated filly with half as
many races, do better?

The afternoon was full of bad omens for Before Dawn's connections, trainer John Veitch, and rider John Velasquez, who
had ridden Before Dawn to a six and three-quarters-length

The Blood-Horse

**Calumet Farm's Before Dawn kept her undefeated record as she
won the Spinaway Stakes for two-year-old fillies.**

maiden victory and a five and a quarter-length win in the Fashion Stakes June 20. She hadn't raced since because of bucked shins.

In Sunday's second race, Velasquez was injured when his horse, Native Truth, apparently broke a leg, fell, and had to be euthanized. Veitch needed a rider, and he settled on Gregg McCarron, jockey Chris McCarron's brother.

Things didn't get better for Veitch as the day progressed. He sent out three horses before the Spinaway. None lit the board, and one of them, Rivalero, was pulled up in the stretch when he bled.

Regardless, Before Dawn was 4-5 in a field of ten two-year-old fillies. And she crushed her competition, winning by seven and three-quarter lengths in 1:09 2/5 for six furlongs, at the time the fourth fastest Spinaway ever. Before Dawn tacked on easy victories in the Astarita Stakes and Matron before running second against colts in the Champagne, beaten four and three-quarter lengths by Timely Writer, and winning the two-year-old filly championship.

Chalk players who bet Before Dawn to win the Spinaway got $3.60 for a two-dollar ticket, probably not enough to get them out for the meet.

15

Triple Crown Lumps

The Travers Stakes, the oldest stakes for three-year-olds in the United States, has not been particularly kind to winners of the Triple Crown races.

Only one of three Triple Crown winners who raced in the Travers won: Whirlaway in 1941. Gallant Fox was second in 1930, and Affirmed placed second in 1978 when he was disqualified for interfering with his arch rival, Alydar, who was placed first.

The Travers, first contested in 1864, was initially conducted at a mile and three-quarters before being shortened to a mile and an eighth in 1895, 1901, 1902, and 1903. It has been run at a mile and a quarter ever since.

Only nine Derby winners in the past fifty-nine years have even started in the Travers. This reflects the difficulty of having a three-year-old precocious enough to race a mile and a quarter in the Kentucky Derby on the first Saturday of May and durable and resilient enough to do it again in the Travers in late August. Just two Derby winners have won: Sea Hero in 1993 and Thunder Gulch in 1995.

When Preakness and Belmont Stakes winner Point Given won the 2001 Travers, it made Preakness winners one for twelve in the Travers the past thirty-four years and Belmont Stakes winners five for twenty the past thirty-two. The first

Runaway Groom upsets a stellar field in the 1982 Travers.

four Belmont Stakes winners who raced in the Travers, Ruthless (1867), Kingfisher (1870), Henry Bassett (1871), and Joe Daniels (1872), all won. The fifth did not. Springbok, described in the 1883 *Horse Breeders' Guide and Handbook* as a "horse of great substance and power, lightly finished all over without a particle of lumber," went to post in a field of seven in the 1873 "Midsummer Derby" as the co-favorite with Tom Bowling. Springbok was racing in second when he fell at the three-quarter-mile pole. Tom Bowling won by thirty yards. Springbok went on to race through the age of six before retiring. He stood for a hundred-dollar stud fee in Kentucky.

In 1875 the winner of the first Kentucky Derby, Aristides, who had been unplaced the year before in the Saratoga Stakes, tried adding the Travers to his resumé but finished third to D'Artagnan. Favored Ozark finished eighth in the field of ten.

The first Preakness winner to compete in the Travers, Cloverbrook, who had also won the Belmont Stakes, finished fifth in the 1877 Travers to heavily favored Baden Baden, who had won the Kentucky Derby and Jersey Derby but ran third behind Cloverbrook in the Belmont.

One hundred and five years later, the match-up of the respective winners of the Kentucky Derby, Preakness, and Belmont Stakes in the 1982 Travers was billed as the first such meeting in Travers history. It was not. In 1918, the year before Sir Barton became the first Triple Crown winner, the Preakness Stakes had been run in two divisions for the only time in its 127-year history. The winner of the first division, War Cloud, joined Kentucky Derby winner Exterminator and Belmont Stakes winner Johren in the 1918 Travers. The 11-10 favorite was Willis Sharpe Kilmer's entry of Exterminator and Sun Briar, who had won the 1917 Saratoga Special and Hopeful on the way to being named champion two-year-old. Sun Briar beat Johren, who carried six pounds more, by a head to take the Travers. War Cloud was six lengths back in third and Exterminator last in the field of four.

Unlike Point Given, these winners of Triple Crown races went off as favorites in the Travers and failed to get the job done:

• 1926 Belmont Stakes winner Crusader was fourth at 4-5 to Mars.

• 1928 Preakness winner Victorian was second at 6-5 to Petee-Wrack.

• 1945 Belmont Stakes winner Pavot was fourth at 4-5 to Adonis.

• 1947 Belmont Stakes winner Phalanx was second at 1-2 to Young Peter.

• 1963 Preakness winner Candy Spots was fourth at 6-5 to Crewman.

• 1974 Preakness and Belmont Stakes winner Little Current was second at even-money to Holding Pattern.

• 1981 Kentucky Derby and Preakness winner Pleasant

Colony was second by a head at 8-5 to Willow Hour.

In 1982 the respective winners of the Kentucky Derby, Preakness, and Belmont Stakes met in the Travers. Only two other three-year-olds went to post. One of them made racing history.

The Kentucky Derby Winner

Arthur B. Hancock III and Leone J. Peters' Gato Del Sol broke last from the eighteen post in a field of nineteen in the 1982 Kentucky Derby and still won going away by two and a half lengths under Eddie Delahoussaye Jr. The 21-1 longshot was trained by Eddie Gregson.

Gato Del Sol did little early in his career to indicate he would reach such heights, finishing third and seventh in his first two starts as a two-year-old at Hollywood Park. But when Southern California racing switched to Del Mar in August, he came to hand quickly, winning a one-mile maiden race by seven lengths. He was third in the Balboa Stakes and won the Del Mar Futurity. Gato Del Sol ran third in the Norfolk Stakes, was second by a half-length in the Hollywood Prevue Stakes, and finished seventh behind Stalwart and the one-eyed wonder Cassaleria in the $500,000 Hollywood Futurity.

At three, the gray son of Cougar II out of Peacefully by Jacinto raced four times before the 1982 Kentucky Derby, winning none of his starts. After running third in an allowance race, he was second by a neck in the San Felipe Handicap, fourth in the Santa Anita Derby, and second by five and a half lengths to Linkage in the Blue Grass Stakes.

After winning the Kentucky Derby, Gregson figured he was better off skipping the mile and three-sixteenths Preakness with his late-runner, focusing on the mile and a half Belmont Stakes instead.

After Gato Del Sol ran a distant second in the Belmont,

Gregson tried the son of Cougar against older horses in the Suburban Handicap. Gato Del Sol was last in the field of eight, sixteen and a half lengths behind the winner, Silver Buck.

Gato Del Sol's connections announced that Gato Del Sol would remain in New York under the care of trainer Howie Tesher, who would try and develop a new running style for the horse and point him to the Travers.

Tesher, indeed, trained some speed into Gato Del Sol, and

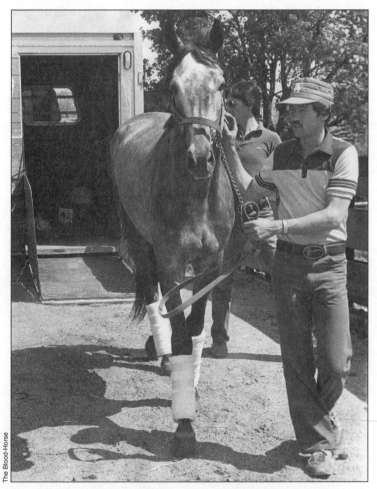

1982 Kentucky Derby winner Gato Del Sol faded to last in the
Midsummer Derby, the Travers Stakes.

the gray colt won an allowance race at Saratoga by three lengths on August 8, thirteen days before the Travers.

Tesher shared his training strategy in a Travers diary he wrote with Matt Graves of the Albany *Times Union*. Among the excerpts:

August 18 — "I'll work him Thursday or Friday. If I breeze him Thursday, it'll be a half mile. I'll blow him out Friday three-quarters of a mile. He's coming up to the race terrific. He'll gallop a mile and a half tomorrow (Wednesday). It gets more exciting every day it gets closer to the race. I just hope the weather holds up. I'm almost positive I wouldn't race him if the track was off. I'd certainly have second thoughts about it."

August 21 (race day) — "He still looks super. We blew out in :36 and 3/5. We know he's ready to race. The way I see the race, Aloma's Ruler will go to the lead. There's no better lead rider in the world then Cordero. Then it's up to Maple (riding Conquistador Cielo) whether he'll go or wait. I think he'll wait. If he does, he'll have to contend with us. If they go head and head, it's going to help us."

The Preakness Stakes Winner

Nathan Scherr's Aloma's Ruler was a late-developing speedster trained patiently and intelligently by John "Butch" Lenzini Jr. Aloma's Ruler raced four times as a two-year-old. His second-place debut at Monmouth Park was followed with three victories at The Meadowlands: a maiden race, an allowance race, and the $25,000 Nutley Stakes. At three Aloma's Ruler won the Bahama Stakes at Hialeah by a head over Distinctive Pro, then was out of action three months and two days after injuring his left front ankle. He was nosed by Happy Hooligan in an allowance race at Pimlico but won the Withers Stakes at Aqueduct and added the Preakness Stakes by a half-length over Linkage, who had skipped the Kentucky Derby.

Lenzini tried stretching Aloma's Ruler out to a mile and a half on a sloppy track in the Belmont Stakes, but the Preakness winner finished ninth by forty-four lengths. Aloma's Ruler recovered to finish third against older horses in the Suburban,

Aloma's Ruler, the 1982 Preakness winner, could only finish second in the Travers.

trouncing Gato Del Sol in the process. Aloma's Ruler won the Jersey Derby by a nose and was second by three-quarters of a length to Wavering Monarch, while spotting him nine pounds in the Haskell Invitational at Monmouth Park.

"The Belmont Stakes is a definite throw-out," Lenzini said the day before the Travers. "If the track is real fast on Saturday, you'll see what Aloma's Ruler is capable of."

The Belmont Stakes Winner

Woody Stephens was an incredibly successful trainer. His five consecutive Belmont Stakes are legendary. Even starting a horse in five consecutive Belmont Stakes is an accomplishment, let alone winning one or two back to back. Odds are Stephens' record will stand a long, long time.

Woody Stephens left a human legacy, too: the fine horsemen his former assistants became. Billy Badgett, David Donk, and Phil Gleaves come readily to mind.

Stephens imprinted on those successful trainers a basic tenet: do right by the horse, no matter how talented it may be. Henryk de Kwiatkowski's Conquistador Cielo had more talent than most. But the son of Mr. Prospector might never have won the first of Stephens' five straight Belmont Stakes if Stephens hadn't known his horse well enough to back off when it mattered most and to step forward when the time was right, even if it meant defying conventional wisdom.

When Conquistador Cielo won the 1981 Saratoga Special at odds of 8-1, Stephens was twenty-eight days short of his sixty-eighth birthday. After finishing fourth by a neck in the Sanford, Cielo suffered a stress (saucer) fracture of his left foreleg and was done for the season.

The three-year-old returned in two seven-furlong allowance races at Hialeah the following spring, winning the second start by four lengths in a quick 1:22 1/5.

Cielo, though, turned up sore the next day. He lost more time after developing a cough in mid-April, and Stephens did not rush him back to make the Triple Crown. "I try to take awfully good care of my horses," Stephens said later that summer.

Cielo recovered and was ready to run in early May. Stephens found a soft landing for his return, an allowance race at Pimlico on May 8, which Cielo won by three lengths. Instead of remaining at Pimlico and competing in the May 15

Preakness, Stephens entered Cielo in an allowance race at Belmont Stakes four days later. Cielo responded with an eleven-length win in 1:34 1/5 for the mile.

Cielo was ready for the next step up, and he took it magnificently. It was not a shock that he won, rather how he won, as the 2-1 favorite against older horses in the Metropolitan Handicap. Breaking from the eleven post in a field of fourteen, Cielo shot to the lead under Eddie Maple, dueled through a first quarter in :22 4/5, and then kissed the field good-bye. By the half in :45, he led by two lengths. He hit the three-quarters in 1:09 and kept right on humming, completing the mile in 1:33, a stakes and track record. He finished seven and a quarter lengths in front of Silver Buck.

In winning his fourth straight race, Conquistador Cielo had run faster in the Met than Kelso, Buckpasser, Arts and Letters, Forego, Cox's Ridge, State Dinner, and Fappiano.

In a bold move, Stephens announced that Conquistador Cielo would be starting in the mile and a half Belmont Stakes

Milt Toby

Conquistador Cielo, the 1982 Belmont Stakes winner, finished third.

five days later. "Unconventional" was one of the more pleasant responses to his plans. Some wondered whether Stephens had leaped into senility overnight. Others were convinced he would make a fool of himself and his horse.

But not everyone doubted him. The Belmont Stakes was televised by CBS that year and odds-maker Jimmy "The Greek" Snyder went on record saying that he loved Conquistador Cielo in the Belmont, especially because the Belmont would be contested on a sloppy track. Cielo had never run on a sloppy or muddy track, but being a son of Mr. Prospector, Snyder said he should love it.

Bettors weren't quite sure what to do, as Cielo again drew the outside post in an eleven-horse field for substitute rider Laffit Pincay Jr., who replaced Maple after the latter cracked six ribs in a spill the day before the Belmont. Mr. Prospector was renowned for producing speed and wet-track runners, but not offspring that could race a mile and a half. Cielo went off the 4-1 second choice; Linkage was the 2-1 favorite; Gato Del Sol, 6-1; and Aloma's Ruler and Royal Roberto were each 7-1.

Pincay shot Cielo extremely wide around the first turn as 44-1 longshot Anemal led briefly on the inside. Then Cielo took over. Pincay allowed him to continue far from the rail on the backstretch, and when 40-1 longshot High Ascent took a run at him with a half-mile remaining, Cielo quickly spurted clear and continued to widen his margin. He won by fourteen lengths under a hand ride over Gato Del Sol, getting the mile and a half in 2:28 1/5. Afterward everyone wanted a piece of Conquistador Cielo.

Stephens pointed to the Travers, one of the few stakes races in New York that had eluded the trainer. To get Cielo there, Stephens used the Dwyer and the Jim Dandy Stakes. In the Dwyer, with Maple back aboard, Cielo cruised to a four-length wire-to-wire win at 1-10 over John's Gold.

Cielo was asked to carry 129 pounds in the Jim Dandy

Stakes, conceding significant weight to three other three-year-olds, though he went off at 1-10 again. Cielo opened a four-length lead on the backstretch and had to work a bit to hold off 114-pound lightweight Lejoli by one length. Conquistador Cielo had won seven straight races.

And then, there were more headlines about Cielo off the track than on.

Syndication and an Injunction

One week before the Travers, Claiborne Farm announced it would syndicate seventy-five percent of Cielo for $36.4 million, forty shares at $910,000 each, with de Kwiatkowski retaining ten shares, two of which would go to Stephens. Inflation might have escalated Cielo's price tag, but the figures were still staggering. In the preceding nine years, a share in Secretariat cost $190,000, Seattle Slew $300,000, Affirmed $400,000, and Spectacular Bid $550,000.

As with Secretariat, syndication meant Cielo would not race as a four-year-old. "Naturally, you hate to give up this kind of horse," Stephens said.

If Cielo's long-range future had been settled, his immediate plans had not.

Eddie Maple had been suspended for seven days by the stewards at Belmont Park for careless riding in a division of the Lexington Handicap on Dew Line, who was disqualified for interference.

Maple appealed, and he almost paid a heavy price for it. The appeal went before the New York State Racing and Wagering Board, which ruled the day before the Travers that the suspension stood, meaning Maple would not be able to ride Cielo in the Travers.

That sent Maple's attorney, Edwin M. Cooperman, scurrying to get a court order that would allow Maple to ride in the

Travers. "I'm trying to find a judge in Nassau County," Cooperman told the Albany *Times Union* the night before the Travers. "I don't know if I can reach him tonight, but if I don't, I'll try tomorrow. I knew they would do this, and I'll be at the track Saturday."

Stephens, of course, was not amused. He had a tentative commitment from Pincay should Maple not get an injunction in time. "They shouldn't hang us up like this," he said. "If Eddie Maple or Laffit Pincay Jr. doesn't ride this horse in the Travers, he doesn't run. We're not about to put some new jockey on him. If we have to scratch Saturday, he'll never run again. The man (de Kwiatkowski) told me to leave him (Cielo) in the Travers until 3 p.m., and if Maple hasn't got an injunction, then scratch the horse."

Keep in mind that Maple was going for an unprecedented third consecutive Travers, following the victories of Temperence Hill and Willow Hour.

On Saturday morning, Maple got an injunction. He would ride Conquistador Cielo, giving Stephens a shot at his first Travers.

The Haskell Invitational Winner

The 1982 Travers field was supposed to number six. But late-developing Wavering Monarch never made it. After finishing third behind Linkage and Gato Del Sol in the Blue Grass Stakes and twelfth in the Kentucky Derby, Wavering Monarch entered the three-year-old championship picture with three straight victories, including his Haskell victory over Aloma's Ruler.

However, Wavering Monarch bruised a foot after throwing a shoe during a workout at Saratoga three days before the Travers. His trainer, George "Rusty" Arnold, originally thought the bruise was superficial. But while X-rays showed no fracture, the bruise continued to bother Wavering Monarch, forc-

Wavering Monarch in a winning Haskell performance.

ing Arnold to scratch his first-ever starter in the Travers. "It's just one of the breaks of the game," he said. "The timing couldn't be worse."

But Arnold would have a rooting interest in the Travers.

The Schenectady Dreamer's Colt

Growing up in Schenectady, New York, Albert Coppola used to jump the fence to get into Saratoga Race Course because he couldn't afford the admission. "That was my lifelong ambition: to get to Saratoga and race horses," Coppola said.

It took a while for Coppola to realize his dream. After serving in the Army in World War II, Coppola attended Siena College in Loudonville, just north of Albany, then transferred to George Washington University in Washington, D.C. He never left the area, starting up the Washington Business School and operating other secretarial schools. He married and had five children. Coppola was fifty-four years old when he met Canadian trainer John DiMario through a friend of DiMario's brother in 1978.

A year later Coppola bought his first horse, a two-year-old named Skit. Skit joined DiMario's barn and won just one race as a four-year-old before breaking a coffin bone.

Coppola, though, was not discouraged and decided to venture to Kentucky to buy a yearling. He visited several major farms while he was there. At Gainesway, he saw Blushing Groom, whose first crop of yearlings was being sold that year, 1980. "I said, 'My God, what a good looking stallion!' " he told William H. Rudy of *The Blood-Horse*.

Coppola leafed through the catalogue for the Fasig-Tipton Kentucky fall sale. "I saw several Blushing Grooms," he told Rudy. "One I liked was the last yearling to be sold on Saturday night."

That yearling was Runaway Groom out of a stakes-winning mare named Yonnie Girl, who had already produced six winners. "I thought it would bring much more than I could pay," Coppola said.

Coppola's opinion was perfectly justified. Blushing Groom's yearlings in his first crop sold for an average of $153,563.

But Runaway Groom was Hip No. 460 in a sale of 460 yearlings, and that worked to Coppola's advantage. He got Runaway Groom for $39,000, the lowest price for a Blushing Groom yearling colt the entire year. "I just hung in there and waited to the end," Coppola said. "The bidding reached the middle thirties, and I then began to bid."

Runaway Groom suffered bucked shins and a virus, and was not ready to run until November of his two-year-old season. DiMario, who was training in New York, wanted Runaway Groom to begin serious training in a better climate. So the colt was shipped to Florida for light training. In April of his three-year-old year he was shipped to Keeneland, where he was entrusted to Wavering Monarch's trainer, Rusty Arnold.

Both Wavering Monarch and Runaway Groom had made their career debuts April 2 at Keeneland in separate races.

Wavering Monarch won easily while Runaway Groom finished second by a nose to Star Drone. Runaway Groom started two more times at Keeneland, finishing second by two and a half lengths before winning his maiden by four lengths.

He did not race again for nearly two months, but he made a winning return, taking an allowance race at Churchill Downs by a length on a sloppy track two weeks after Conquistador Cielo's fourteen-length romp in the Belmont Stakes.

Runaway Groom was a Canadian-bred and was kept eligible for the Canadian Triple Crown.

Reunited with DiMario, Runaway Groom stepped up to stakes company for the first time in the $150,000-added Queen's Plate. Dismissed at 38-1 in a field of eighteen, Runaway Groom ran second, two and a half lengths behind Son of Briartic.

Runaway Groom shipped back to New York to win an allowance race in his grass debut. Then he was on the road again, finishing second by a half-length to Determinant in the Heresy Stakes at Woodbine. That race set him up well for the second leg of the Canadian Triple Crown, the mile and a half, $75,000-added Prince of Wales Stakes at Fort Erie. Runaway Groom beat Icy Circle by a head, with Son of Briartic third.

DiMario will never forget what Coppola said after the race: "Now for the Travers." DiMario thought, "My God, what's he talking about?"

The Horse That Rarely Won

For a colt who finished his three-year career still eligible for a non-winners-of-four allowance race, Lejoli did pretty darn good for trainer Leon Blusiewicz, earning $211,585. At two Lejoli was second in the Primer Stakes at Pimlico and the Juvenile Stakes at Belmont and third in both the Sanford and Hopeful stakes at Saratoga.

Chapter 15

After finishing thirteenth in the Flamingo, Lejoli was fourth in the Arkansas Derby, ninth in the Blue Grass Stakes, sixth in the Belmont Stakes, fourth in the Jersey Derby, third in the Haskell, and second in the Jim Dandy. He was competitive enough to give his optimistic connections another chance for glory in the Travers.

The Race

The second-largest crowd in Saratoga history, 41,839, turned out to see the 113th running of the $221,500 Travers Stakes on August 21. The sky was cloudy; the temperature unseasonably cold.

Conquistador Cielo would go off as the odds-on favorite at 2-5 despite wearing front bandages for the first time. There had been rumors before the Travers that Cielo had suspensory problems.

From the rail out: Gato Del Sol was 4-1; Lejoli, 14-1; Runaway Groom with rider Jeff Fell, 12-1; Conquistador Cielo; and Aloma's Ruler, 5-1 under Angel Cordero from the outside five post.

Aloma's Ruler and Cielo broke first and second and were quickly clear of the other three. On the outside of Cielo, Aloma's Ruler led by a half-length on the clubhouse turn before Cielo countered.

Cielo and Aloma's Ruler were doing their interpretation of Jaipur and Ridan's epic Travers battle twenty years earlier. Maple and Cielo were on the inside. Cordero had Aloma's Ruler exactly where he wanted him, on Cielo's outside.

"Conquistador was the one I had to beat," Cordero said eighteen years later. "Everything worked out well for me. I had him pinned on the rail. I wanted to keep him inside of me. It was heavier on the inside. He had no chance to run his race. He was never going to settle. That was my strategy."

Whether Maple had a strategy was difficult to discern. Because from the moment they left the gate, Cielo wanted to go. Maple would not let him loose, and he also could not get him to take back. "My horse fought me all the way," Maple said.

Cielo's past performance line for the Travers would indicate that with a single word: rank.

Conquistador Cielo took a brief lead on the backstretch, before Aloma's Ruler responded, moving in front by three-quarters of a length. Four lengths back, Gato Del Sol was on the outside, racing evenly with Lejoli. Runaway Groom, who had hit his head on the starting gate, trailed.

Cielo fought back and narrowed Aloma's Ruler's lead to a head going into the far turn. They had covered six furlongs in 1:10 3/5. Midway on the turn, Cielo was just a head behind Aloma's Ruler. Behind them, Gato Del Sol couldn't keep pace and Lejoli was a clear third. Farther back, Runaway Groom was beginning to roll, and he had little trouble passing Gato Del Sol.

At the top of the stretch, Aloma's Ruler increased his lead to a half-length, before Cielo yet again came back for more. Cielo regained the lead at the three-sixteenths pole by a head and was a neck ahead at the eighth pole when Aloma's Ruler surged again, taking a narrow lead. Fans fixed their eyes on these two horses giving everything they had and could only wonder, Did Cielo have anything left?

Cordero didn't think so. "I thought I had it at the eighth pole," he said. "I was riding against Conquistador Cielo all the way because it looked like a two-horse race. Everything came out the way I planned. I had him all the way where I wanted him. I didn't have to go to Plan B."

There was no Plan C. Just as Aloma's Ruler finally put Cielo away maybe fifty yards from the wire, Cordero, as well as most of the crowd that had been focusing on their battle, saw a gray horse charging down the middle of the track.

A gray closer? For an instant, the mind said, Gato Del Sol, the gray closer who had won the Kentucky Derby. It wasn't. Gato Del Sol had faded and would finish last by nine and a quarter lengths. "I could see it was Runaway Groom," Cordero said. "I was surprised he ran that big that day. He ran both of us down."

It was over in seconds. Runaway Groom hit the wire a half-length in front of Aloma's Ruler, who beat Conquistador Cielo by three-quarters of a length. Fell had only used his whip four times in the stretch. "The race was made for a come-from-behind horse like mine," Fell said. Runaway Groom paid $27.80, still the fifth-highest win payoff in Travers history,

Runaway Groom returning to the winner's circle.

after covering the mile and a quarter on a fast track in a modest 2:02 3/5, the last quarter-mile in a pedestrian :26 4/5.
Coppola could not have cared less: "I thought we might be
able to finish third or maybe fourth. Winning this race is
incredible."

There would be no more races for either Cielo or Aloma's
Ruler. Cielo had strained a ligament in his left front ankle.
Stephens announced Cielo's retirement the day after the
Travers. "I decided it would be in the best interest of the
horse," Stephens told William Leggett of *Sports Illustrated*. "He
didn't have the best of it yesterday, being on the inside and all.
If I had to do it over again, I probably would have had him go
to the lead instead of taking back. He was too rank, and a
horse can't run like that."

Conquistador Cielo, though, had seven wins and one third
in eight starts in 1982 and was rightfully voted champion
three-year-old and Horse of the Year. Stephens, whose only
previous Travers starter, Smarten, had finished a distant second in 1979 to General Assembly, did get his Travers winner
with Forty Niner, who beat Seeking the Gold by a nose in a
thrilling 1988 Midsummer Derby.

Aloma's Ruler was training for the Super Derby in September
when he pulled a suspensory ligament in his left front leg.
Lenzini said it was not related to his earlier injury, but Aloma's
Ruler never raced again.

Runaway Groom won his next start, the Breeders' Stakes at
Woodbine, by three-quarters of a length before losing his final
eight races, six as a four-year-old. One of the losses was a
fourth in the 1983 Del Mar Invitational Handicap behind Bel
Bolide and Gato Del Sol.

Gato Del Sol chipped a bone in his left knee in the Travers
and did not start again in 1982. He did, however, return for
three more seasons, winning two of seventeen starts on grass
and one of five on dirt.

Lejoli won the 1982 Winter Quarters Handicap at The Meadowlands, and in his final start the 1983 J. Edgar Hoover Handicap at Pimlico.

Those five horses' only link was a Saturday afternoon at Saratoga when they staged an unforgettable Travers.

16

Not a Secret Anymore

Lady's Secret, Secretariat's most accomplished offspring and the 1986 Horse of the Year, made forty-five starts in her four-year career. Four pivotal ones took place at Saratoga. In the first she upset a champion-to-be. In the second she showed she could beat older fillies and mares. Her victory over males in a grade I stakes in the third paved the way to her 1986 Horse of the Year title. And then there was her fourth Saratoga start, the one just about everyone wishes had never happened.

Hall of Fame trainer D. Wayne Lukas had personally arranged the mating of his mare, Great Lady M., to Secretariat, which produced Lady's Secret. The gray filly was born on Lukas' farm in Oklahoma. "I raised her on that ranch," Lukas told Tim Layden of the Albany *Times Union* in 1987. "I was responsible for her breeding. I mean, she's a family deal."

Owned by Eugene Klein, who also owned the NFL's San Diego Chargers, Lady's Secret took time to develop, though she had won her debut in a dead heat, with Bonnie's Axe, as the 7-5 favorite in a two-year-old filly maiden race at Belmont Park, May 2, 1984. The comment in her chart says, "Drifted out."

Lukas entered Lady's Secret in the Astoria Stakes, and she fought hard on the lead before weakening to fifth. She made her next six starts at two in California, the first at Hollywood Park in the Landaluce Stakes, named for Lukas' undefeated filly. At two Landaluce won all five of her starts, four of them graded stakes, by a combined forty-six and a half lengths, before contracting an infection and dying in her trainer's arms. It would have been a great Hollywood script if Lady's Secret had won the Landaluce, but she finished fourth, beaten by nine lengths. Lady's Secret then won a minor stakes and ran fourth in another before running third by a head in the Anoakia Stakes and a distant fifth in the grade I Oak Leaf. She won her final start at two, the Moccasin at Hollywood Park.

Lukas freshened her briefly and then raced her in twenty-one of twenty-three consecutive months. This display of durability earned Lady's Secret the nickname "The Iron Lady."

She began her three-year-old season by winning just two of her first seven starts. Lady's Secret appeared to be a cut below the best three-year-old fillies in 1985, running second in the Prioress Stakes to Clock's Secret, then fourth by eleven lengths to Mom's Command in the Comely Stakes.

Mom's Command went on to sweep the New York Filly Triple Crown, winning the Acorn, Mother Goose, and the Coaching Club American Oaks.

Lady's Secret would do even more. In her next twenty-five starts, all in stakes and seventeen of them grade Is, Lady's Secret won eighteen times. But, given Mom's Command's success, it took a little time for people to notice Lady's Secret. Then she beat Mom's Command.

First, though, Lady's Secret won three ungraded stakes: the Bowl of Flowers by seven lengths at Belmont Park, the Regret Handicap by three and a half at Monmouth Park, and the Rose Stakes by four and three-quarters back at Belmont. Yet she would go off at 10-1 in her next race.

First Two Saratoga Starts

The knock on Lady's Secret, who was entered in the seven-

Barbara D. Livingston

Lady's Secret ran some of her best — and worst — races at Saratoga.

furlong Test Stakes against Mom's Command and eight other three-year-old fillies, was her perceived inability to go more than six furlongs. She had tried four times and won none of them (three at seven furlongs and one at a mile and a six-teenth). Her best effort in those four losses was her third by a head in the seven-furlong Anoakia Stakes at Santa Anita.

That was why Lady's Secret was 10-1 in the Test. Mom's Command, riding a five-race winning streak, was 1-2, carrying highweight of 124, three pounds more than Lady's Secret.

If there were an equine dictionary and you looked up "perfect trip," you might see Lady's Secret's race in the 1985 Test Stakes. Ridden for the second time by Jorge Velasquez, already her ninth different rider, Lady's Secret broke first out of the nine post and assumed a perfect stalking spot behind dueling leaders Mom's Command and Majestic Folly. She moved up willingly as the two fillies in front of her ripped off a half in :44 4/5. Majestic Folly, on the outside of Mom's Command, gained the lead, but Velasquez had already moved up Lady's Secret three-wide on the turn. Majestic Folly fought on, but

Lady's Secret took the lead at the sixteenth pole and won by
two lengths in 1:21 3/5, only a fifth of a second off White Star
Line's 1978 stakes record.

Behind her, in a great display of courage, Mom's Command
had come on again and beaten Majestic Folly by a neck for
second.

In silencing her distance critics, Lady's Secret had won her
fourth straight stakes. Instead of asking Lady's Secret to go a
mile and a quarter in the Alabama, Lukas entered the gray filly
in the Ballerina at seven furlongs against older females. Sent
off as part of a favored entry under her ninth different jockey,
Don MacBeth, Lady's Secret sat second until the far turn,
gained a narrow lead at the top of the stretch, and fought off
Mrs. Revere to the wire, winning by a nose in 1:22 3/5.

The next day Mom's Command won the Alabama by four
lengths. She never raced again.

Lukas did a masterful job stretching out Lady's Secret. In the
mile Maskette at Belmont Park, she romped wire to wire by
five and a half lengths. In the mile and an eighth Ruffian
Handicap she wired five rivals by four lengths as part of an
entry. Lukas then asked her to go a mile and a quarter in the
Beldame, and she again won wire to wire by two lengths.

She had won eight straight stakes races. A victory in the
ninth, the Breeders' Cup Distaff at Aqueduct, would have
clinched at least the three-year-old filly championship and
given her a shot at Horse of the Year. But she ducked out at the
start of the race under Velasquez. She recovered and led for the
first mile of the mile and a quarter stakes before Life's Magic,
her stablemate also owned by Klein, roared past her under
Angel Cordero Jr. to win by six and a quarter lengths. Lady's
Secret was a clear second by three lengths over Dontstop
Themusic. The Lukas entry, which included a third filly,
Alabama Nana, had gone off at 2-5. Mom's Command
received the three-year-old filly championship off seven wins

and two seconds in nine starts. Lady's Secret had ten wins, five seconds, a fourth, and a fifth in seventeen starts. But there would be next year.

Remarkably, Lady's Secret would post nearly identical numbers as a four-year-old: ten wins, three seconds, and two thirds in fifteen starts.

After finishing second in the 1985 La Brea Stakes under Chris McCarron for the first time, Lady's Secret started 1986 with consecutive wins in the El Encino, La Canada, and Santa Margarita Invitational Handicap. Lady's Secret was second by a neck to Love Smitten in the Apple Blossom Handicap at Oaklawn Park and then won the Shuvee Handicap by three and a half lengths under Pat Day, her eleventh different rider.

Lukas felt Lady's Secret had a chance at Horse of the Year, and he knew she would have to beat males to do it. He had tried it once, and Lady's Secret was second by a neck in the 1985 Determine Stakes at Bay Meadows early in her three-year-old season. The Metropolitan Handicap was a different matter, but Lukas decided to take a shot. Lady's Secret raced well but weakened late to finish third.

Her next two starts were against her own sex. Again the heavy favorite, she finished second to Endear in the Hempstead Handicap and won the Molly Pitcher Handicap by six and a quarter lengths at Monmouth Park.

Third Saratoga Start

Again, Lukas entered Lady's Secret against males, this time in the August 2 Whitney Handicap. She dominated six rivals, winning by four and a half lengths at 6-5 on a sloppy track, a performance that advanced her bid for Horse of the Year honors.

She tried males in her next two starts and raced well without winning. After finishing third by three and a half lengths behind Roo Art and Precisionist in the Philip H. Iselin

Handicap, she was second by four and three-quarters lengths to Precisionist in the Woodward.

Lady's Secret completed her season by winning four grade I stakes, all at odds-on: the Maskette by seven lengths, the Ruffian Handicap by eight lengths, the Beldame by a half-length over Coup de Fusil when she drifted out, and the Breeders' Cup Distaff by two and a half lengths. She was 1986 champion handicap mare and only the fourth female named Horse of the Year. It would have been a great time to call it a career.

Instead, Lukas brought her back for her five-year-old season.

The wisdom of that decision was questioned after her very first start in 1987. Sent off the 4-5 favorite in the Donn Handicap against six males, she led early and then stopped like she had never stopped before. She finished sixth, thirty-two and a half lengths behind the winner.

Lady's Secret was undaunted by the slop.

Bob Coglianese/NYRA

Something seemed terribly wrong, but Lukas insisted to the press that she was fine, gave her three months off, and brought her back in an allowance race at Monmouth.

She had never raced in allowance company, proceeding from a maiden race in her debut into stakes company. She had made forty straight starts in stakes company, the last twenty-three of them graded.

Lady's Secret easily won her allowance race on a sloppy track and finished second by two lengths to Reel Easy in the Molly Pitcher. She then dominated a field of overmatched fillies and mares, winning an allowance race at Monmouth by seven lengths.

Then she headed for Saratoga.

Last Saratoga Start

Exactly six years after Genuine Risk, one of the great fillies of the 1980s, appeared in the first race at Saratoga, an allowance race she won by eight and a quarter lengths at 1-10, Lady's Secret appeared in the first race at Saratoga, a mile and an eighth allowance, on a sloppy track. Chris McCarron flew in from California to ride Lady's Secret, who had worked a blazing four furlongs in :46 3/5 and went off at 3-10. "Anything less than a win would be disappointing," Lukas told Layden of the *Times Union*.

Then how was this? Starting from the two post in a field of five, Lady's Secret broke on top. Heading into the far turn, this great champion bolted to the outside fence and refused to race, McCarron eventually pulling her up to a stop.

"She acted like she wanted to go back to the barn instead of being on the track," McCarron said. "That fence was moving up on us awful fast and she scraped it. My boots were hitting the fence as we were moving."

Nevertheless, Lukas and Klein insisted nothing was wrong.

"It's a mental problem with her drifting out like that. Maybe she needs a psychiatrist," the trainer said.

Lukas and son Jeff, his assistant trainer, were barbecued by the press for failing to draw the conclusion that Lady's Secret was done with racing. Syndicated columnist Andy Beyer wrote: "The Lukases were virtually the only people in racing

Trainer D. Wayne Lukas and owner Eugene Klein.

who didn't recognize it, or didn't think that Lady's Secret deserved to bow out in a fashion befitting a champion. "

Here's how she bowed out:

She had to show she could negotiate a turn in front of the stewards before she could race again at a New York Racing Association track. Dr. Manuel Gilman, then a Jockey Club steward, explained, "It's for the protection of the public. We want to make sure she can get around turns properly. It's mainly for the bettors to prevent the same thing from happening again."

Lukas withdrew his plans of racing Lady's Secret in the John A. Morris Handicap later in the meet and retired her.

It may be the only time in Saratoga history that a champion's odds-on loss did that horse some good.

17

Come Back, Alysheba

In the four years following Runaway Groom's 1982 victory in the Travers, only two winners of Triple Crown races, Deputed Testamony and Danzig Connection, competed in the Midsummer Derby. In 1983 Preakness winner Deputed Testamony finished fourth behind Play Fellow and favored Slew o' Gold. In 1986 Danzig Connection, the last of Woody Stephens' five consecutive Belmont Stakes winners, finished third and was placed second behind Wise Times when second-place finisher Broad Brush was disqualified.

You didn't have to be Dick Tracy to figure out why the nation's best three-year-olds were skipping the Travers. The Travers' purse had stagnated at $250,000. Meanwhile, the purse for the Haskell Invitational Handicap, known as the Monmouth Invitational Handicap through 1982, increased from $200,000 to $300,000 in 1985. Both 1985 Kentucky Derby winner Spend a Buck and Belmont Stakes winner Creme Fraiche skipped the Travers and raced in the Haskell, finishing second and third behind Skip Trial. Danzig Connection lost the 1986 Haskell to Wise Times.

The 1987 Haskell purse would be increased to $500,000. Risking a Travers of second-class status, the New York Racing Association in 1987 quadrupled its purse to one million dollars, making it the richest race in New York racing history. "We just felt we had to keep up," said NYRA's vice president of racing, Lenny Hale, the man most responsible for the drastic increase.

The reaction was immediate. What the New York Racing Association got in 1987 was a Travers' field of dreams, arguably the most contentious and talented collection of three-year-olds the race had ever seen.

There were Alysheba, winner of the Kentucky Derby and Preakness, and Bet Twice, the horse who beat him in both the Belmont Stakes and Haskell. Their respective trainers, Hall of Famers Jack Van Berg and Warren "Jimmy" Croll Jr., had never started a horse in the Travers. Neither had legendary California trainer Charlie Whittingham, who skipped the $150,000 Del Mar Derby to run his Swaps Stakes winner, Temperate Sil, whom he co-owned, in the Travers. "I can win

Java Gold upsets one of the most contentious Travers fields.

easy out there for $150, but you don't get many chances to run for a million-dollar pot," the Hall of Famer told Tim Layden of the Albany *Times Union*.

There were the first- and second-place finishers in the Whitney Handicap earlier in the Saratoga meet, Mack Miller's Java Gold and LeRoy Jolley's Gulch. Jim Dandy Stakes winner Polish Navy would go in the Travers, as would undefeated Fortunate Moment, winner of the American Derby at Arlington Park. Cryptoclearance, who had been second in the Belmont Stakes and third in the Jim Dandy, was in too. The final horse in the Travers field of nine would be Gorky, a rabbit Jolley entered to help ensure a fast pace for Gulch, who had only been beaten in the Whitney by three-quarters of a length. Gorky had raced in the Whitney, too, and fulfilled his mission by battling two speed horses into submission, Seldom Seen Sue and Gone West.

Alysheba vs. Bet Twice, Round Five

There were story lines galore in the Travers; none more talked about than the fifth meeting between Alysheba and Bet Twice. They had split their first four confrontations. In the Kentucky Derby, thanks to a miraculous ride by Chris McCarron, Alysheba won by three-quarters of a length over Bet Twice, who came out into Alysheba in mid-stretch, causing him to stumble badly. McCarron not only stayed on but was able to get Alysheba going again, and the son of Alydar accomplished what his sire could not: victory in a Triple Crown race. Two and a half months later, Alysheba's owner was giving McCarron an ultimatum.

Alysheba had taken the Preakness, beating Bet Twice by a half-length, to move to the threshold of the Triple Crown. In the Belmont Stakes, however, Bet Twice blew Alysheba and everyone else away, winning by fourteen lengths.

Cryptoclearance was second by a nose over Gulch, with Alysheba, who endured a brutal trip, a neck back in fourth. Despite Bet Twice's immense winning margin, McCarron was severely criticized. It was not without justification. McCarron had gotten Alysheba into trouble twice and was forced to steady him and then check him sharply. Was it worth fourteen lengths? Probably not.

But Alysheba lost his next race, the Haskell, too, by a neck to Bet Twice after racing in tight quarters on the first turn.

Three days before the Travers, Alysheba's co-owner, Clarence Scharbauer, announced, "We're going to let Chris ride him one more time, but we won't let him ride anymore if he doesn't give him a good ride in the Travers. He made some bad mistakes in the last two races. He knows that. But you have to remember what he did in the Kentucky Derby and the Preakness."

The next day McCarron responded. "If you don't feel the pressure, you have no feeling," he said. "This is the most important race of the summer."

Time for Java?

Mack Miller was on a heck of a roll. First he won the Whitney against older horses with Java Gold. Next he was inducted into the Racing Hall of Fame. Then he had the opportunity to give his long-time owner, Paul Mellon of Rokeby Stables, his fourth Travers, following the victories of Quadrangle (1964), Arts and Letters (1969), and Java Gold's sire, Key to the Mint (1972).

Java Gold had missed the spring classics while fighting a virus that held on for ten weeks. Since returning, he had won four of five starts, none more impressive than his win in the Whitney over older horses. But in the Whitney, Java Gold carried just 113 pounds, getting four from Gulch, who was sec-

ond, and fourteen from top-weighted Broad Brush, who'd finished third. In the Travers everybody carries 126 pounds. "The
weight is a concern; sure it is," Miller told Tim Wilkin of the
Albany *Times Union*. "I would hope he can carry it. There are a
lot of questions to be answered yet."

Preparations

On Monday of Travers week, Bet Twice worked a sharp five
furlongs in :59. But Temperate Sil blazed the same distance the
next day in :57 1/5, the second fastest five-furlong work of the
meet, topped only by Groovy's :56 4/5 ten days earlier. Java
Gold then worked six furlongs in 1:11, getting his final quarter
in :23 1/5. Fortunate Moment, an unraced two-year-old who
had won all six of his starts at Arlington Park, including the
American Derby, went five furlongs in :58 1/5, equaling the
third fastest workout of the Saratoga meet. His trainer, Harvey
Vanier, was hoping to repeat his Travers success with Play
Fellow four years earlier.

Barbara D. Livingston

**Alysheba, the Kentucky Derby and Preakness winner, didn't like the
sloppy going and finished unplaced.**

The New York Racing Association fielded 250 media requests for the Travers, double to triple the norm. ABC televised the Travers live.

Anticipation was unabashed. "A lot of people have told me this is as good a race involving three-year-olds that they've seen in a long time," Croll said. "There are probably five or six horses that could win this, and I have one of them. That's a good thing to be going in with, especially in a one-million-dollar race. This might be the best crop of three-year-olds in the last twenty years."

Van Berg said, "This is probably the most talented field assembled in many years."

Post positions were drawn and a morning line set. In post position order, the field lined up as follows:

1 - Polish Navy, Randy Romero, 10-1
2 - Cryptoclearance, Angel Cordero Jr., 15-1
3 - Java Gold, Pat Day, 5-2
4 - a-Gulch, Jose Santos, 10-1
5 - Fortunate Moment, Earlie Fires, 15-1
6 - Alysheba, Chris McCarron, 2-1
7 - Temperate Sil, Bill Shoemaker, 8-1
8 - Bet Twice, Craig Perret, 3-1
9 - a-Gorky, Antonio Graell, 10-1

a - Gulch and Gorky were coupled as an entry

Friday afternoon, August 21, 1987, was a glorious sunny day. However, the Travers was run the next day, and the forecast predicted heavy rain.

Java Gold had won four of five starts on off tracks, the lone loss to Polish Navy as a two-year-old. Neither Alysheba nor Bet Twice had raced on a sloppy track. Temperate Sil's sire, Temperence Hill, won the Belmont Stakes on a muddy track and the Suburban Handicap on a sloppy track. Temperate Sil, though, had lost both starts on off tracks. Cryptoclearance had won the Everglades Stakes on a sloppy track. Gulch had won the Tremont and the Wood Memorial on muddy tracks and run third on a sloppy track in the Gotham Stakes.

It poured on Travers morning, though the sun broke through briefly during the afternoon. That didn't matter a heck of a lot when a downpour started minutes before the horses went to the gate. The track was listed as sloppy.

In *The Blood-Horse*, Dan Mearns called the day "flatteringly described as miserable."

Yet the 118th Travers attracted the fourth-largest crowd in Saratoga history, 45,055. Alysheba was the 5-2 favorite; Java Gold, 3-1; Bet Twice, 4-1; Temperate Sil, 5-1; and Cryptoclearance 7-1.

Temperate Sil and Gorky jumped out of the gate and raced as if the Travers were a sprint, flying by themselves through six furlongs in 1:10, the second fastest three-quarters in Travers history. Only North Sea had gone faster, reaching six furlongs in 1:09 3/5 in the 1972 Travers won by Key to the Mint.

At one point on the backstretch, Temperate Sil and Gorky had separated themselves from the rest of the field by twelve lengths.

Then they were engulfed around the far turn as Polish Navy and Bet Twice rocketed past them side by side.

Polish Navy was the stronger of the two and took the lead, but Cordero had Cryptoclearance in full stride rallying from last, as did Pat Day on Java Gold after they went five-wide on the far turn.

Cryptoclearance made the front and opened a length and a half lead, before Java Gold quickly drew even and then clear, winning by two lengths. "When I got in front of Cryptoclearance, I felt like I had the race won," Day said. "I knew all the horses I passed weren't coming back."

Behind Cryptoclearance the field was strung out. Polish Navy was nearly seven lengths back in third, followed by Gulch, Bet Twice, Alysheba, Fortunate Moment, Temperate Sil, and Gorky.

Alysheba had been beaten twenty and a quarter lengths, and not even a disgruntled owner could blame McCarron this time. "On the first turn, I was trying to get him to run, but he wasn't taking the bit at all," McCarron said. "When he got hit in the face with the slop, he didn't like it and just stopped trying. He was climbing all the way. I don't know if mud caulks would have helped any. I just knew he wasn't happy out there."

Alysheba proved the Travers was a throw-out in his final two starts. He won the Super Derby by a half-length over Candi's Gold and then turned in a sensational performance in the Breeders' Cup Classic, losing by a nose in the last stride to Ferdinand, who would be named Horse of the Year. Alysheba was three-year-old champion over Java Gold, who followed his Travers victory by beating older horses in the Marlboro Cup by two and a quarter lengths and running second to Creme Fraiche in the Jockey Club Gold Cup. He suffered a broken foot in the race and was retired.

Alysheba returned at four to win seven of nine starts: the Strub, Santa Anita Handicap, San Bernardino Handicap, the Iselin Handicap, Woodward, Meadowlands Cup, and Breeders' Cup Classic by a half-length over Seeking the Gold. Alysheba's two losses were a fourth in the $600,000 Pimlico Special to his rival Bet Twice and a second in the Hollywood Gold Cup to Cutlass Reality. Alysheba was 1988 champion handicap horse and Horse of the Year. In his twenty-six lifetime starts, he had posted eleven wins, eight seconds, two thirds, three fourths, a fifth in his career debut, and one distant sixth in his only start at Saratoga.

18

Keep Off the Grass

Unlike the Travers and Alabama, Saratoga's turf stakes have relatively recent origins though some of them began life on the dirt.

The Bernard Baruch Handicap, first run in 1959, is the oldest of Saratoga's turf stakes. The Diana Handicap appeared as a turf race in 1974 but had its first running on the dirt in 1939. In 1975 the Sword Dancer Invitational was born, though it was contested at Aqueduct its first two years and at Belmont Park from 1977 through 1991. The Saranac Handicap — originally a dirt race dating to 1901 — joined the roster of turf stakes in 1978. The Lake Placid Handicap was started in 1984. A year later came the National Museum of Racing Hall of Fame Handicap and the Fourstardave Handicap — originally the Daryl's Joy, then renamed for the New York-bred who won a race at Saratoga for eight straight years. The Ballston Spa Breeders' Cup Handicap began in 1989, the Lake George Stakes and Glens Falls Handicap both in 1996.

The Bernard Baruch was named for the financier who advised presidents on economic matters for more than forty years. Born in Camden, South Carolina, on August 19, 1870, Bernard Mannes Baruch was eleven when his family moved to New York City, where he attended City College. He graduated when he was nineteen, took a job as an office boy in a small

New York City brokerage house, and, just seven years later, owned one-eighth interest in the firm. After buying a seat on the New York Stock Exchange, he quickly became a millionaire and began his own firm. He also owned a winning Thoroughbred named Happy Argo.

Though the Sword Dancer is a grade I stakes, the grade II Bernard Baruch has attracted a disproportionate number of turf champions because it has been around a lot longer.

And like other Saratoga races, the Bernard Baruch has caused the undoing of favorites and champions.

Assagai, the 1966 champ, won that year's Baruch by three lengths and then was second in 1967 to Fort Marcy, who would be named 1967 and 1970 grass champion. Hawaii won the 1969 Baruch by four lengths on the way to his grass title the same year.

Manila and Steinlen, grass champions in 1986 and 1989, contested the Bernard Baruch at the same incredibly low odds of .30-1 in the 1987 and 1990 renewals, respectively. Neither one got the job done.

In 1987 jockey Angel Cordero Jr. upset Manila with long shot Talakeno, then rode Manila to win the Arlington Million in his next start, that champion's final race. Thirteen years later, Cordero said, "I think if Talakeno ran against Manila ten times, Manila would win nine."

Manila, a son of Lyphard out of the Le Fabuleux mare Dona Ysidra, was bred and initially owned by E.M. Cojuangco Jr., a confidant of former Filipino President Fernando Marcos. American Bradley Shannon purchased Manila after the colt's winless two-year-old season of three starts. Ironically, the first two were at Saratoga, both on dirt, when he was seventh under Jean Cruguet and second under Cordero. Cordero rode Manila in his final two-year-old start on the dirt at Aqueduct, where Manila was second by a length and a quarter.

Trainer LeRoy Jolley intended to race Manila on grass in the colt's three-year-old debut at Hialeah, but the race was taken off the grass. Manila won by eight lengths under Roger Velez. He would never race on dirt again.

With his strong grass pedigree, Manila surprised no one by winning his turf debut, an allowance race at Keeneland, by seven and a quarter lengths. Moved up to stakes company, Manila was second in the Forerunner Stakes at Keeneland and a troubled second as part of the favored 7-10 entry in the Saranac Stakes at Belmont Park.

Manila did not lose again in 1986, winning the Cinema Handicap by two and a half lengths at Hollywood Park.

Jose Santos rode Manila in the colt's next five races, all victories: the Lexington Stakes at Belmont Park, the United Nations Handicap at Atlantic City; the Ballantine Scotch Classic at The Meadowlands; and the Turf Classic at Belmont Park.

In the Breeders' Cup Turf at Santa Anita, Manila went off the third choice at nearly 9-1 despite his five-race winning streak. The entry of Theatrical and the great mare Estrapade went off as the 5-2 second choice. The 1-2 favorite was Dancing Brave, named Europe's Horse of the Year after his record-setting victory in the Prix de l'Arc de Triomphe.

The top four contenders finished first through fourth — in the opposite order of their odds. Dancing Brave was an uninspiring, non-threatening fourth, beaten six and three-quarters lengths. Estrapade was collared late by Theatrical, who went after Estrapade on the turn and passed her in mid-stretch.

Behind them was Manila, who had advanced on the inside around the far turn from fifth into third. But Santos couldn't find room on the inside of the tiring Estrapade and had to check and alter course. Manila regained his momentum and surged powerfully to battle Theatrical to the wire. Forty yards from the finish, Theatrical's rider, Gary Stevens, dropped his whip as Manila edged clear to win by a neck.

The 1986 grass championship was a no-brainer. Manila had

raced nine times on turf, winning seven of them and finishing second in the other two. His winning streak was six, all graded stakes.

At four, Manila kept right on winning, with scores in the Elkhorn Stakes at Keeneland, the Early Times Turf Classic at Churchill Downs, and the United Nations Handicap.

His nine-race winning streak had been woven at seven different tracks across the country.

On August 6, 1987, ten days before his next start in the Bernard Baruch Handicap, Manila had a public workout at Saratoga. He broke the turf course record, going a mile in 1:34 3/5. That was a fifth of a second faster than Secretariat's mile work on dirt eight days before his stunning defeat in the 1973 Whitney Handicap. Maybe it's not a good thing to break a track record before a stakes race.

Manila's final work for the Bernard Baruch was a bullet five furlongs in 1:00 2/5, the fastest of the day at that distance.

Only three other horses challenged Manila, who carried high weight of 127 pounds. One of the three was Happy Valley Farm's Talakeno, trained by Dick Dutrow. Talakeno carried 115 pounds, including Cordero, who was seeking his twelfth consecutive Saratoga riding title, one he would not get. The other two starters were Spellbound and Duluth, who each got in with 114 pounds.

A jockey does not get to Cordero's rarefied status without doing homework. And Cordero knew Manila's top priority was not the Bernard Baruch, rather the Arlington Million twenty days later. "Going into the race, I know he was a big favorite, but I thought I had a chance to beat him," Cordero said. "It was a small field. I wanted to be behind him and close to him because he was prepping for the Arlington Million. This was the time to beat him."

Could Talakeno do it? Though he'd won the now defunct Seneca Handicap on grass at Saratoga the previous year under

Cordero, Talakeno had won just one of five starts in 1987: the Blue Larkspur Stakes at Belmont Park on June 5. In his last race before the Bernard Baruch, Talakeno was fifth in the Daryl's Joy. Bettors dismissed Talakeno at 7-1. Manila was 3-10.

The day of the Bernard Baruch was an August Saratoga steamer, ninety degrees — not a good sign for Manila. Jolley earlier had scratched Manila from the Red Smith Handicap at Belmont Park because of the extreme heat. With the Arlington Million just twenty days away, and Manila's last race being July 15 in the United Nations, Jolley had few options.

Besides, Manila had beaten much tougher competition. He just had not done it at Saratoga. In the paddock before the Bernard Baruch, Manila was lathered and a handful to saddle.

Spellbound, trained by Jack Van Berg and ridden by Jerry Bailey, set the pace with Manila just off his flank in second. Right behind Manila on the outside was Duluth. Cordero had Talakeno down on the hedge inside of Duluth as Spellbound set slow fractions, a quarter-mile in :24 3/5 and a half in :48.

Then they got serious.

Jacinto Vasquez asked Manila to take on Spellbound, and Manila tried as the tempo quickened. The third quarter was a blistering :22 4/5 and the fourth in :23 2/5. Manila made steady, slow progress on Spellbound, but he was working awfully hard to do so, finally getting by him at the eighth pole.

Cordero, meanwhile, had gotten Talakeno's attention on the turn with a couple cracks of the whip. As Duluth tried advancing outside of Manila early in the stretch, Cordero split the two and went after Manila.

Manila wrested the lead but Talakeno wore him down and won by a half-length. The final time was an unremarkable 1:47 2/5. What was remarkable was Cordero and Talakeno standing in the winner's circle instead of Vasquez and Manila.

Manila's connections were mystified. "He didn't fire at all," Vasquez said. "He should have been playing with these horses.

He should never have gotten beaten by this kind. He's superior. He just never ran at all."

Jolley wasn't exactly pleased with Manila's performance and resorted to using double negatives. "If he can't beat these bad-(expletive) horses, he can't beat nothing," Jolley said. "You don't expect that kind of performance from him. He just didn't run an eighth of a mile."

In the Arlington Million, with Cordero in the saddle instead of Vasquez, Manila beat Sharrood by a length and a half as the even-money favorite with Theatrical another three and a quarter lengths back in third.

Manila did not race again, breaking a bone in his left front leg two months before his scheduled retirement. Theatrical won his final three races of the year, the Turf Classic, Man o' War, and Breeders' Cup Turf, all grade I stakes, and was named 1987 grass champion. He had seven wins, one on a disqualification, and two seconds, getting disqualified and placed fourteenth in one of them, in nine starts that year. Manila's 1987 record was four wins and one second in five starts. The only time they met was in the Arlington Million.

Talakeno never reached the Arlington Million, but he did win another Saratoga stakes in 1987, taking the Saratoga Breeders' Cup as the favorite under Cordero. The victory ended a twenty-five-race losing streak that cost Cordero his twelfth consecutive riding title. Since he subsequently won the 1988 and 1989 titles, the 1987 one would have given him fourteen straight. The jockey who beat Cordero in 1987 to win his only Saratoga riding title was one of Manila's former jockeys, Jose Santos.

Cordero, though, remains proud of his flawless ride on Talakeno to upset Manila. "Some of these horses, if there are twenty jockeys around, fifteen could win on that horse that day," Cordero said in 2000. "Some horses need a certain kind of ride to win. You feel like you accomplished something. You feel big. You knocked out the champion of the world."

Another grass champion came to Saratoga the very next year. His name was Steinlen. Bred in Great Britain and owned by Wildenstein Stable, the son of Habitat out of Southern Seas, by Jim French, did not make his debut until his three-year-old season, in 1986. His first ten starts were in France under the tutelage of Patrick-Louis Biancone. After losing his first three starts, Steinlen won four straight, then was third twice before running fifth in his first group stakes.

Steinlen shipped to the United States and landed in trainer Bobby Frankel's stable in California in the fall of 1987.

Talakeno defeats turf champion Manila in the 1987 Bernard Baruch.

Steinlen made his U.S. debut in an allowance race at Santa Anita on October 30 and finished seventh as the 3-1 favorite, less than two months after Manila's final race.

After switching barns to D. Wayne Lukas, Steinlen strung together three straight victories, the last two the El Rincon Handicap and the Premiere Handicap. Steinlen then finished second in the John Henry Handicap, before winning the Inglewood Handicap and running second by a length to Skip Out Front in the American Handicap on July 4, 1988.

Lukas shipped Steinlen cross country to upstate New York for the first of Steinlen's three visits to Saratoga.

He made quite an impression, disputing the pace the entire way in the Bernard Baruch under Pat Day before getting beaten by a half-length by My Big Boy. Off that brave performance, Steinlen was the 2-5 favorite in the Budweiser Breeders' Cup Handicap. It was almost a repeat of his previous start. He battled on the lead the whole way and held on to win by a neck over Iron Courage.

At age six, Steinlen returned to Saratoga and wound up with a championship. With Cordero aboard for the only time, Steinlen took the first division of the Daryl's Joy Stakes by two and a half lengths. Santos was aboard in the Bernard Baruch, and Steinlen was the overpowering five-length winner. That gave Steinlen three wins and a strong second in four career Saratoga starts.

More important, it set him up perfectly for his fall campaign. He won the Arlington Million by a half-length, the Budweiser Breeders' Cup Handicap at Keeneland by a head, and the Breeders' Cup Mile at Gulfstream Park by three-quarters of a length over Sabona. Steinlen had posted seven wins, including five straight, three seconds and a third in eleven starts and was named 1989 male grass champion.

He would race again in 1990 at the age of seven and make one more trip to Saratoga for his third appearance in the Bernard Baruch. Only four challenged the 126-pound high-weight, including Rokeby Stable's Who's to Pay, who would get sixteen pounds from Steinlen, and the speedy River of Sin, getting eleven. The other two starters were Foreign Survivor and Green Book.

Who's to Pay's appearance in the Bernard Baruch was quite accidental. It was only the second grass start of his career. "The truth is, I had no place to run him," his Hall of Fame trainer, Mack Miller, said. "I tried a couple of allowance races, but they didn't fill. I said, 'What the hell, I'll run him in the Bernard Baruch.' "

It wasn't a crazy notion. Though 10-1 on the morning line, Who's to Pay went off the 4-1 second choice in the Bernard Baruch. One of the reasons may have been his new jockey, Jean-Luc Samyn, who did not learn he had the mount until the morning of the race. Long renown for his abilities on grass, Samyn is known as "Samyn on the green."

While Who's to Pay had a new rider, Steinlen had a new development. Steinlen had raced with the diuretic Lasix, a medication for bleeders, in his two prior starts, but Lasix was not allowed in New York. Even so, Steinlen went off at 3-10, the exact same odds as Manila three years earlier.

After the break Steinlen seemed to be in a fine stalking position under Santos shadowing the front-running River of Sin into the far turn, while Who's to Pay was back in fifth. Steinlen took over the lead readily at the head of the stretch, but Who's to Pay had used a quick three-wide brush to move into third.

Steinlen had a two-length lead, but Who's to Pay had little difficulty running him down, drawing away to a two-length

Who's to Pay defeating Steinlen in the Bernard Baruch.

victory in 1:48 2/5. The comment for Steinlen in his past performance line was "not good enough."

Who's to Pay's performance was good enough, giving Miller the last of his seven Bernard Baruch victories, one he never expected. "Can you imagine, I beat Steinlen," he said.

Samyn was a bit surprised with Who's to Pay, too. "Sure I'm surprised, because it was a champion we beat," he said.

In his next start Steinlen finished third by six and a half lengths in the Arlington Million. He concluded his career with a distant last on dirt in the Jockey Club Gold Cup at 14-1 and a solid fourth in the Breeders' Cup Mile at Belmont Park, only a length and a half off the winner, Royal Academy, and a half-length in front of the horse in sixth, Who's to Pay.

The 1994 Bernard Baruch attracted two great grass horses, champion Paradise Creek and his nemesis of two years, Lure. Both had minimal previous experience at Saratoga. Paradise Creek had been fourth on dirt in the 1991 Hopeful Stakes and then won the 1992 National Museum of Racing Hall of Fame Stakes on grass as the 6-5 favorite. The following year, Lure won the 1993 Daryl's Joy Stakes by three lengths at 1-5 on turf.

Lure and Paradise Creek had already met six times with Lure winning the first four meetings and Paradise Creek the last two. They met for the seventh and final time in the Bernard Baruch. In their final confrontation, Lure went off the slightest of favorites at even money; Paradise Creek at 1.10-1. Lure bravely held off Paradise Creek the length of the stretch to win by a length, ending Paradise Creek's six-race win streak. Paradise Creek was named champion turf horse over Lure that year, making Lure one of the best horses never to win a championship.

19

Don't Jump to Conclusions

Steeplechase racing, first conducted in North America in Canada in 1838, has been a part of Saratoga racing for more than sixty-five years. Jungle King, the 1937 steeplechase champion, set a tone for future jump champions at Saratoga: successful in most races, but not perfect.

Jungle King fell in the 1935 Beverwyck Handicap at 8-5, then won an allowance race by forty lengths. A year later, he won the Beverwyck as part of an entry that went off at .08-to-1.

Other champions, Elkridge (1942 and '46), Rouge Dragon (1944), Top Bid (1970), and Life's Illusion (1975), were beaten stakes favorites at Saratoga too.

Three champions who dominated steeplechase racing in the 1980s and '90s, accounting for twelve championships, including seven in a row, had mixed success at Saratoga. The first, Mrs. Bunny Murdock's Zaccio, was trained by Hall of Famer W. Burling "Burly" Cocks. The second, William Pape's Flatterer, was trained by Cocks' former assistant, Jonathan Sheppard, who also wound up in the Hall of Fame. The third, Mrs. Walter Jeffords' Lonesome Glory, was literally given away before he ever raced, then achieved greatness thanks to the patience of trainer Bruce Miller.

The three champion jumpers shared another distinction. They all lost as stakes favorites at Saratoga.

Zaccio, the champion from 1980-82, compiled the best record at Saratoga of any multiple jump champion: five victories and three seconds in eight starts over the jumps.

Zaccio's first two Saratoga starts were in allowance races as a three-year-old in 1979. He won the first by nine and a quarter lengths at 3-2, then lost the second by a neck to Parson's Waiting at .70-1.

The following year Zaccio paved the way to his first championship with nearly identical stakes wins at Saratoga, taking the 1980 Lovely Night Handicap by one and three-quarters lengths as the 1.30-1 favorite and the New York Turf Writers Handicap by one and a quarter lengths as the 1.10-1 betting choice. But Zaccio ended 1980 on a down note, losing his rider in the Temple Gwathmey Handicap at Belmont Park.

Zaccio lost his lone jump race at Saratoga in 1981, running second by four and a half lengths as part of the favored 6-5

Champion steeplechaser Zaccio (on the inside) starred at Saratoga.

entry in a handicap race while carrying 164 pounds, eighteen more than the winner, Codicioso.

The following year, his loss as the 8-5 favorite in the Lovely Night Handicap cost Zaccio a rare hat trick at Saratoga. Carrying 159 pounds in that race, Zaccio led late, but Quiet Bay, one of three Sheppard horses in the field, rolled by after the final fence to win by two lengths.

After the Lovely Night, Zaccio won a handicap by sixteen lengths, then, carrying 161, he gamely held off Give a Whirl by a neck while spotting him fifteen pounds in the New York Turf Writers Cup.

Zaccio did not race in 1983, but he returned in 1984 to win one of three allowance races before retiring. By then there was a new champion, one trained by Jonathan Sheppard.

Sheppard has dominated steeplechase racing for two decades yet also continues to have success on the flat. In 2001 he saddled Augustin Stable's gray six-year-old With Anticipation to multiple stakes victories on the turf.

Though he's also trained such flat runners as Storm Cat, Sheppard will be forever known as a steeplechase trainer. How could he not be? He was the leading steeplechase money-winning trainer twenty-two times, including eighteen in a row, and the leading trainer in victories twenty-one times.

Sheppard, born near Newmarket, England, came to the United States in 1961 at the age of twenty and hooked up with Burly Cocks, working for him on Cocks' farm in Unionville, Pennsylvania, and then riding for him for two years before turning to training.

Sheppard's first two champions were Athenian Idol in 1973 and Augustin Stable's Cafe Prince, who won consecutive titles in 1977 and 1978.

Flatterer, one of the greatest jumpers of all time, eclipsed both of them, winning sixteen of twenty-two steeplechase races and four consecutive championships from 1983 through

1986. Before being pulled up in the 1987 Breeders' Cup Steeplechase at 4-5 in his final start, he had finished out of the money just once. At Saratoga.

Flatterer won an allowance race in his first Saratoga jump start in 1983, then moved up to stakes company in the New York Turf Writers Handicap. Carrying 140 pounds, the lowest weight of his entire jumping career, Flatterer went off as part of a 9-10 entry, coupled with another Sheppard trainee, Augustin Stable's Double Reefed. Flatterer was never involved at any point in the race, checking in fourth by ten and a quarter lengths behind Double Reefed. The comment in Flatterer's past performance line for that race read "Jumped poorly."

In every other start he jumped magnificently. Flatterer followed his failure at Saratoga by winning the final four races of his four-year-old season, including the (American) Grand National Handicap, the Temple Gwathmey, and the Colonial Cup, earning the first of four consecutive championships.

Not wanting Flatterer to start in the 1984 New York Turf Writers Handicap off a three-month layoff, Sheppard gave Flatterer a race on the flat. He was seventh, but the race tightened him and helped him win the New York Turf Writers.

Flatterer tacked on wins in the Brook Handicap carrying 167 pounds and the Colonial Cup with 160 to earn his second title.

In 1985 Flatterer was so good that the 1985 New York Turf Writers Handicap at Saratoga failed to fill because no other horse would challenge him. Subsequently, the stakes was conducted as a flat grass race at Belmont Park, and Flatterer was third by five and three-quarters lengths. Then he won his third consecutive Colonial Cup by seventeen lengths under 162 pounds. He was champion again.

In 1986 Flatterer won his forth title. In one memorable start he carried 176 pounds to a seven-length victory in the National Hunt Cup Handicap in the Radnor Races at Malvern, Pennsylvania. No steeplechase horse before or since has ever carried more to the winner's circle in the United States.

Flatterer made five starts in 1987. He finished second by a length and a half in the Champion Hurdle at Cheltenham in Great Britain, then tried to win the Middleburg Handicap under 178 pounds. He could not, finishing last in the field of five, six and a half lengths behind the winner, Gogong.

Flatterer won the Iroquois Memorial and an allowance race by six lengths before being pulled up in the Breeders' Cup.

It's hard to believe a horse could top Flatterer's four championships, but Lonesome Glory did, winning in 1992, '93, '95, '97, and '99. But Lonesome Glory almost never made it to the races. He was one of nine horses Walter M. Jeffords left to his wife, Kay, when he died in 1989. And she gave him away.

"She had given Lonesome Glory to her daughter, who had show horses," Lonesome Glory's trainer, Bruce Miller, said. "They were not able to get him broken. He was very skittish and scared. And so a trainer with Mrs. Jeffords at that time, Andy Elder, recommended that she send him to me to break him."

And Miller, whose daughter Blythe and son Chip would develop into two of steeplechase racing's greatest riders, had his problems with Lonesome Glory, too. "He was very, very hard to break," Miller said. "After a long period of time, he was still very skittish, and we really didn't know what direction to go."

The answer was steeplechasing. "It's a long, slow process, and it takes a lot of patience," Miller said. "Mrs. Jeffords had never had a steeplechase horse at that time. She was wondering whether she should sell him late in his three-year-old season."

She didn't, and in 1991 Lonesome Glory quickly showed the wisdom of her decision. After a fifth, third, and fourth in three flat turf races, the son of Transworld won his jumping debut by two lengths at 6-1. He was on his way. Lonesome Glory posted four more wins, the last by a head at 20-1 in the Sport of Kings Challenge at Cheltenham in Great Britain, and was named 1992 steeplechase champion.

Lonesome Glory's five championships were a result of patience.

In his first start at Saratoga, in the 1994 New York Turf Writers Handicap, Lonesome Glory ran third by seven and a half lengths to Mistico at equal weights (168). Another third, behind Warm Spell in the Breeders' Cup Grand National, was the likely reason Warm Spell was named 1994 champion.

Two Saratoga victories helped Lonesome Glory regain the title in 1995. After carrying 164 pounds to a one-length victory at even money in the A.P. Smithwick Handicap, Lonesome Glory took the New York Turf Writers Handicap by a neck at 6-5 over Mistico carrying six pounds more, 166 to 160.

Lonesome Glory lost his final three Saratoga starts. In 1997, though he would again be named champion, he was fourth at 2-1 in the A.P. Smithwick and third as the even money favorite in the New York Turf Writers Handicap. At age ten the following summer Lonesome Glory finished sixth as the 6-5 favorite in the 1998 New York Turf Writers Handicap.

Yet he would capture another championship at age eleven by winning both of his two starts in 1999, both grade I stakes, the non-wagering Carolina Cup and the Royal Chase at Keeneland under Blythe Miller, who rode Lonesome Glory in his final twenty-nine jump races. "He was just a special horse," she said.

Despite the trouble her dad had breaking him. All it took was a leap of faith.

20

Same Old Saratoga

Through the late nineties and into the new millennium, the unparalleled quality of racing at Saratoga remained unchanged, even as the meet expanded to thirty-six days. Simulcasting brought Saratoga racing into venues all over the continent. And champions kept on losing.

Carolyn Hines' Skip Away, the 1996 three-year-old champion, 1997 and '98 handicap champion, and 1998 Horse of the Year, made just two high-profile starts at Saratoga, finishing third in both as a heavy favorite.

In his two races before the 1996 Travers, Skip Away won the Ohio Derby by three and a half lengths and the Haskell Invitational by one length.

In his two races after the 1996 Travers, Skip Away won the Woodbine Million by four lengths and shocked Cigar, and the racing world, by winning the Jockey Club Gold Cup by a head over the defending Horse of the Year.

Skip Away went off the 7-5 favorite in the 1996 Travers under Jose Santos and was in a good spot at third midway down the backstretch behind dueling leaders Louis Quatorze, the winner of the Preakness and Jim Dandy Stakes, and Prince Heaven. Alongside Skip Away was Dr. Caton, who was already starting to tire. Will's Way was by himself in fifth, another length and a half back in the field of seven.

The pace was quick: three-quarters of a mile in 1:10.67, and Skip Away seemed to be in an ideal position when Santos tried rushing through on the inside of Louis Quatorze and Prince Heaven in a sudden thrust. Skip Away got within a half-length of Louis Quatorze, but there wasn't enough room on the inside to continue. Santos was forced to snatch Skip Away back.

Meanwhile, with Prince Heaven about ready to call it a day, an alert Jorge Chavez had already moved Will's Way up on the outside of Skip Away to go after Louis Quatorze, in effect getting the trip Skip Away would have inherited had Santos simply held his ground.

Will's Way and Louis Quatorze engaged in a stretch-long battle, with Will's Way finally edging clear to a three-quarters-length win. Skip Away rallied again and finished third, one length behind Louis Quatorze. Santos never rode Skip Away again, replaced by Shane Sellers and later Jerry Bailey.

In 1997, for the second straight year, Skip Away came to Saratoga hoping to extend his winning streak to three, following victories in the Massachusetts and the Suburban handicaps.

Formal Gold and Will's Way had run two-three behind Skip Away in the Mass Cap and three-two behind him in the Suburban. When all three entered the Whitney, people expected a great race, and they got it, though Skip Away, sent off the even-money favorite despite spotting Formal Gold five pounds and Will's Way eight, was never involved. There was no excuse this time as he finished third by six and a half lengths to Will's Way, who gamely out-dueled Formal Gold by a nose.

Skip Away lost to Formal Gold twice more, finishing second to him in both the Iselin Handicap at Monmouth Park and the Woodward Stakes at Belmont Park, but then won the Jockey Club Gold Cup by six and a half lengths and the Breeders' Cup Classic by six lengths.

The Hineses expected to win Horse of the Year, but they were fortunate to win the handicap championship over

Barbara D. Livingston

**Champion Skip Away lost the Travers and the Whitney
in successive years to Will's Way.**

Formal Gold, who had beaten Skip Away in four of six meetings that year. The 1997 Horse of the Year was the undefeated two-year-old Favorite Trick, who had won all eight of his starts, including the Saratoga Special and Hopeful Stakes.

In 1998 Favorite Trick, now in Hall of Fame trainer Bill Mott's barn, weakened to eighth in the Kentucky Derby but came back to win the Jim Dandy Stakes by a nose over Deputy Diamond in a courageous effort. That made him three for three at Saratoga, an undefeated record that lasted twenty days until Favorite Trick ran fifth by two lengths to Secret Firm as the 6-5 favorite in the King's Bishop Stakes on Travers Day.

Escena, bred and owned by the late Allen Paulson and trained by Mott, did even worse than Skip Away at Saratoga. Skip Away was zero for two. She went zero for four. As a three-year-old in 1996, she ran fifth by eleven and a half lengths to Capote Belle in the Test Stakes as the 7-5 favorite, then second by four lengths to Yanks Music in the Alabama at 7-2.

Escena returned to Saratoga in 1998 riding a four-race win streak, having taken the Apple Blossom Handicap at Oaklawn Park by two and a half lengths, the Louisville Breeders' Cup Handicap by four lengths, the Fleur de Lis Handicap by six lengths at Churchill Downs, and the Vanity Invitational by two lengths at Hollywood Park.

Bettors made her 3-10 in the Go for Wand Handicap. Escena was beaten in the final stride of the mile and an eighth stakes by Aldiza, who carried ten pounds less. Off her brave defeat, Escena went off at 4-5 in the Personal Ensign Handicap at Saratoga twenty-six days later. She finished sixth by six lengths to Tomisue's Delight.

Escena salvaged her season, and the handicap mare championship, by winning the 1998 Breeders' Cup Distaff by a nose over Banshee Breeze. Fortunately for her connections, the race was at Churchill Downs, not Saratoga.

In 1999 Joan G. and John W. Phillips' Eclipse champion

Aldiza defeats champion Escena in the final strides of the Go for Wand Handicap.

grass mare Soaring Softly won seven of her eight races. The one she didn't get was at Saratoga.

Much of trainer Jimmy Toner's 1999 season was hellish: the discovery that he had skin cancer; a barn fire at Belmont Park that took the lives of three of his horses; and having another filly, Call Nine One One, nearly lose her life after an impressive allowance victory at Saratoga. Through it all, he remained focused on a goal: to win the initial Breeders' Cup Filly & Mare Turf at Gulfstream Park.

Earlier in the nineties, Toner's top turf mare, Memories of Silver, lost her chance at a championship when she was defeated in two California stakes races, the Yellow Ribbon and Matriarch, at the end of the 1997 season, races New York-based Toner would have skipped had there been a Breeders' Cup turf race for fillies and mares.

Soaring Softly would get an opportunity that Memories of Silver had not, even though at the start of her four-year-old season she was unraced on grass. On dirt the daughter of Kris S. out of the Key to the Mint mare Wings of Grace had two wins, a second, and three thirds in eight starts.

Her progress on grass in 1999 was phenomenal. She won allowance races at Gulfstream Park and Keeneland before stepping up to stakes company and winning the Vineland Handicap at Garden State, the Sheepshead Bay Handicap at Belmont, and the New York Handicap.

Toner freshened her and pointed to the Breeders' Cup. The return spot he selected for her was a difficult one, the Diana Handicap at Saratoga. In a talented field of nine, she went off the 2-1 favorite despite her seven-week layoff. She raced evenly, finishing fifth by three and three-quarters lengths to Heritage of Gold.

Toner reasoned that she needed the race, but he also changed jockeys from Mike Smith to Jerry Bailey. Soaring Softly then won the Flower Bowl Handicap by a length at

Belmont Park and the first Breeders' Cup Filly & Mare Turf by three-quarters of a length as a tepid 7-2 favorite from the twelve post in a fourteen-horse field at Gulfstream Park.

Her loss in the Diana cost her a perfect eight-for-eight season.

Saratoga sported a new look in the year 2000. Thanks to eight million dollars spent by the New York Racing Association, Saratoga had three new admission gates and new jockeys' quarters. Defeated champions in stakes races were not new.

Chilukki, the 1999 two-year-old champion filly, went off the 8-5 favorite in the 2000 Test Stakes. She was sixth by six and three-quarters lengths to Dream Supreme, who also won the grade I Ballerina Stakes against older fillies and mares.

The next day Heritage of Gold challenged Beautiful Pleasure, the 1-5 favorite and 1999 champion older mare, on a sloppy track in the Go for Wand Stakes.

Skip Dickstein

Heritage of Gold upsets Beautiful Pleasure in the Go for Wand.

One to five seemed a tad low. A year earlier Beautiful Pleasure had upset champion older mare Banshee Breeze at Saratoga, and Heritage of Gold's undefeated record in 2000 included a victory over Beautiful Pleasure.

That all seemed irrelevant as Beautiful Pleasure, who was four for five on wet tracks, splashed into the far turn with a seemingly insurmountable lead of seven lengths.

Suddenly, however, Heritage of Gold, who had never raced on a wet track, didn't seem to mind the footing. Suddenly, she found her best stride and began to rally, cutting Beautiful Pleasure's lead in half. She then proceeded to whittle the lead to two lengths, then one, and then ran right past Beautiful Pleasure to win by a length.

The defeat was so stunning that it was still in the mind of Beautiful Pleasure's rider, Jorge Chavez, after Beautiful Pleasure returned to defeat Heritage of Gold in the Personal Ensign Handicap at Saratoga twenty-six days later as the .90-to-1 favorite. "I got a big disappointment the last time, really a broken heart," Chavez said quietly in the winner's circle.

Perfect Sting, second by a half-length at 5-2 to Nani Rose in the Lake George Stakes at Saratoga the year before, overcame a difficult trip to win the 2000 Diana Handicap by three-quarters of a length at 3-5 on the way to her female grass championship, one she clinched by winning the Breeders' Cup Filly & Mare Turf.

Two days earlier, with a backdrop of torrential rain from coal black clouds, streaks of lightning, and frightening echoes of thunder, City Zip and Yonaguska dead-heated in the 2000 Hopeful Stakes with Macho Uno in between them, all of a neck back in third. Macho Uno subsequently won the Breeders' Cup Juvenile and was named two-year-old champion colt.

In the summer of 2001, Macho Uno was the Graveyard's first victim.

Macho Uno had not raced since the Breeders' Cup Juvenile, and trainer Joe Orseno brought him back for his three-year-old debut in allowance company on opening day. He lost at even money under Jerry Bailey after racing erratically in the final yards and getting nailed at the wire. Orseno added blinkers for Macho Uno's next start, and the son of Holy Bull responded by winning the Pennsylvania Derby impressively.

One could only wonder if Point Given — the colt Macho Uno had beaten by a nose in the 2000 Breeders' Cup Juvenile — would be knocked off, too, when he showed up for the Travers. In his three-year-old season, Point Given had won the San Felipe, Santa Anita Derby, Preakness, Belmont Stakes, and Haskell, five victories sandwiching his fifth-place finish in the Kentucky Derby.

Baffert sent Point Given's stablemate, Congaree, the easy winner of the grade I Swaps Stakes in his last start, to contest Saratoga's traditional prep for the Travers, the Jim Dandy Stakes. Congaree not only finished third at 2-5 to Scorpion but also injured his knee and was retired.

In between Macho Uno's and Congaree's defeats, Albert the Great, one of the top older horses in the country, lost the Whitney at 4-5 to Lido Palace, who beat Albert the Great again in the Woodward Stakes at Belmont Park six weeks later.

There were other high-profile casualties of the 2001 Saratoga meet. Although 2001 champion sprinter Squirtle Squirt won the grade I King's Bishop Stakes as the 3-2 favorite, Xtra Heat, fated to be 2001 champion three-year-old filly, was a game second at 2-1 to favored Victory Ride in the grade I Test Stakes. Beautiful Pleasure returned to lose two more stakes at Saratoga as the favorite, the Go for Wand and Personal Ensign handicaps. Cashier's Dream, a top contender for two-year-old filly honors, suffered her first loss in the Adirondack Stakes at 3-5 to You but returned to win the Spinaway Stakes impressively. Dream Supreme went off at odds of 1-2, hoping to repeat her 2000 victory in the grade I Ballerina, but was third to the 21-1 longshot in the field of five, Shine Again, trained by Allen

Jerkens. Praise the Prince solidified his claim as top steeple-chaser by winning the A.P. Smithwick at 3-5, only to return and lose the New York Turf Writers Cup at 2-5 to It's a Giggle, trained by Jonathan Sheppard.

But the 2001 meet will most likely be remembered for the Travers, when an all-time record Saratoga crowd of 60,486 came to see Point Given, who had looked vulnerable in his previous start, the Haskell, but still managed to win.

The overflow crowd in the paddock included New York Governor George Pataki and his wife, Libby. Point Given, known to be playful and mischievous at times, stood calmly waiting to be saddled, his head held high as he watched the people watching him. The 17-hand giant then went out and won the Travers easily, as his sire Thunder Gulch had done, by three and a half lengths at 3-5.

But a tendon injury was discovered soon after the race, and Point Given was retired. He was named three-year-old champion colt and 2001 Horse of the Year.

He will never be a Graveyard victim.

Other champions will. It happens every summer at Saratoga.

Chronology of Upsets

Aug 7, 1897 .... Archduke beats Hamburg at 1-3 in Grand Union Hotel Stakes
Aug. 6, 1910 .... Sir John Johnson beats Maskette at 1-2 in Delaware Handicap
Aug. 20, 1910 .... Novelty beats Iron Mask at 1-1 in Hopeful Stakes
Aug. 4, 1915 .... Star Jasmine beats Roamer at 3-5 in Champlain Handicap
July 31, 1916 .... Stromboli beats Regret at 4-5 in Saratoga Handicap
Aug. 13, 1919 .... Upset beats Man o' War at 1-2 in Sanford Stakes
Aug. 12, 1924 .... Priscilla Ruley beats Princess Doreen at 2-5 in Alabama Stakes
Aug. 10, 1926 .... Rapture beats Edith Cavell at 6-5 in Alabama Stakes
Aug. 14, 1926 .... Mars beats Crusader at 4-5 in Travers Stakes
Aug. 18, 1928 .... Petee-Wrack beats Victorian at 6-5 in Travers Stakes
Aug. 9, 1930 .... Jamestown beats Equipoise at 3-5 in Saratoga Special
Aug. 16, 1930 .... Jim Dandy beats Gallant Fox at 1-2 in Travers Stakes
Aug. 29, 1936 .... Granville beats Discovery at 2-5 in Saratoga Cup
Aug. 17, 1940 .... Nasca beats Level Best at 3-5 in Spinaway Stakes
Aug. 24, 1940 .... New World beats Whirlaway at 6-5 in Grand Union Hotel Stakes
Aug. 7, 1942 .... *Bonnie Ann beats Vagrancy at 1-5 in Alabama Stakes
Aug. 14, 1942 .... Elkridge beats Speculate at 6-5 in North American Steeplechase
Aug. 14, 1943 .... Eurasian beats Bourmont at 4-5 in Travers Stakes
Aug. 8, 1944 .... Vienna beats Twilight Tear at 1-20 in Alabama Stakes
Aug. 11, 1945 .... Adonis beats Pavot at 4-5 in Travers Stakes
Aug. 15, 1945 .... Trymenow beats Stymie at 7-5 in Whitney Handicap
Aug. 21, 1946 .... Hypnotic beats Bridal Flower at 6-5 in Alabama Stakes
Aug. 30, 1946 .... Replica beats Rouge Dragon at 1-2 in Saratoga Handicap
Aug. 9, 1947 .... Rico Monte beats Stymie at 2-5 in Whitney Handicap
Aug. 16, 1947 .... Young Peter beats Phalanx at 1-2 in Travers Stakes
Aug. 14, 1948 .... Ace Admiral beats My Request at 4-5 in Travers Stakes
Aug. 12, 1950 .... Lights Up beats Bed o' Roses at 6-5 in Travers Stakes
Aug. 23, 1950 .... Busanda beats Next Move at 3-5 in Alabama Stakes
Sept. 1, 1951 .... Cousin beats Tom Fool at 3-5 (e) in Hopeful Stakes
Aug. 11, 1952 .... Count Flame beats Tom Fool at 4-5 in allowance race
Aug. 16, 1952 .... One Count beats Tom Fool at 3-2 in Travers Stakes
Aug. 19, 1952 .... Busanda beats Kiss Me Kate at 4-5 in Diana Handicap
Aug. 20, 1952 .... Flirtatious beats Grecian Queen at 2-1 in Spinaway Stakes
Aug. 28, 1952 .... Busanda beats Kiss Me Kate at 1-1 in Saratoga Cup
Aug. 21, 1953 .... War Rhodes beats King Commander at 6-5 in Lovely Night Hurdle
Aug. 12, 1954 .... Escargot beats King Commander at 1-1 in North American Steeplechase
Aug. 18, 1954 .... Lavender Hill beats Evening Out at 6-5 in Diana Handicap
Aug. 20, 1954 .... Carafar beats Neji at 1-1 in Lovely Night Hurdle
Aug. 23, 1954 .... Gandharva beats High Voltage at 9-5 in Spinaway Stakes
Aug. 20, 1955 .... Social Outburst beats Parlo at 4-5 (e) in Saratoga Handicap
Aug. 22, 1955 .... Register beats Doubledogdare at 1-1 in Spinaway Stakes
Aug. 24, 1955 .... Rico Reto beats High Voltage at 2-5 in Alabama Stakes
Aug. 22, 1956 .... Searching beats Parlo at 6-5 in Diana Handicap
Aug. 25, 1956 .... Paper Tiger beats Dedicate at 1-1 in Saratoga Handicap
Aug. 25, 1957 .... Renegade beats Dedicate at 6-5 in Saratoga Handicap
Aug. 4, 1958 .... Rich Tradition beats Quill at 8-5 in Schuylerville Stakes
Aug. 13, 1958 .... First Minister beats Intentionally at 1-1 in Grand Union Hotel Stakes
Aug. 17, 1960 .... Bronzerullah beats Hail to Reason at 1-1 in Saratoga Special
Aug. 22, 1960 .... Tempted beats Quill at 1-2 in Diana Handicap
Aug. 15, 1961 .... Primonetta beats Bowl of Flowers at 1-2 in Alabama Stakes
Aug. 16, 1961 .... Battle Joined beats Jaipur at 3-4 in Saratoga Special
Aug. 11, 1962 .... Firm Policy beats Cicada at 4-5 in Alabama Stakes
Aug. 1, 1963 .... Barbwolf beats Lamp Chop at 3-2 in Test Stakes
Aug. 10, 1963 .... Tona beats Lamb Chop at 2-5 (e) in Alabama Stakes
Aug. 17, 1963 .... Crewman beats Candy Spots at 1-2 in Travers Stakes
Aug. 7, 1964 .... Nautilus beats Amber Diver at 3-2 in Beverwyck Steeplechase
Aug. 19, 1964 .... Candalito beats Queen Empress at 4-5 in Adirondack Stakes
Aug. 26, 1964 .... Candalito beats Queen Empress at 1-1 in Spinaway Stakes
Aug. 27, 1964 .... Nautilus beats Amber Diver at 3-5 in Saratoga Steeplechase Handicap
Aug. 2, 1965 .... Indulto beats Impressive at 8-5 in Flash Stakes

Aug. 5, 1965.............. Cestrum beats Queen Empress at 3-5 in Test Stakes
Aug. 12, 1966............. Indulto beats Impressive at 1-1 in Jim Dandy Stakes
Aug. 4, 1967.............. Spooky Joe beats Mako at 1-1 in Beverwyck Steeplechase
Aug. 24, 1967............. Prides Profile beats Straight Deal at 6-5 in Diana Handicap
Aug. 24, 1967............. Spooky Joe beats Mako at 1-1 in Saratoga Steeplechase Handicap
Aug. 8, 1968.............. National Anthem beats Top Bid at 4-5 in Saratoga National Hurdle
Aug. 11, 1968............. Queen's Double beats Ta Wee at 1-1 in Spinaway Stakes
Aug. 5, 1971.............. Lucky Traveler beats Forward Gal at 7-5 in Test Stakes
Aug. 14, 1971............. Lauries Dancer beats Forward Gal at 5-2 in Alabama Stakes
Aug. 16, 1971............. Debby Deb beats Numbered Account at 4-5 in Adirondack Stakes
Aug. 1, 1973.............. Wichita Oil beats Riva Ridge at 1-2 in allowance race
Aug. 4, 1973.............. Onion beats Secretariat at 1-9 in Whitney Handicap
Aug. 24, 1973............. Prove Out beats Forego at 3-5 in allowance race
Aug. 9, 1974.............. Golden Don beats Halo at 9-10 in Bernard Baruch Handicap
Aug. 10, 1974............. Quaze Quilt beats Chris Evert at 1-2 in Alabama Stakes
Aug. 17, 1974............. Holding Pattern beats Little Current at 1-1 in Travers Stakes
Aug. 6, 1976.............. Crag's Corner beats Straight and True at 4-5 in Lovely Night Hurdle
Aug. 3, 1977.............. El Portugues beats Honest Pleasure at 2-5 in allowance race
Aug. 6, 1977.............. Nearly On Time beats Forego at 4-5 in Whitney Handicap
Aug. 25, 1977............. Happy Intellectual beats Life's Illusion at 6-5 NY Turf Writers Steeplechase
Aug. 3, 1979.............. Cafe Prince beats Martie's Anger at 2-5 (e) in Lovely Night Hurdle
Aug. 11, 1979............. It's in the Air beats Davona Dale at 1-5 in Alabama Stakes
Aug. 18, 1979............. General Assmbly beats Davona Dale at 5-2 in Travers Stakes
Aug. 23, 1979............. Leaping Frog beats Cafe Prince at 2-5 (e) in NY Turf Writers Steeplechase
Aug. 24, 1979............. Parson's Waiting beats Zaccio at 3-5 in allowance hurdle
Aug. 8, 1980.............. Davona Dale beats It's in the Air at 6-5 in Ballerina Stakes
Aug 9, 1980............... Love Sign beats Sugar and Spice at 6-5 in Alabama Stakes
Aug. 16, 1980............. Temperence Hill beats Plugged Nickle at 9-5 in Travers Stakes
Aug. 1, 1981.............. Fio Rito beats Winter's Tale at 3-2 in Whitney Handicap
Aug. 5, 1981.............. Love Sign beats Highest Regard at 2-5 in Ballerina Stakes
Aug. 15, 1981............. Willow Hour beats Pleasant Colony at 8-5 in Travers Stakes
Aug. 6, 1982.............. Quiet Bay beats Zaccio at 8-5 in Lovely Night Hurdle
Aug. 21, 1982............. Runaway Groom beats Conquistador Cielo at 2-5 in Travers Stakes
Aug. 13, 1983............. Play Fellow beats Slew o' Gold at 2-1 in Travers Stakes
Aug. 18, 1983............. Double Reefed beats Flatterer at 4-5 (e) in NY Turf Writers Steeplechase
Aug. 18, 1984............. Madame Forbes beats Ambassador of Luck at 4-5 in Revidere Stakes
Aug. 1, 1985.............. Lady's Secret beats Mom's Command at 1-2 in Test Stakes
Aug. 24, 1985............. Basie beats Life's Magic at 4-5 (e) in Delaware Handicap
Aug. 10, 1987............. Lady's Secret bolts at 1-5 in an allowance race
Aug. 14, 1987............. I'm Sweets beats North Sider at 4-5 (e) in Ballerina Stakes
Aug. 16, 1987............. Talakeno beats Manila at 1-5 in Bernard Baruch Handicap
Aug. 22, 1987............. Java Gold beats Alysheba at 5-2 in Travers Stakes
Aug. 11, 1989............. Three Way beats Rhythm at 4-5 in a maiden race
Aug. 12, 1990............. Who's to Pay beats Steinlen at 1-5 in Bernard Baruch Handicap
July 23, 1994............. Twist Afleet beats Heavenly Prize at 3-2 in Test Stakes
Aug. 7, 1994.............. Boundary beats Cherokee Run at 3-5 in A Phenomenon Handicap
Aug. 13, 1994............. Heavenly Prize beats Lakeway at 3-10 in Alabama Stakes
Aug. 13, 1995............. Classy Mirage beats Inside Information at 2-5 in Ballerina Stakes
July 27, 1996............. Capote Belle beats Escena at 7-5 in Test Stakes
Aug. 24, 1996............. Will's Way beats Skip Away at 7-5 in Travers Stakes
Aug. 2, 1997.............. Will's Way beats Skip Away at 1-1 in Whitney Handicap
Aug. 16, 1997............. Runup the Colors beats Ajina at 3-5 in Alabama Stakes
Aug. 21, 1997............. Bisbalense beats Lonesome Glory at 1-1 in NY Turf Writers Steeplechase
Aug. 2, 1998.............. Aldiza beats Escena at 3-10 in Go for Wand Stakes
Aug. 15, 1998............. Cetewayo beats Chief Bearhart at 6-5 in Sword Dancer Invitational
Aug. 22, 1998............. Banshee Breeze beats Manistique at 1-2 in Alabama Stakes
Aug. 27, 1998............. Hokan beats Lonesome Glory at 6-5 in NY Turf Writers Steeplechase
Aug. 28, 1998............. Tomisue's Delight beats Escena at 4-5 in Personal Ensign
Aug. 29, 1998............. Secret Firm beats Favorite Trick at 6-5 in King's Bishop Stakes
Aug. 29, 1998............. Coronado's Quest beats Victory Gallop at 6-5 in Travers Stakes
Aug. 11, 1999............. Intidab beats Artax at 7-1 in A Phenomenon Handicap
Aug. 14, 1999............. Honor Glide beats Yagli at 3-5 in Sword Dancer Invitational
Aug. 27, 1999............. Beautiful Pleasure beats Banshee Breeze at 3-5 in Personal Ensign Handicap
July 27, 2000............. City Zip beats Yonaguska at 3-5 in Sanford Stakes
July 29, 2000............. Dream Supreme beats Chilukki at 8-5 in Test Stakes

Chronology of Upsets

July 30, 2000.............. Heritage of Gold beats Beautiful Pleasure at 1-5 in Go for Wand Stakes
Aug. 4, 2000............... Personal First beats Trippi at 1-2 in Amsterdam Stakes
Aug. 19, 2000............. Jostle beats Secret Status at 4-5 in Alabama Stakes
Aug. 24, 2000............. Ninepins beats Campanile at 4-5 in NY Turf Writers Steeplechase
Aug. 30, 2000............. Shadow Caster beats Richter Scale at 9-5 in Forego Handicap
July 25, 2001.............. Wicked Will beats Macho Uno at 1-1 in an allowance race
July 28, 2001.............. Lido Palace beats Albert The Great at 4-5 in Whitney
July 29, 2001.............. Serra Lake beats Beautiful Pleasure at 6-5 (e) in Go for Wand
Aug. 4, 2001............... Scorpion beats Congaree at 2-5 in Jim Dandy
Aug. 13, 2001............. You beat Cashier's Dream at 3-5 in Adirondack
Aug. 25, 2001............. Shine Again at 21-1 beats Dream Supreme at 1-2 in Ballerina

* *was disqualified*   *(e) - part of an entry*

Champions at Saratoga

Horse	Wins-Starts	As Favorite Wins-Starts	Horse	Wins-Starts	As Favorite Wins-Starts
Affectionately	1-2	1-2	Counterpoint	1-1	1-1
Affirmed	*3-4	*2-3	Countess Diana	3-4	2-2
Ajina	0-1	0-1	Cozzene	1-4	1-2
Alysheba	0-1	0-1	Crafty Admiral	0-2	0-0
Ambassador of Luck	1-4	1-3	Criminal Type	1-1	1-1
Amber Diver	5-20	1-8	Crusader	1-3	1-2
Ancestor	3-11	0-3	Damascus	1-1	1-1
Artax	0-2	0-0	Dark Mirage	2-2	0-0
Arts and Letters	2-3	2-2	Davona Dale	1-3	0-2
Askmenow	1-2	0-0	Dearly Precious	1-1	1-1
Assagai	1-3	1-2	Decathlon	0-2	0-1
Athenian Idol	3-6	1-3	Dedicate	1-5	1-3
Aunt Jinny	0-1	0-0	Dehere	3-3	3-3
Autobiography	0-3	0-1	De La Rose	2-3	1-2
Bald Eagle	1-1	1-1	Deputy Minister	0-1	0-0
Banshee Breeze	2-3	1-2	Desert Vixen	3-3	3-3
Barnabys Bluff	2-5	1-2	Devil Diver	3-6	2-5
Battlefield	3-5	3-5	Devil's Bag	1-1	1-1
Bayou	0-2	0-0	Discovery	8-12	7-9
Beautiful Pleasure	3-5	2-3	Doubledogdare	0-1	0-1
Bed o' Roses	1-4	1-2	Double Jay	1-1	1-1
Before Dawn	1-2	1-1	Dr. Fager	2-2	2-2
Beldame	2-6	2-2	Dr. Patches	1-3	1-2
Ben Brush	1-2	0-1	Easy Goer	3-3	3-3
Benguala	2-6	0-1	El Chico	5-5	5-5
Bimelech	2-2	2-2	Elkridge	5-12	3-7
Black Maria	3-14	2-5	Epitome	0-1	0-0
Blue Peter	2-2	2-2	Equipoise	4-5	4-5
Bold Forbes	1-1	1-1	Escena	0-4	0-3
Bold Lad	1-1	1-1	Evening Out	2-3	1-2
Bon Nouvel	3-10	3-4	Exterminator	5-14	1-7
Boston Harbor	0-1	0-0	Fairy Chant	0-6	0-1
Bowl Game	0-2	0-0	Family Style	1-2	1-1
Bowl of Flowers	0-1	0-1	Fast Attack	0-1	0-0
Bridal Flower	0-3	0-1	Favorite Trick	3-4	3-4
Brother Jones	1-3	0-0	First Flight	0-2	0-2
Buckpasser	2-2	2-2	First Landing	2-2	2-2
Bushranger	0-2	0-0	Flanders	2-2	1-1
But Why Not	1-1	1-1	Flatterer	2-7	2-3
Cafe Prince	4-10	3-5	Flat Top	0-2	0-1
Canonero II	0-1	0-0	Fly So Free	1-3	0-1
Capot	1-3	1-3	Foolish Pleasure	1-1	1-1
Capote	0-1	0-1	Forego	0-2	0-2
Career Boy	4-8	4-4	Fort Marcy	1-3	1-1
Carry Back	1-1	1-1	Forty Niner	2-3	0-0
Cavalcade	0-3	0-1	Forward Gal	1-4	0-2
Challedon	1-1	1-1	Gallant Bloom	0-1	0-0
Chateaugay	1-2	1-1	Gallant Bob	0-1	0-0
Cherokee Run	0-2	0-1	Gallant Fox	2-4	1-2
Chief Bearhart	0-1	0-1	Gallorette	3-8	2-4
Chief's Crown	*3-4	*3-4	Gamely	*5-6	3-3
Chilukki	1-2	1-2	Genuine Risk	1-1	1-1
Chris Evert	0-2	0-1	Go for Wand	2-2	2-2
Cicada	2-4	1-2	Gold Beauty	1-1	1-1
Cigar	0-1	0-0	Golden Attraction	3-4	2-2
Colin	2-2	2-2	Gran Kan	1-6	0-2
Conniver	0-5	0-0	Granville	3-5	2-2
Conquistador Cielo	2-4	1-2	Grecian Queen	0-5	0-1

Champions at Saratoga

Horse	Wins-Starts	As Favorite Wins-Starts	Horse	Wins-Starts	As Favorite Wins-Starts
Grey Lag	1-4	1-2	Martie's Anger	1-8	0-1
Groovy	1-1	1-1	Maskette	3-4	3-4
Guilty Conscience	1-1	1-1	Meadow Star	2-2	2-2
Gulch	2-5	2-2	Mercator	0-1	0-1
Hail to Reason	2-3	2-3	Miss Request	0-6	0-2
Hamburg	2-3	2-3	Misty Morn	1-3	1-2
Hansel	0-2	0-0	Moccasin	4-4	3-3
Hawaii	1-1	1-1	Mom's Command	1-3	1-2
Heavenly Cause	0-2	0-1	Mongo	0-1	0-0
Heavenly Prize	3-4	2-3	My Juliet	1-1	1-1
Henry of Navarre	4-4	4-4	Myrtle Charm	1-1	1-1
Hermis	6-8	3-3	Nadir	2-2	1-1
Hidden Lake	1-1	1-1	Nashua	2-2	1-1
High Voltage	0-2	0-2	Native Dancer	6-6	5-5
Holy Bull	1-1	1-1	Needles	1-1	0-0
Honest Pleasure	1-2	0-1	Neji	1-2	1-2
Housebuster	2-2	2-2	Never Bend	1-2	1-1
Idun	2-3	2-2	Next Move	0-1	0-1
Imp	1-4	1-2	North Sider	0-1	0-1
Impressive	1-5	0-3	Not Surprising	2-4	1-1
Inside Information	0-1	0-1	Now What	1-6	0-1
Intentionally	0-1	0-1	Numbered Account	3-4	3-4
It's in the Air	2-3	1-2	Oedipus	3-14	1-5
Jaipur	3-4	2-3	Office Queen	0-1	0-0
Jam	2-9	0-2	Old Rosebud	3-5	2-3
Jimmy Lorenzo	0-1	0-0	Omaha	0-4	0-0
John Henry	1-3	1-1	One Count	1-1	0-0
Johnny D.	1-2	1-2	Open Fire	3-5	3-4
J. O. Tobin	0-1	0-0	Open Mind	1-2	1-1
Jungle King	5-20	5-8	Our Boots	0-1	0-0
Just a Game	1-1	1-1	Our Mims	1-1	0-0
Kelso	4-4	4-4	Outstandingly	0-1	0-1
Key to the Mint	2-2	2-2	Pan Zareta	0-1	0-0
King Commander	2-9	1-2	Paradise Creek	1-3	1-1
Kiss Me Kate	1-4	1-3	Parka	0-1	0-0
Lady Maryland	1-3	0-0	Parlo	1-3	0-2
Lady Pitt	*0-4	*0-1	Pavot	1-2	0-0
Lady's Secret	3-4	2-3	Perfect Sting	1-2	1-1
Lakeville Miss	0-2	0-0	Personal Ensign	1-1	1-1
Lamb Chop	1-3	1-3	Personality	1-2	1-1
La Prevoyante	5-5	5-5	Petrify	0-1	0-1
Late Bloomer	1-3	1-2	Phalanx	0-4	0-2
Laugh and Be Merry	0-1	0-0	Pleasant Colony	0-1	0-1
Leallah	0-1	0-0	Plugged Nickle	2-3	1-2
Lemhi Gold	0-3	0-0	Point Given	1-1	1-1
Lemon Drop Kid	3-5	2-3	Polynesian	0-4	0-1
Level Best	1-3	1-2	Pompoon	0-2	0-1
Life's Illusion	3-5	2-3	Porterhouse	*0-1	*0-1
Life's Magic	1-3	1-2	Primonetta	1-1	0-0
Little Current	0-2	0-2	Princess Doreen	2-8	1-4
Lonesome Glory	2-6	2-4	Protagonist	1-3	0-0
Lord Avie	0-2	0-0	Proud Delta	1-2	0-0
Macho Uno	1-2	1-1	Queena	3-3	1-1
Mako	3-8	2-4	Queen Empress	1-5	1-4
Manila	0-3	0-1	Queen of the Stage	1-1	1-1
Man o' War	5-6	5-6	Quick Pitch	5-13	0-1
Maria's Mon	1-3	1-1	Quill	0-3	0-2
Marica	1-1	1-1	Regal Gleam	0-2	0-0
Mar-Kell	2-4	0-1	Regret	5-6	5-6
Market Wise	0-3	0-1	Relaxing	0-1	0-0

Champions at Saratoga

Horse	Wins-Starts	As Favorite Wins-Starts	Horse	Wins-Starts	As Favorite Wins-Starts
Rhythm	1-2	0-1	Tom Fool	6-9	3-6
Riva Ridge	2-3	1-2	Top Bid	3-13	3-5
Roamer	9-18	5-8	Top Flight	3-4	3-3
Rockhill Native	*0-1	*0-1	Top Knight	2-2	1-1
Rouge Dragon	3-5	3-4	Turkoman	0-2	0-1
Roman Brother	1-2	1-2	Twenty Grand	2-2	2-2
Rose Jet	1-4	0-1	Vagrancy	1-3	1-2
Royal Governor	0-10	0-0	Vanlandingham	0-1	0-1
Rubiano	1-2	1-1	Victory Gallop	1-2	1-2
Ruffian	1-1	1-1	Vitriolic	1-3	0-0
Run the Gantlet	0-1	0-0	Wajima	1-1	1-1
Sacahuista	2-4	2-2	War Admiral	4-4	4-4
Safely Kept	1-1	0-0	War Battle	0-5	0-1
Saratoga Dew	0-1	0-0	Warm Spell	4-5	1-2
Sarazen	3-7	3-4	War Plumage	1-1	0-0
Seabiscuit	2-4	1-1	Waya	1-1	0-0
Seattle Slew	1-1	1-1	Wayward Lass	0-2	0-2
Secretariat	3-4	2-3	What a Summer	1-1	1-1
Sensational	0-4	0-1	What a Treat	2-6	1-1
Serena's Song	0-1	0-0	Whirlaway	4-6	4-5
Shadow Brook	3-13	2-4	Winning Colors	2-2	2-2
Shipboard	3-6	1-2	Xtra Heat	0-1	0-0
Shuvee	3-7	3-5	Yanks Music	1-1	0-0
Sickle's Image	1-1	0-0	Zaccio	5-9	5-7
Silent Screen	1-2	0-0	Zev	5-7	5-6
Silverbulletday	1-1	1-1			
Sir Barton	2-6	2-2	* - Record includes a disqualification from a win		
Skip Away	0-2	0-2			
Sky Beauty	*3-4	*2-3			
Slew o' Gold	1-2	1-2			
Smart Angle	2-2	1-1			
Smoke Glacken	1-1	0-0			
Snow Knight	1-1	1-1			
Soaring Softly	0-1	0-1			
Soothsayer	1-3	1-1			
Speculate	2-4	2-4			
Stage Door Johnny	0-1	0-1			
Stagehand	0-5	0-0			
Star de Naskra	1-1	1-1			
Steinlen	3-5	3-4			
Storm Song	1-3	0-1			
Straight and True	0-6	0-2			
Straight Deal	1-5	0-2			
Stymie	2-6	1-2			
Sun Beau	0-3	0-0			
Sunshine Forever	0-2	0-0			
Surfside	2-3	2-3			
Susan's Girl	0-1	0-0			
Swale	1-2	0-0			
Sweep	1-3	1-3			
Sword Dancer	2-3	2-2			
Sysonby	3-3	3-3			
Talking Picture	3-3	1-1			
Ta Wee	2-4	2-4			
Tea-Maker	6-15	2-4			
Temperence Hill	1-3	0-0			
Tempest Queen	0-2	0-1			
Tempted	4-7	2-3			
The Mast	1-3	0-0			
Thunder Gulch	1-1	1-1			

Index

Affirmed 63, 69, 116, 143, 145, 183, 193
Aloma's Ruler..............9, 188-189, 192, 194, 198-201
Alydar 70, 145-146, 163, 183, 213
Alysheba 211-219
Amber Pass...178
Angle Light 121-123, 134
Archduke...19
Arts and Letters...................................63, 191, 214
Baden Baden 185
Banner Gala 169-170
Banshee Breeze...238, 241
Beau Gar..127
Beautiful Pleasure 12-13, 240-242
Bed o' Roses 95
Before Dawn 180-182
Best Turn 143
Bet Twice...212-218
Black Maria 42-44, 47
Blue Larkspur 71, 223
Bold Hour...110, 166
Bold Lad...130
Bold Ruler 95, 113, 115, 117
Bold Venture 66, 68
Boot to Boot...45-46
Bowl of Flowers...............89-92, 95, 101, 204
Bramalea 93-94
Bridal Flower..77
Bright Rex 173
Broad Brush 211, 215
Buckpasser 104-110, 126, 191
Bull Dog 70, 79
Bundler 139
Busanda 104-105
Cafe Prince...231
Call Nine One One 239
Candy Eclair 144, 146-147
Canonero II...124, 128
Capt. Moore..16
Captain Alcock...32, 34
Cassaleria 186
Challedon...68
Chance Shot 47-48
Cherokee Frolic.......................................162, 170
Chief's Crown 143
Chilukki..240
Chris Evert 139-143, 145
Cicada 89, 92-95, 101, 116
Cigar...72, 235
Citation...72, 121
City Zip 26, 241
Classy Mirage 127
Clock's Secret 204
Cloverbrook...184-185
Concern 109, 215
Conquistador Cielo 9, 12, 14, 63, 161, 167,
                     170, 173, 188, 190-194, 197-201
Cougar II 137, 186
Cousin...79-82
Cox's Ridge 163, 191
Crack Brigade...54-55
Creme Fraiche 211, 218

Crusader..45-46, 55, 185
Cryptoclearance 213-214, 216-218
Damascus...108-110
Dancing Brave..221
Dangerous...46
Davona Dale 12, 139, 143-144, 146-149
De La Rose..178
Dedicate...86-87
Dehere..26, 102
Deputed Testamony 211
Deputy Minister...179
Desert Vixen 102, 118
Determinant...197
Discorama 162, 170
Discovery 66-68, 70, 100, 239
Display..........................40-41, 45-46, 48, 204, 206
Dr. Fager...109-113, 163
Duluth 222-223
Easy Goer 102, 124
Ed Crump...27
Edith Cavell 41-42, 44
El Chico..102
Elkridge...229
Endear..207
Escena 237-238
Espino 41
Exterminator...35, 185
Fair Play 27, 30-31
Fairway Phantom.......................................176-177
Falcon Almahurst...156
Favorite Trick 64, 237
Fictional Chief 175
Fiesta Libre 143
Fifth Marine 118
Find........16, 25, 42, 74, 78, 119, 122, 131, 152, 166,
                           179, 194, 221
Fio Rito 163-166
Firestone 170
Firethorn..66
Firm Policy..93-94
First Landing...116
Five Star Flight...176-177
Flatterer...229, 231-233
Flower Bowl 89, 239
Fly So Free...63
Forego 136, 141, 191
Foreign Survivor 226
Formal Gold...236-237
Fort Marcy...118, 220
Fortunate Moment 213, 215-216, 218
Forty Niner..201
Friar Rock..27
Funloving...89
Gallant Bloom...113
Gallant Fox 9, 12-13, 50-65, 69, 77, 115, 183
Gallant Knight 55
Gallo Blue Chip 151
Gallorette...76-78
Gamely 95, 112-114, 143, 149, 177, 231, 236
Gato Del Sol...................186-187, 192, 194, 198-201
Gay Serenade 97

General Assembly 147, 201
Genuine Risk.......26, 148-149, 161, 170-172, 178, 209
Glorious Song 162
Go for Wand 12, 114, 238, 240, 242
Golden Broom 31-32, 34
Gorky...213, 216-218
Granville...65-70
Green Book 226
Green Glade 113
Groovy 215
Gulch.........................183, 213-214, 216-218, 243
Gun Bow 98
Hamburg...............................12-13, 19-20, 25-26
Hannibal 81
Happy Hooligan 188
Hawaii 220
Heavenly Prize 105
Heritage of Gold 239-241
Herschelwalker.......................................167, 173
High Ascent 192
High Voltage 12, 14, 87
Highest Regard.......................................149, 168
Hill Gail 81-82
Hitting Away...91
Holding Pattern 143, 185
Holy Bull 242
Honest Pleasure 171
Icy Circle...197
Impressive........................55, 80, 106-107, 214, 239
Initial 17, 24, 239
Inside Information 12
It's in the Air 145-149
Jaipur.......................95, 108, 110, 179, 198
Jameela...178
Java Gold 212-218
Jersey Lightning...25
Jim Dandy ...9, 51-52, 56-64, 166-167, 169, 174, 176,
                    192, 198, 213, 235, 237, 242
Jim Gaffney...56
Johnny D. 168
Johren 24, 185
Jungle King 229
Justin Passing...158
Kelso 101-104, 107, 126, 163, 191
Key to the Mint...........118, 123, 163, 214, 217, 239
King's Bishop 115, 128, 237, 242
Kiss Me Kate...85
Knight Errant..22
Knightly Spiced...168
La Prevoyante 102, 118
Lady Digby...17
Lady M 203
Lady Suffolk 15
Lady's Secret...203-210
Lamb Chop...........................12, 89, 95-98, 101, 113
Landaluce...203-204
Lejoli.............167, 172-173, 180, 193, 197-199, 202
Lemhi Gold.................................166-167, 176
L'Alezane...118
L'Carriere...163
Life's Illusion...229
Life's Magic...206
Linda's Chief.......................................120, 122
Linkage.............................186, 188, 192, 194
Little Current 140, 143, 185

Lizzie W 16
Lonesome Glory 229, 233-234
Lord Avie..174, 176-177
Louis Quatorze.................................64, 235-236
Love Sign 148-149, 168, 178
Lovely Night 168, 230-231
Lure 228
Lyphard...220
Macho Uno 241-242
Mack Lobell..151
Majestic Folly...205-206
Malicious 103-104
Man o' War 8, 10, 12, 25, 29-38, 41, 44-47, 53, 56,
                    115, 126, 137, 224
Manila 12, 220-225, 227
Marguerite....................................49, 53
Mars 32, 45-46, 185
Maskette 12-13, 20-22, 147-148, 171, 206, 208
Mayanesian 172-173, 179-180
Memories of Silver 239
Menow...79
Mettlesome 71
Miss Keeneland 71
Miss Musket 140
Misstep...47, 49
Missy's Mirage...127
Mistico 234
Misty Gallore 148, 171
Misty Morn 14, 87
Moccasin 102, 204
Mom's Command 204-206
Mr. Prospector.................................146, 190, 192
Mrs. Revere 206
My Big Boy...226
Mystical Mood 162, 172
Nalee 96-97
Nashua 86, 97, 163, 165, 167, 176, 178
Native Dancer 79, 84-85, 99-100, 102, 112-113, 116
Native Truth...182
Nearly On Time 136
Nevele Pride 151
Never Bow 127
New World 69
Next Move 104-105
Niatross...151-160
Noble Nashua 163, 165, 176, 178
North Sea 128, 217
One Count.......................................82, 84-85
Onion 9, 12, 117, 127-130, 132, 134-138
Our Mims...118, 144
Our Native 123
Out of Hock 179-180
Overproof..119
Paper Tiger...87
Paradise Creek...228
Parlo 85
Parson's Waiting 230
Pavot...75-76, 185
Petee-Wrack 48-50, 53, 185
Pensive 71
Perfect Sting 241
Personal Ensign 238, 241-242
Phalanx 185
Play Fellow...211, 215
Pleasant Colony........................166, 174-178, 185

251

Index

Polish Navy.................................213, 216-218
Point Given....................................242-243
Pompey...45-46
Poppycock...146
Precisionist......................................207-208
Primonetta...90-92
Prince Fortune 166, 176-177
Prince Heaven................................235-236
Priscilla Ruley..41
Prismatical.......................................169-170
Prove Out.............................127, 136-137
Quadrangle 214
Quaze Quilt.......................................141-142
Quebec...119
Queena...102
Questionnaire..76
Quill...87
Rapture..42-43
Reel Easy 209
Regret..........................25-28, 92, 204
Reigh Count...48-49
Rhythm...8
Rico Monte 74, 77-78
Rico Reto........................14, 86-88
Ridan..........................93, 95, 102, 198
Ring of Light................................163, 165
Riva Ridge.........115-116, 121, 123-126, 132, 135-136
Roamer...........................22-24, 85, 91
Rosemont..68
Round Table...7
Round View 77
Royal Academy 228
Royal Stranger..48
Royal Vale..85
Ruffian 147, 171, 206, 208
Rule by Reason 132, 134-135
Runaway Groom..........9, 184, 196-201, 211
Ruthless...184
Saratoga Dew 163
Say Florida Sandy..................................163
Sea Hero 183
Seabiscuit..68
Seattle Slew 116, 193
Secret Firm 237
Secretariat 9, 12, 115-126, 128-137, 143, 147, 159, 193, 203, 222
Seeking the Gold..........................201, 218
Semprolus...13
Sensational............................131, 177, 218
Sensitive Prince.....................................127
Sham.......................................122-124
Sharrood..224
Shipping Magnate 172-173
Shuvee.....................................114, 118, 207
Silent Screen..166
Silver Buck 187, 191
Sir Barton 19, 35-36, 51, 185
Sir Gaylord..116
Sir John Johnson 13, 21-22
Skip Away 235-237

Skip Out Front 226
Slew o' Gold..211
Soaring Softly..............................238-239
Somethingroyal 115
Spectacular Bid................116, 147, 193
Spellbound......................................222-223
Spicy Living 95-97
Sportin' Life 166-167
Star Shoot......................................45, 56
State Dinner...................................163, 191
Steinlen.....................12, 220, 225-228
Stupendous 107, 112, 129
Stymie....................12, 14, 73-78
Sugar and Spice.............................148-149
Summer Guest 118-119, 137
Summing...................166, 169, 174, 176
Sun Falcon 58-60, 62
Swaps 86, 90, 163, 212, 242
Sword Dancer 109, 219-220
Sysonby....................................85, 102
Ta Wee..111
Talakeno.........................220, 222-225
Talking Picture 102, 118, 140
Temperence Hill......161-162, 171, 176, 178, 194, 216
Tempted 169
The Liberal Member...............163, 165, 178
The Swimmer..................................32, 34
Theatrical..221, 224
Thunder Gulch 183, 243
Tim Tam..143
Timely Writer....................167, 180, 182
Tom Fool................79-85, 97, 100, 104-105
Tomisue's Delight 238
Top Bid...229
Traffic Cop 128
Transworld 233
Trenton Time...............154-155, 157-158
Trove...162, 172
True Knight 126, 132
Trymenow...75-76
Twilight Tear....................................70-72
Upset 8, 10, 12, 19, 25, 28-29, 31-32, 34-38
Vagrancy 95
Victorian 7, 11, 48-49, 185
Vienna..72
War Admiral.........................38, 102, 104
War Cloud..185
Warm Spell..234
Wavering Monarch 189, 194-197
West Coast Scout 132, 134
Whichone...................54-57, 59-62
Whirlaway.........................69, 126, 183
White Star Line......................................206
Will's Way 235-236
Willow Hour 166-167, 170, 174-177, 186, 194
Winter's Tale.................................163, 165
Yanks Music 237
Yonaguska 241
Young Peter...185
Zaccio....................................229-231

Sources

Champions, Daily Racing Form

The 1990 American Racing Manual, Daily Racing Form

The 2000 American Racing Manual, Daily Racing Form

They're Off! Horse Racing at Saratoga, by Edward Hotaling

The Noble Animals, by Landon Manning

Saratoga, Saga of an Impious Era, by George Waller

Saratoga Stakes Histories 2000

The New York Racing Association Media Guide

The Travers Stakes Media Guide

The Kentucky Derby Media Guide

The Preakness Media Guide

The Breeders' Crown Media Guide

Acknowledgments

So many people helped me in so many ways research this book. At the head of the list is my wife, Anna, who made countless trips to the library to go through miles of microfilm. She searched and found literally hundreds of old newspaper articles about the near nine hundred horses and hundreds of people mentioned in *Graveyard of Champions*.

Tom Gilcoyne, the historian of the National Museum of Racing and Hall of Fame, devoted hours of work to help me, always asking, "What's next?" He also shared stories about the Saratoga races he had seen growing up. Carol Crandell helped me in the museum library, too. Phyllis Rogers of Keeneland Library also researched horses and sent me clips. Ken Davis of the *Daily Racing Form* looked up statistics for me.

Mark Cusano, Dan Hayes, and the staff of "Down The Stretch," an extremely well-done weekly television show out of Schenectady, New York, not only found video of old races for me, but spliced them together and put them on tape so I could watch many of the races I wrote about.

My buddy Joan Lawrence of the NTRA sent me volumes of clips that were extremely helpful. So was Kathleen Adams.

Judy Marchman at Eclipse Press dug up dozens of magazine articles, and Diane Viert of *The Blood-Horse* also helped immensely. So did Fran LaBelle and his media relations staff at the New York Racing Association. Thanks, also, to Mike Flynn and the staff at the New York Thoroughbred Breeders Inc.

Angel Cordero Jr., Ron Turcotte, Eddie Maple, Jerry Bailey, and Phil Johnson were valuable resources, as was that wonderful trainer, Allen Jerkens, who also contributed the foreword.

I thank my editors and my good friend and proofreader, Yale Sussman.

Finally, I thank Anna and our son, Bubba (a.k.a. Benjamin), for listening to countless rewrites and helping with the index, as well as the table of champions' performances at Saratoga.

About the Author

BILL HELLER, a freelance writer in Albany, New York, won the 1997 Eclipse Award for magazine writing for his story, "The Times They Are a-Changin'," in *The Backstretch* magazine. He also is a three-time winner of the John Hervey Award for harness racing magazine writing. Heller won the 1999 Bill Leggett Breeders' Cup magazine writing award and a 2000 first-place writing award from American Horse Publications. He currently writes for the *Thoroughbred Times, The Backstretch,* and *Mid-Atlantic Thoroughbred.*

Heller has authored twelve other books, including *Personal Ensign, Forego,* and *Go for Wand,* all in the Thoroughbred Legends series; *Obsession — Bill Musselman's Relentless Quest; Overlay, Overlay; The Will To Win — The Ron Turcotte Story; Travelin' Sam, America's Sports Ambassador; Billy Haughton — The Master;* and *Playing Tall — The 10 Shortest Players in NBA History.*

Other Titles *from* ECLIPSE PRESS

At the Wire
Horse Racing's Greatest Moments

Baffert
Dirt Road to the Derby

The Calumet Collection
A History of the Calumet Trophies

Cigar
America's Horse (revised edition)

Country Life Diary
(revised edition)

Crown Jewels of Thoroughbred Racing

Dynasties
Great Thoroughbred Stallions

Etched in Stone

Four Seasons of Racing

Great Horse Racing Mysteries

Hoofprints in the Sand
Wild Horses of the Atlantic Coast

Horse Racing's Holy Grail
The Epic Quest for the Kentucky Derby

Investing in Thoroughbreds
Strategies for Success

Lightning in a Jar
Catching Racing Fever

Matriarchs
Great Mares of the 20th Century

Olympic Equestrian

Ride of Their Lives
The Triumphs and Turmoils of Today's Top Jockeys

Royal Blood

Thoroughbred Champions
Top 100 Racehorses of the 20th Century

Women in Racing
In Their Own Words

THOROUGHBRED
Legends®
S E R I E S

Affirmed and Alydar

Citation

Dr. Fager

Forego

Go for Wand

John Henry

Man o' War

Nashua

Native Dancer

Personal Ensign

Round Table

Ruffian

Seattle Slew

Spectacular Bid

Sunday Silence

Swaps

A Division of The Blood-Horse, Inc.
PUBLISHERS SINCE 1916